# Education Studies

## An issues-based approach

### Third edition

Editors
Will Curtis
Stephen Ward
John Sharp
Les Hankin

# Education studies

## An issues-based approach

## Third edition

Los Angeles | London | New Delhi
Singapore | Washington DC

Learning Matters
An imprint of SAGE Publications Ltd
1 Oliver's Yard
55 City Road
London EC1Y 1SP

SAGE Publications Inc.
2455 Teller Road
Thousand Oaks, California 91320

SAGE Publications India Pvt Ltd
B 1/I 1 Mohan Cooperative Industrial Area
Mathura Road
New Delhi 110 044

SAGE Publications Asia-Pacific Pte Ltd
3 Church Street
#10–04 Samsung Hub
Singapore 049483

Editor: Amy Thornton
Development editor: Geoff Barker
Production controller: Chris Marke
Project management: Deer Park Productions,
Tavistock, Devon
Marketing manager: Catherine Slinn
Cover design: Wendy Scott
Typeset by: C&M Digitals (P) Ltd, Chennai, India
Printed and bound in Great Britain by: Henry Ling
Limited at The Dorset Press, Dorchester, DT1 1HD

First published in 2006 by Learning Matters Ltd.
© 2014 the editors and authors

**Library of Congress Control Number: 2013947939**

**British Library Cataloguing in Publication Data**

A catalogue record for this book is available from
the British Library

ISBN: 978-1-4462-6742-4 (hbk) and
ISBN: 978-1-4462-6743-1 (pbk)

# Contents

# Editors

**Will Curtis** is Director of Part Time and 2+2 Programmes in the Centre for Lifelong Learning at the University of Warwick.

**Stephen Ward** is Emeritus Professor of Education at Bath Spa University where he was formally Dean of the School of Education and Head of Education Studies.

**John Sharp** is Professor of Education and Head of Doctoral Studies at Bishop Grosseteste University in Lincoln.

**Les Hankin** led the development of the Education Studies degree pathway at Liverpool Hope University.

# Contributors

**Kate Adams** is Reader in Education at Bishop Grosseteste University in Lincoln.

**Nick Allsopp** is Head of Academic Practice at Loughborough University.

**Anna Beck** is a PhD student in the School of Education at the University of Glasgow.

**Pat Beckley** is the Academic Coordinator for the 3–7 cohorts on the PGCE Primary course at Bishop Grosseteste University.

**Andrea Bullivant** works for Liverpool World Centre, a Development Education Centre liaising with schools and other education contexts to raise awareness of global and social justice issues.

**Mark Chater** is Director of Culham St Gabriel's, an independent educational trust supporting research, development and innovation in religious education.

**Jim Crawley** is Programme Leader for Lifelong Learning, and a Teaching Fellow at Bath Spa University.

**Howard Gibson** lectures at Bath Spa University, focusing on areas where political philosophy, language and educational issues meet.

**Suanne Gibson** is based at Plymouth University where she leads the BA Education Studies degree.

**Nasima Hassan** is Principal Lecturer and Head of Education and Community at the University of East London.

**Denis Hayes** was formerly Professor of Primary Education and is now a freelance education writer.

**Clive Hedges** is a Senior Lecturer in education at Teesside University.

**Victoria Holt** is Coordinator for the Global Citizenship Project in the Faculty of Education at Liverpool Hope University.

**Elizabeth Hopkins** is a Senior Lecturer in education at Bishop Grosseteste University.

**Anesa Hosein** is currently a Lecturer in Higher Education at the University of Surrey.

**Viv Kerridge** is Senior Lecturer, specialising in applied drama, at Bishop Grosseteste University.

**Jane McDonnell** is Senior Lecturer in Education at Liverpool John Moores University.

**Barbara Murphy** lectures in Education Studies at Bishop Grosseteste University.

**Mark Murphy** is Reader in Education, School of Education, University of Glasgow.

**Stephen Newman** is a Senior Lecturer in Education and Continuing Professional Development at Leeds Metropolitan University.

**Alice Pettigrew** currently works as a Researcher at the Institute of Education, University of London.

**Namrata Rao** is currently a Lecturer in Education Studies at Liverpool Hope University.

**Ruth Sayers** is Dean for School of Culture, Education and Innovation at Bishop Grosseteste University.

**Keira Sewell** is Lecturer in Primary Education at the University of Southampton.

**Feng Su** is a Lecturer in Education at Liverpool Hope University.

# Acknowledgements

Every effort has been made to trace the copyright holders and to obtain their permission for the use of copyright material. The publisher and author will gladly receive any information enabling them to rectify any error or omission in subsequent editions.

# Introduction to the third edition

Education is something that we tend to take for granted as what happened to us in school. But when we come to study it we find that there are many different ideas about what education and schooling should be. This book gets to grips with the question of what it means to study education as a university subject. We look at the nature of learning, education in the community and the implications for schools of the government's education policies.

What is education and why is it so important? Where does education take place and when? How is education studied? These are fairly obvious questions to ask, you'd think, but they are actually quite difficult to answer. Go right ahead and try for yourself or, better, try with a group of friends. It's not so easy, is it? Behind the questions lie the great scope, diversity and complexity of Education Studies as a subject discipline itself. It explores the processes of learning and teaching and the social, cultural, political and historical contexts in which they occur. It is this very scope, diversity and complexity that makes Education Studies such an exciting university subject.

## About this book

This book, first published in 2006, has been popular with students and successful in contributing to the development of Education Studies as a university subject. It is intended to inform and support your own learning and personal and professional development as you go about studying education. It will help whether you are in the first or final year of a formal course of Education Studies, training to be a teacher, or even undertaking research at a higher level for a master's degree or doctorate. We hope that you will be introduced to the book as a 'core text' by your tutors in an intellectually rigorous and systematic manner in lectures, seminars and tutorials. You might also find it essential as a background reader for self-study.

## Features of the book include:

- 20 chapters written and presented in an authoritative and informative yet readable and accessible way by contributors from a great many institutions around the country, each bringing their own interest and expertise to bear on the issues raised and considered;
- up-to-date revisions to 10 of the chapters in the second edition;
- 10 entirely new chapters which introduce the latest thinking on current educational topics;
- research boxes and pause-for-thought boxes to help promote critical reflection and analysis and a deep exploration of ideas;
- fully referenced text to provide further reading for those who wish to pursue the content of chapters further.

# Themes in education

The book looks carefully at the all-encompassing themes that shape the educational landscape and which influence our increasingly uncertain lives. Globalisation, with all its opportunities and threats, is explored in terms of market forces, cultural and ethnic dominance and the responses society must make as it changes and adapts to meet new challenges. The motifs of lifelong learning, citizenship, faith and inclusive regard for all members of society are interwoven here. All entail the mantle of responsibility as citizens and, for some of us, as leaders. Coursing through all the universal themes set out in these chapters is a concern for identity and the fulfilment of the individual.

Education Studies and teacher training are not the same, but they are related. Whether you go on to teach or to make a career in one of the newer education professions, you will certainly find the chapters interesting and informative and free of the narrow confines of the compliance-driven culture typical of most courses leading to Qualified Teacher Status. This is important in an increasingly vocationalised world driven by measurable outcomes and generic transferable skills. Questioning the very basis upon which any educational practice is established, that is, understanding its theoretical, philosophical and ideological underpinning, is as important as getting trained to deliver one. Academic critique of policy and practice is what Education Studies is about, and this book will guide and inform you in your thinking and discussion.

# Chapter 1

# What is education?

## Keira Sewell and Stephen Newman

### Introduction

Ask anyone what education means and the answers are likely to be varied. Many primary-aged children might suggest that it helps them to learn, whereas secondary-aged children often think that education helps to get a job. Adults have different views, often based on their own experiences of the education system. Thus the term 'education' is not an easy one to define, often being wrapped up with the ideas of schooling, learning and training. This chapter examines the debates about the nature of education and the possible definitions or meanings of education. It looks at the different ways philosophers have thought about education and it asks you to do some philosophical thinking of your own about the different language-games played by educational thinkers and policy-makers.

## Defining education

The notion of education has taxed the minds of philosophers since the times of Plato and Socrates. Despite the multitude of definitions put forward, Matheson and Wells (1999) have argued that we are still no nearer reaching one that is wholly satisfactory. Gregory (2002) has suggested education is concerned with equipping minds to make sense of the physical, social and cultural world, while Peters (1966) has proposed that when we use the term 'education' it brings with it the implication that there is an 'intention to transmit', in a 'morally acceptable' way, something considered worthwhile; such beguiling simplicities having found expression in more recent political rhetoric (Gove, 2011). Yet, can we really equip young minds with the ability to make sense of a world which will look very different in ten or twenty years from now? Who determines what is, and what is not, worthwhile and on what do they base such decisions? What is meant by Peters's phrases 'intention to transmit' and 'morally acceptable'? It is no easier to answer these questions if we take Hirst's (1965) view that liberal education has value for an individual because it fulfils the mind rather than fulfilling vocational or utilitarian needs.

One of the difficulties in defining education lies in the interchangeability of those terms associated with it. Where some may see the term 'schooling' as synonymous with the term 'education', or suggest that the relationship between learning and teaching is causal (e.g. Carr, 2003), Gregory (2002) has indicated that the terms are distinct and that the relationship between the two cannot be assumed. Indeed, it is this distinctiveness that enables individuals to determine their own education on leaving a schooling system that they may believe has failed them.

# What is education? Schooling, education, learning, training

The argument that the notions of schooling and education are distinct raises the question of whether education can simply be assigned to *product*, or whether it is the *process* of education that is of paramount importance. However, if education is regarded as a process, a further question arises: what should this process entail? There may initially appear to be a strong argument in support of learning playing a fundamental role, particularly if learning is taken to mean the acquisition of knowledge, understanding or skills that were not previously held. Perhaps the starting point for this debate should therefore be learning rather than education; that is, that the type of learning taking place may determine whether we refer to education as training or even schooling.

This regress of questions continues in the notion of training. Becker (1964) described training as focusing on the development of technical abilities that are linked to specific vocations or are generic across the field of employment. Cohen (1982) described it as applying to a specific and limited learning goal. Thus attention turns to the nature of technical abilities, what defines limited learning goals, and whether training promotes a different kind of learning from education.

Papadopoulous (1998) acknowledged the many possible interpretations of the term 'education', arguing that it can be regarded as an all-embracing term, serving a number of different purposes in ways that recognise both product and process. He has suggested that education is variously seen as promoting:

- economic prosperity;
- employment;
- scientific and technological progress;
- cultural vitality in a society increasingly dominated by leisure activities;
- social progress and equality;
- democratic principles;
- individual success.

# A philosophical approach

The remarks thus far have illustrated that there is little, if any, consensus about any one precise meaning of the term 'education'. Not only does the term seem to have many meanings but the search for criteria for the term that are relevant for all the meanings it has also seems fraught with difficulty. It seems far from easy to identify any core attribute that each and every use of the term 'education' must share.

An alternative approach that may be helpful takes as its starting point the reminders provided by Wittgenstein, particularly those provided in his *Philosophical Investigations* (Wittgenstein, 1953). Wittgenstein suggested that most terms get their meanings from the contexts – the 'language-games' – in which they are used. He proposed that most words do not have fixed meanings and hence uses; rather, they are like tools in a toolbox and can be used for varied purposes. If someone makes a mistake in their use of a term, then the relevant criteria from the appropriate 'language-game' can be made explicit in an attempt to provide clarification. Thus the judgement of whether a use is appropriate comes from the context in which the word is used.

Instead of considering the term 'education', let us consider the term 'chair' as an apparently more straightforward example. Is there a core or central meaning of that term? Perhaps your instinctive first thoughts lead you to think that there is. But a chair may differ in size, shape or colour; it may have legs, it may have none. A chair may seat one person, or maybe more than one. 'Chair' might be used to mean a professorial post in a university, or a person convening a meeting. Interestingly, however, in spite of this diversity of meanings, there is no apparent confusion when this term is used in our everyday language. This is, in everyday life, far from being a puzzling or surprising fact. This example suggests that the criteria for deciding whether the use of the term 'chair' is appropriate come from the context, rather than from the term 'chair' itself.

The notion that words do not have fixed meanings is closely allied to that which suggests that words can have more than one meaning. Take as a further example the term 'games'. Wittgenstein suggested that the uses of this term form a network where there may be overlaps of meaning between some of the uses, but that there is nothing in common to all of the uses. Wittgenstein also suggested that this network of similarities can be characterised by the phrase 'family resemblances'. The same notion can be taken to represent a series of related 'language-games', each 'consisting of language and the actions into which it is woven'; as before, some of these 'language-games' are closely related, others are not.

---

*Pause for thought* | meanings and contexts

The word 'red' (like other ordinary words) takes its meaning from the way in which it is actually used. The use of the word depends not just on an object being described, but also on context. Think, for example, of the differences between the uses of 'red' in the phrases 'red paint', a 'red pillar box', someone with 'red hair' or 'being in the red'. Consider the uses of the term 'white' in 'white coffee', 'white wine', 'white skin' and 'white paint'. Try to make up some phrases of your own using the word 'deep', but where 'deep' has different meanings.

---

# The meanings of 'education'

Having considered some of the examples with which Wittgenstein highlighted the issue of meanings, let us return to consider the implications for attempting to define 'education'. With these ideas in mind, we can see that if the social context provides the structure for understanding the use of language and meanings then, in asking the question *What is education?*, we may expect a range of diverse answers, depending on the contexts in which the question is asked. We should not expect 'education' to have one fixed meaning; rather we may expect the term to have many meanings, meanings that may change.

Does this mean that we can never define what we mean by education? Not at all. But, according to Wittgenstein, such a definition would be context-specific and probably given for a special purpose. Thus, one interpretation of the term 'education' in *this* context may be to conceptualise education as involving developing expertise in various 'language-games'. At a general level this may be all that can be said; such an interpretation being descriptive rather than prescriptive, and explicitly context-specific. In this sense, to engage in education is indeed to be involved in a social process of meaning-making.

Consider, for example, trainee teachers. The purpose of their training is to prepare them to meet the professional competences expected from someone entering the teaching profession. However, Lang (1995) has argued that we cannot assume a commonality in the individual belief systems of trainees and that teacher education must be reflective, providing opportunities for trainees to examine and explore the values, beliefs and attitudes that underpin their approach to education and identify those factors that may determine how they resolve conflict. Such an approach, it is argued, enables them to move beyond mute acceptance of policy and procedure to a deeper understanding of the philosophies and principles that underpin these and an appreciation of the extent to which their own values and beliefs support or inhibit putting them into practice. Newman (1999) supported this distinction, characterising teacher *training* as a means of developing a beginning teacher's ability merely to follow the rules of a 'language-game', and teacher *education* as a way of developing:

*a critical practitioner: someone who is capable of thinking about what they do, justifying and explaining it where appropriate, and adapting their playing and their understandings [of language-games] to varying circumstances.*

(p.159)

Such an approach would seem to be in marked contrast to that which envisages the development of new teachers as one to be best based in school *to help develop … teaching skills and … learn about key teaching methods* (Department for Education, 2012).

As a further example, consider the teacher who needs to manage a bully/victim problem. Training might equip them with the skills to follow school policy and procedure but not to address some of the deep-rooted values and beliefs that affect the way they feel. Education, it is suggested, can explore these feelings and, while not always promoting change, at the very least can raise awareness of the presence of these feelings, of the ways in which they may determine responses, and help to develop the ability to articulate and justify particular actions in a way appropriate to the context (that is, to the 'language-game' being played).

# Education for differences

If education has many meanings which vary according to context, then it would be appropriate to consider the notion that education should not be limited to any one definition. Such a decision frees us to consider the range of educational opportunities available to us throughout our lives.

On one level it is likely that all of us will have experienced the traditional contexts of formal education. These contexts are normally long term, extending from primary through to higher education, and include institutions such as schools, colleges and universities. They frequently involve a government-set or institutionally-devised curriculum, and assessments that lead to nationally or internationally accepted awards or qualifications. Such outcomes appear to be valued by all generations, even though younger generations no longer see qualifications as a passport to high level or even stable employment (Aro et al., 2005).

Despite the high esteem in which the outcomes of formal contexts are held, however, for some, these traditional contexts of formal education, far from being neutral in their approach, seek to impose a particular view of knowledge, of language, of relationships and of reasoning on those who attend them (Giroux, 1985). Schools are thus regarded as instruments of social control (Freire, 1972), serving to reinforce the interests of a particular dominant group and to work against the interests of those who are less influential. This perception of traditional contexts of education as authoritarian (Meighan, 2005) perhaps helps to explain the increasing interest in alternative forms of education, such as home tuition, spearheaded by such groups as Education Otherwise. Just how alternative these approaches are is often determined by the curriculum offered and the methods and contexts of delivery. As Webb (1990) has noted, provision at home may vary considerably in terms of motive, method and aims, ranging from delivery of the statutory curriculum through to a much more individually determined learning programme available in a variety of environments including museums, galleries, science centres, field study centres, or even on extended trips around the world. While the first type of provision might appropriately be described as home schooling, the latter types are more likely to be identified as non-formal or informal education.

Even within the traditional contexts of so-called formal education there are examples of different forms of education. Thus, for example, some schools (such as Summerhill, or Forest Schools) may not subscribe to all that others may consider to be the characteristics of formal education and suggest that alternative approaches to delivering a curriculum may be further explored. Similarly, activities such as yoga classes, cookery classes, music lessons and evening classes may take place within the physical confines of a school but may sometimes be characterised as non-formal in their purpose. Other examples could include driving lessons, youth clubs, guide and scout groups, play schemes and holiday camps.

Informal education might be characterised as describing contexts that are neither formal nor non-formal. Examples might include museums, galleries and science centres, which see their function as public education rather than education limited to a specific client group. Both non-formal and informal education can perhaps often be characterised by an emphasis on choice in that they provide opportunities into which learners can opt, and which may sometimes include opportunities for learners to set their own learning outcomes.

Perhaps some contexts that deliver or support the delivery of statutory curricula are best described as 'alternative' forms of formal education. These include Playing for Success, Learning by Achievement, field study centres and themed museum visits. Such contexts often support learning in a way that could not be achieved within the classroom and often rely heavily on the theory that learners learn best when immersed *in situ* where they have access to specific artefacts, experiences and approaches. However, the description of a year-long trip by a family across Europe, designed to provide access to such experiences as learning a new language, exploring a different culture, trying new foods, and so on, as an 'alternative form of formal education' would not seem appropriate. While possibly contributing to the statutory curriculum, such experiences go far beyond it, often resulting in outcomes that are difficult to quantify. Yet it could be argued that the development of additional skills, knowledge and understandings of the whole family could not be achieved in any other way. To also describe such learning as informal seems unsatisfactory as the objectives of such a trip may be clearly defined and the route planned to specifically achieve these.

Other approaches, such as e-learning, provide opportunities to access information in a place other than the classroom, thus providing access to the curriculum for a range of learners at different times. Technologies, such as the internet, may also enable learners to access learning contexts that may otherwise be impossible; for example, viewing the Antarctic via a webcam at Davis Station. Access to the World Wide Web also opens up a wealth of opportunities for individualised informal learning that allows learners to determine their own interests and outcomes (Rowlinson, 2012). Some uses of such resources, we may wish to argue, are educational; others not. Such arguments may depend on our view of education and the purpose it serves, and on the contexts in which those arguments take place. Playing on a computer game, for example, may develop children's ICT skills but not all may wish to describe such an activity as educational. Other uses of the internet by some children may be even more controversial. (See Chapter 18.)

The past two decades have seen the rapid growth of a new generation of enterprises such as the Eden Project (in Cornwall), the Jorvik Viking Centre (in York), Magna (in Rotherham), Dynamic Earth (in Edinburgh), Eureka! (in Halifax) and Odyssey (in Belfast). These can be characterised by their clear objectives (often related to collective citizenship and the promotion of change), the utilisation of a resource base (physically impressive, exciting and incapable of being replicated in schools), the adoption of an interactive approach, and an ability to respond to a wide range of clients. In exploring the distinct nature of these enterprises, Peacock (2005) suggests the term 'peri-formal' as a means of identifying their unique contribution to education which neither formal nor informal contexts can achieve.

## Research box

### how do different users employ interactive resources?

Much has been made of the interactive, hands-on nature of activities in constructivist, child-centred learning within schools and this debate has informed the ongoing development of museum education. However, the extent to which such an approach can develop conceptual knowledge and understanding is a matter for debate; museums and other 'peri-formal' providers recognise that different users engage with resources in different ways. One example of this was demonstrated by research carried out by Fernández and Benlloch (2000) in Spain, who looked at participant use of the travelling interactive display '*Ver para no creer*' ('seeing, not believing'). The focus of their research was the collection of quantitative behavioural data relating to the duration of visit, duration of group conversations and reading behaviour. Their results indicated that different users interact with the exhibit in markedly different ways. Lone users approach the exhibit calmly, reading the information at appropriate points to enable them to make sense of their interactions. Groups of adults have a much more light-hearted approach, with one of the group members usually dominating the interaction while others in the group read the display panel and observe their actions. Children in groups normally commence interaction without reading the display panels while the adults in their group attempt to guide their actions in order to help them manipulate the exhibit rather than explaining the concepts underpinning it. Conversations are brief and limited to 'doing' rather than 'understanding'. Once the exhibit has been experienced they move on. Learners therefore appear to take what they want at that moment from the activity offered, suggesting that less formal contexts for education not only have to address the needs of a broader range of learners, but that they also may have difficulties in ensuring learning is both 'hands-on' and 'brains-on'.

Meighan and Siraj-Blatchford (2003) discussed the notion of flexitime education that allows learners to spend part of their time in a formal education context, such as a school, and part elsewhere. Such an initiative enables learners to take advantage of the range of learning contexts available, including e-learning. In the United States, there is increasing interest in the development of independent study programmes, designed to meet the needs of individual learners, and in the development of learning systems that have as a central premise the notion that learning can take place anywhere and can be directed by the learners themselves. Meighan and Siraj-Blatchford have recognised the benefits of these approaches. They also pointed out that the notion of flexitime is not readily accepted. While current legislation allows a child to be educated at home or at school, permission for each flexitime arrangement requires separate negotiation. It could be argued that legislation in the UK inhibits the development of flexible approaches such as these. Perhaps some of the responsibility lies with the legislation laid down in the Education Reform Act 1988, which devolves funding to schools based on numbers of pupils in school, the 'bums on seats' approach. As a consequence, schools may be unwilling to formalise a flexitime arrangement or maintain places for pupils on extended trips, no matter how educational such arrangements may be. The extent to which schools may use visits to other educational environments to support curriculum delivery is also influenced by the need to fund such visits, either through the limited budget available or by relying on voluntary contributions from parents or carers. While many museums (e.g. the Natural History Museum in London) have removed or reduced entry prices for educational parties, the cost of transport to and from such venues may preclude schools from making full use of the opportunities they offer.

It seems probable that developments in the use of information and communication technology will facilitate online and virtual access to many such resources, thus helping to widen participation and extend access to these facilities. Good use is already being made of this in education programmes for children in the Australian outback, and Meighan (2000) reported on the success of 'cyber schools' in Canada. If Gregory's (2002) view of education is accepted, an education that hopes to enable learners to make sense of the physical, social and cultural world must at least keep pace with the changes in that world, and many would see change as both necessary and inevitable. However, while it would seem obvious that educational institutions will need to make full use of funding strategies, educational policies and technological initiatives in order to initiate change, it is important to remember that education is deeply embedded in national culture (Wood, 2004). Attempts at educational change will need to reflect this and, as a consequence, approaches used in one country may not necessarily be transferable to another. Despite the increase in home education in countries such as the United States, the UK, Australia and Canada, for example, this approach is still rare in the Netherlands (Bluk, 2004), perhaps because parental expectations demand that education takes place in schools.

## Summary and conclusions

It is evident that strategic thinking that goes well beyond current educational policy will be required to make best use of the educational opportunities available to us in the UK. At present, government funding is used mainly to support formal educational environments, such as schools, leaving other providers, such as the 'peri-formal', to rely on grants, funding by industry, or the National Lottery.

Given that the term 'education' has a variety of meanings and that education can take place in many contexts, those who seek to open up the opportunities afforded by adopting more

*(Continued)*

*(Continued)*

flexible and context-specific descriptions of education will need to be able to argue their case, to be able to play the various 'language-games' of policy-makers, funding agencies, opinion-shapers, educators and others. Traditional views of education may then be replaced by a recognition that a diversity of approaches is possible, where the criteria of education will vary depending on the context, and where explanation, persuasion and justification have an accepted and expected place.

## References

Aro, M, Rinne, R, Lahti, K and Olkinuora, E (2005) Education or learning on the job? Generational differences of opinions in Finland. *International Journal of Lifelong Education*, 24(6): 459–74.

Becker, GS (1964) *Human Capital: a theoretical and empirical analysis, with special reference to education*. New York: National Bureau of Economic Research.

Bluk, H (2004) Performance in home schooling: an argument against compulsory schooling in the Netherlands. *International Review of Education*, 50(1): 39–52.

Carr, D (2003) *Making Sense of Education*. London: RoutledgeFalmer.

Cohen, B (1982) *Means and Ends in Education*. London: George Allen and Unwin.

Department for Education (2012) 'Get into teaching'. Available at **www.education.gov.uk/ get-into-teaching/teacher-training-options.aspx** (accessed 13 April 2013).

Fernández, G and Benlloch, M (2000) Interactive exhibits: how visitors respond. *Museum International*, 52(4): 53–9.

Freire, P (1972) Education: domestication or liberation? reprinted in Lister, I (1974) *Deschooling*. Cambridge: Cambridge University Press.

Giroux, HA (1985) Introduction, in Freire, P, *The Politics of Education: culture, power and liberation*. London: Bergin and Garvey.

Gove, M (2011) 'Michael Gove to Cambridge University'. Available at **www.education.gov. uk/inthenews/speeches/a00200373/michael-gove-to-cambridge-university** (accessed 13 April 2013).

Gregory, I (2002) The aims of education, in Davies, I, Gregory, I and McGuinn, N (eds) *Key Debates in Education*. London: Continuum.

Hirst, PH (1965) Liberal education and the nature of knowledge, in Archambault, RD (ed) *Philosophical Analysis and Education*. London: Routledge and Kegan Paul.

Lang, P (1995) Preparing teachers for pastoral care and personal and social education: to train or educate? *Pastoral Care*, 13(4): 18–23.

Matheson, D and Wells, P (1999) What is education?, in Matheson, D and Grosvenor, I (eds) *An Introduction to the Study of Education*. London: David Fulton.

Meighan, R (2000) *Natural Learning and the Natural Curriculum*. Nottingham: Educational Heretics Press.

Meighan, R (2005) *Comparing Learning Systems: the good, the bad, the ugly, and the counterproductive*. Nottingham: Educational Heretics Press.

Meighan, R and Siraj-Blatchford, I (2003) *A Sociology of Educating*. London: Continuum.

Newman, S (1999) *Philosophy and Teacher Education: a reinterpretation of Donald A. Schön's epistemology of reflective practice*. Aldershot: Ashgate.

Papadopoulous, G (1998) Learning for the twenty-first century: issues, in Delors, J (Chair) *Education for the twenty-first century: issues and prospects. Contributions to the work of the*

*International Commission on Education for the twenty-first century*. Paris: United Nations Educational, Scientific and Cultural Organisation.

Peacock, A (2005) The emergence and characteristics of peri-formal education, Paper presented at the seminar on non-formal education, King's College, London, June 2005.

Peters, RS (1966) *Ethics and Education*. London: George Allen and Unwin.

Rowlinson, J (2012) The Internet and Children: Access and Usage. Available at **www.safekids.co.uk/childreninternetaccessusage.html** (accessed 13 April 2013).

Webb, J (1990) *Children Learning at Home*. Lewes: Falmer Press.

Wittgenstein, L (1953) *Philosophical Investigations*. Oxford: Blackwell.

Wood, K (2004) International perspectives: the USA and the Pacific Rim, in Ward, S (ed) *Education Studies: a student's guide*. London: RoutledgeFalmer.

# Chapter 2

# The mystery of learning

## John Sharp and Barbara Murphy

### Introduction

Learning is widely regarded as a lifelong activity which may occur intentionally or otherwise in a range of different learning environments, including schools, colleges, universities and the workplace. At times, of course, learning takes place with remarkable ease. Committing a simple fact to memory and being able to recall it on demand, or completing a relatively simple practical task successfully having been shown how to do it only once or twice, rarely presents much of a challenge. More often than not, however, what we are expected to learn, or indeed have to learn, is considerably difficult and requires effort. But what have we learnt if, for example, we take copious notes during a lecture and then repeat them back in an examination? Have we learnt something better if we get good grades in assessed coursework? Have we learnt anything at all if we cannot transfer our knowledge from one context to another? This chapter examines how we come to know what we know by reviewing evidence from within the fields of neuroscience, cognitive psychology and education itself. It also looks critically at learning styles and the growing use of learning style questionnaires as a practitioner-based activity in schools.

## What do we mean by learning?

According to Driscoll (2000), most authors share a common view of learning which can be defined as a *persistent change in human performance or performance potential* that cannot be ascribed to growth or maturation. Fortunately, the results of learning are often observable in the outcomes of human behaviour and taxonomies of learning outcomes are well known. Bloom's taxonomy of learning outcomes, for example, consists of six levels of activity which start with a demonstration of knowledge before working their way through comprehension, application, analysis and synthesis to evaluation (Bloom et al., 1956). The higher the taxonomic level, the more advanced the learning and intellectual challenge involved. By way of contrast, Gagné's taxonomy of learning outcomes is broader and considers learning in terms of a variety of cognitive, social, affective and psychomotor factors (Gagné, 1985). While Driscoll's definition of learning is valuable in helping to identify learning in terms of human performance and potential, it does not help to understand how knowledge is acquired in the first instance.

## Learning and the brain

The origin and acquisition of knowledge in humans has been a matter of intense philosophical debate which can be traced back at least to Plato. Historically, views have tended to fall within one of three main camps. Nativists considered all individuals to be born with the knowledge they needed and that anything else was acquired by some innate or inherited characteristic; empiricists considered all individuals to acquire knowledge from experience; and rationalists considered all individuals to acquire knowledge by engaging in reasoning. Today, individuals are considered to be born at least partly 'hard-wired' with an architecture of the mind which facilitates cognition, rather than with a mind full of knowledge *per se*. Understanding that architecture is fundamental to understanding how we learn.

Summarising from the work of Greenfield (1997), the human brain is a creamy-brown coloured organ which reaches full development in late adolescence or early adulthood. Visual inspection of the brain reveals three immediately obvious components, each of which can be identified just prior to birth.

- The cerebrum.
- The cerebellum.
- The brain stem (which runs into the vertebrae or bones of the neck and spine as the spinal cord).

The cerebrum, the outermost layer of which is referred to as the cerebral cortex, is particularly striking and consists of two almost symmetrical and highly convoluted cerebral hemispheres (Figure 2.1). These hemispheres, together with their frontal, temporal, parietal and occipital lobes, are connected by a number of inter-cortical nerve fibres including the corpus callosum. Different regions of the brain, including the sub-cortical structures hidden from view by the cerebral cortex itself, are responsible for the bewildering array of different brain functions, from the receipt and processing of information from receptors located all over the body (the sensory areas) to the co-ordination of almost every action that the body performs, voluntarily or involuntarily (the motor

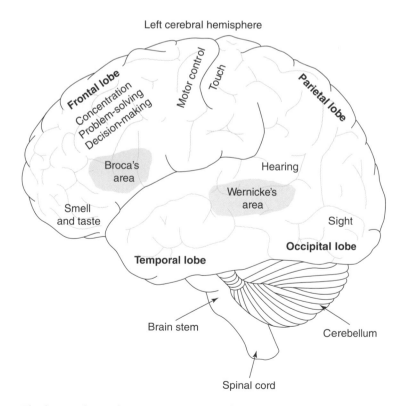

**Figure 2.1** The human brain showing main structural components and functional areas

areas). Some regions carry out combined functions that link sensory and motor information and are active when interpreting experiences, concentrating, problem-solving, decision-making and reasoning (the association areas). Brain function also determines just 'who we are'.

While the techniques available to study learning and the human brain are wide and varied, non-invasive neuro-imaging has proved particularly productive. Positron emission tomography (PET) scans, for example, have revealed that different regions of the brain are active when carrying out related but subtly different language tasks, including hearing words (Wernicke's area and the auditory cortex), speaking words (the motor cortex), seeing words (the visual cortex) and generating words (Broca's area). PET scans have also revealed that language development and comprehension are sometimes lateralised and gender-specific. That is, they involve both hemispheres of the brain in subtly different ways and to subtly different degrees in men and women, statistically at least. But knowing about which areas of the brain are active as we perform very specific experimental or laboratory tasks is one thing. Determining the exact nature of that activity and how it results in learning is something else.

According to O'Shea (2005), the adult brain as a whole, but particularly the cerebral cortex, is densely packed with cells of different types, including an estimated 100 billion neurons. Neurons come in different shapes and sizes and do different jobs. A 'typical' brain cell, however, measures less than about one-tenth of a millimetre across and consists of:

- a squat cell body or soma which contains the nucleus;
- a number of dendrites which branch out from the cell body and taper;
- a single axon which extends outwards from the cell body and ends in an array of synaptic terminals or synapses.

What appears to distinguish neurons from other cells in the human body is their ability to network with each other and communicate. This is made possible by a whole series of signals that begin with action potentials or electrical currents generated in the bodies of neurons themselves, which are then transmitted along their axons. These action potentials arrive at synaptic terminals where they stimulate the release of chemicals called neurotransmitters. As neurotransmitters cross the gap or synaptic cleft between the axon of one neuron and the dendrite of another, synapses are said to 'fire'. This electrochemical means of communication between neurons forms the neuroscientific basis of learning. Even learning a simple fact, however, is a process thought to involve not two but entire populations of neurons distributed around the brain and networked in ways that we cannot even begin to imagine. But there is little point in learning something if you simply forget it. The constant firing of synapses and the connections they make allow certain synapses to become temporarily strengthened, forming short-term memories which may last only a few seconds. Further firing, however, results in a remodelling of synapses themselves which become strengthened on a more permanent basis. The adaptability of neurons and the brain to learn and remodel itself in this way is referred to as 'plasticity'. The effects of plasticity are particularly evident in neuro-imaging studies of the brains of musicians, which reveal enhanced development in areas that correspond to how particular instruments are played (Weinberger, 2005).

Compelling as it may seem, and despite all of the advances made within the field of neuroscience in recent years, the working of the human brain is simply far too complex to formulate any sensible, practical, everyday educational application even in its broadest sense at this time. Indeed, the range of 'neuro-myths' surrounding the brain and education remain an endless source of entertainment to neuroscientists themselves (Bruer, 1997; Byrnes and Fox, 1998; Blakemore and Frith, 2002; Geake and Cooper, 2003; Goswami, 2004).

*Pause for thought* | fact or fiction?

In his book *The brain's behind it*, Smith (2002) has pointed out that it is incumbent upon educators to show responsibility to ask more precise questions of neuroscientists and their findings, and vice versa, if only to question and eradicate the great variety of neuroscientific and educational fallacies that have arisen over the years. Together with a friend or a group of colleagues, consider what you believe to be the truth or otherwise in some of Smith's examples:

- The brain cells you get at birth are those you have for life.
- There are critical periods within which specific brain development occurs.
- You use only 10 per cent or less of your brain.
- Your brain is like a sponge.
- Stress stops you learning.
- Your memory is perfect.
- Your left brain is logical, your right brain creative.
- Listening to Mozart makes you intelligent.
- Children can concentrate for only two minutes more than their chronological age.
- Male and female brains are so different we ought to teach boys and girls in different ways.

Now consider the personal and educational implications of your beliefs. Of course, not all of these statements are true ... but which ones? Would you be surprised to find out that most are actually half-truths, distortions or just plain wrong? Take a look at Smith's commentary on the matter and reflect upon the significance of his findings. For more information on this topic, consult Geake (2009) and Goswami (2008, 2011).

# Modelling memory

While the complexities of learning and memory formation at the level of the neuron are considerable, learning and memory are widely regarded as emergent properties of the human brain which can be investigated in other more readily observable ways. From a series of highly controlled laboratory-based experiments and recourse to how computers work as a suitable metaphor, the limitations of which are well understood if often overlooked, psychologists have modelled the human cognitive system in terms of at least three interconnected storage areas. These include:

- sensory memory;
- short-term or working memory;
- long-term memory.

Summarising from the work of Eysenck and Keane (2010), learning and memory formation not only involve the processing and storage of information but other features, including attention, perception, encoding and retrieval (Figure 2.2).

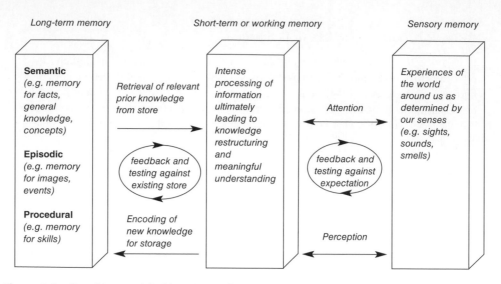

**Figure 2.2**  Cognitive model of learning and memory

In their studies of learning and memory, cognitive psychologists often explore declarative or 'knowing that' knowledge, the main focus of our attention here, using the schema construct (the cognitive psychologist's equivalent of a neuronal network). A schema of an object such as a book, for example, is an idealised knowledge package that contains all of the information elements associated by an individual with that object. Because a schema is regarded as an organising structure for knowledge, it is convenient to consider a schema's information elements to be represented in memory in terms of concepts. In classical theories of concept formation, concepts have attributes. Attributes define what it is to be a member of a concept and concept learning takes place by association (similarity, contiguity and contrast). Explanation-based views of concepts and concept formation, however, are more useful when dealing with the complexities of attributes and the relations that exist between them which together give rise to higher levels of cognitive functioning. Theories of knowledge acquisition based upon the schema construct and the semantic networks they form assume that schema are not static and that their content, the arrangement of that content and the relations between information elements change as knowledge acquisition and concept learning take place (the cognitive psychologist's equivalent of plasticity). Of course, human learning involves more than information processing. People also deal with meaning and making sense of the world and the events going on around them. Interestingly, the most influential factor affecting the rate, accuracy and effectiveness of knowledge acquisition and concept learning, including what we forget, is what a learner already knows.

Cognitive psychologists have long used information processing as a means to explore potential instructional sequences and events for teaching. According to Gagné and Driscoll (1988), as one of many possible examples, these include:

- gaining attention (alertness);
- activating motivation by introducing objectives (expectancy);
- stimulating the recall of prior knowledge (retrieval to short-term or working memory);
- presenting stimulus materials (selective perception);
- providing learning guidance (encoding and entry to long-term memory storage);
- eliciting performance (responding);

- assessing performance and providing feedback (reinforcement);
- enhancing retention and transfer (cueing retrieval).

*Pause for thought* | the condition of learning

Think of a lecture or tutorial you have attended recently, a seminar you have led, or a class you have taught. On reflection, can you identify any of the instructional events outlined by Gagné and Driscoll (1988)? Did they occur in any particular order? Consider the learning environment you found yourself in or created for others, the tasks you were asked to complete or gave others to do, and the social organisation and interactions of the people present. Can you define any effective teacher characteristics involved? What about the learners? What does all of this tell you about cognition and the condition of learning?

# Learning in an educational context

If the picture of learning painted in earlier sections seems somewhat clinical, we only have to look towards schools, classrooms and a curriculum area like science to add a little 'mess' (DEMOS, 2004). Science is a particularly valuable curriculum area to consider, as learning theory in science education has advanced far beyond the global theorists such as Piaget and Vygotsky into constructivism in a domain-specific way (Driver et al., 1994). Research into children's ideas in science education seeks to consider how children conceptualise the objects, events and phenomena of science by eliciting their knowledge and understanding of them. Much work in this area, and across the primary and secondary age phases in particular, has demonstrated repeatedly that scientific knowledge cannot be transmitted easily from one individual to another (e.g. didactically from teacher to child) but must be constructed through acts of personal and social cognition by learners themselves (Duit and Treagust, 2003). The emergent properties of knowledge acquisition and concept learning in science education are now well established.

- Children form their own ideas about the world in which they live long before any formal teaching takes place in school.
- Children's ideas frequently differ from the science taught at school and the ideas of scientists themselves.
- Children's ideas can be strongly held and resistant to change even in the most supportive, caring and stimulating of teaching and learning environments.
- Children's ideas can and do change as a result of learning science at school, but often in unanticipated ways.
- Children often share similar ideas as a result of shared experiences, the use of language and interpersonal relationships.

More importantly, perhaps, the emergent properties of knowledge acquisition and concept learning in science resonate well with the features of learning and memory presented earlier from within the fields of neurosciences and cognitive psychology and established links have already been made, if only in the broadest and most qualitative way (Anderson, 1997; Mayer, 2002).

## the chaos in learning science

Basing their work on constructivist premises, and extrapolating from the non-linear principles of dynamical systems theory and chaos, Luffiego et al. (1994) have presented an advanced schema-based model of learning science involving the evolution of a conceptual schema in order to describe the state of a learner's cognitive system before, during and after teaching or instruction. While the application of dynamical systems theory and chaos to matters of an educational nature might at first seem unusual, their extension from the realms of mathematics and computing into many other disciplines has met with some success, particularly in terms of explaining the sometimes odd behaviour and predisposition of evolving systems that tend towards disorder and unpredictability, however brief that tendency might be (i.e. learning is limited, selective and incomplete). According to Luffiego et al., the human cognitive system is an open, dynamic and non-linear system capable of selecting, storing and processing information, and this system exhibits extreme variability between individuals as a result of the sensitivity of initial cognitive states (the 'butterfly effect'). Luffiego et al. have suggested that the conceptual schema within most cognitive systems are in fact powerful information 'attractors', for they exhibit general stability and resistance to change and give rise ultimately to 'final-states' of knowledge (which emerge as children's ideas). As a result, learning science may take place along similar or widely divergent and unpredictable pathways resulting in errors and misconceptions as well as scientific conceptualisation. At the very least, Luffiego et al. have provided a new language of learning, at best a whole new paradigm within which to explore science education and other curriculum areas in new and exciting ways.

However, learning science as a process of conceptual change (or learning in any other cognate discipline for that matter) may be overly simplistic. Science at school is an intellectual, practical, creative and social endeavour which seeks to help children and older students better understand and make sense of the world in which they live. Science education involves them in thinking and working in particular ways in the pursuit of reliable scientific knowledge. If, as Driver et al. (1994) have suggested, children are to be enculturated into science, then intervention and negotiation of meaning with a teacher are essential if the tools and conventions of the scientific community are to be made fully available. As Driver et al. have also noted, *the challenge is one of how to achieve such a process of enculturation successfully in the round of normal classroom life,* particularly when *the science view that the teacher is presenting is in conflict with the learners' prior knowledge schemes* (1994: p.7). This, of course, places considerable demands on the curricular expertise of teachers. Linder (1993) has also argued from both cognitive and phenomenographic perspectives that individuals could construct a repertoire of conceptions of objects, events and phenomena ('domains of knowledge'), the one eventually chosen and used depending on the context, social, scientific or otherwise, for which it is required ('mode of perception'). Linder has proposed that learning by 'conceptual appreciation' might be more appropriate than learning by conceptual change.

But teaching, like curriculum development, is also strongly influenced by culture and ideology, not just how children learn (Millar and Osborne, 1998; Sharp and Grace, 2004). Hodson (1998), for example, has suggested that with child-centred, process-driven or discovery-led pedagogies it is often commonplace to find, say, children at school in Key Stage 1 constructing a knowledge of the world around them which is far from scientific, but that anything is allowed to count as science provided the children are working co-operatively and in a warm and friendly learning environment. As Hodson correctly noted, however, not all investigations and enquiries are scientific and not all forms of knowledge and understanding arising from them are equally valid from a scientific point of view. In secondary schools too, while it is accepted that practical work undoubtedly contributes towards securing interest, curiosity and progress in science, scientific knowledge and understanding cannot always be developed through practical work alone.

# VAK or VAK-uous?

In much the same way as metacognition, or learning how to learn, has grown in prominence as an effective learning strategy in educational circles over the years, the whole concept of learning styles has made an equally impressive recent appearance. Despite a long history and solid research pedigree from within the field of cognitive psychology, the apparent trivialisation of learning styles and their determination in schools throughout the UK is perhaps something of a concern (Sharp et al., 2008). Much of this trivialisation revolves around the notion that an individual's preferred learning style can somehow be reduced to only one of three independently assessed modalities – visual, auditory or kinaesthetic – and that this can be identified using a simple instrument in the form of a self-assessment questionnaire. More worrying is the notion that the outcome from such a simple questionnaire could then be used to inform teaching or curriculum development to better match an individual's learning needs.

Often implicit within this position is a view that working within a learner's preferred learning style will ultimately lead to improvements in various cognitive and intellectual abilities. Some sources go further, suggesting that there is a clear link between learning styles and 'multiple intelligences theory', when actually neither rests on firm foundations (Franklin, 2006), or that justification for learning styles can be found in how the brain works (Perks, 2004). In a special issue of the journal of *Educational Psychology* devoted to learning style issues, Cassidy (2004) has already pointed out that *whilst educators in all fields are becoming increasingly aware of the critical importance of understanding how individuals learn, it is equally important that any attempts to integrate learning style into educational programmes are made from an informed position*. With background provided by Cassidy and the extensive review provided by Coffield et al. (2004), we aim the following criticisms at VAK as it appears in schools to stimulate discussion and debate.

## Origin and terminology

Despite the history of learning styles research, which can be traced back through the psychology literature for some 40 years or more, the exact origin or source of derivation of VAK and VAK instrumentation used in schools remains uncertain. Indeed, the range of instruments to be found and the variation between them can be quite startling. Few have found their way into schools with any indication of provenance and few come with any literature explaining how they should be used and interpreted. Even those that do, including the commercially available VAK questionnaires found on the internet, need to be interrogated critically. While the closest learning styles questionnaire with a school-centred focus is thought to be the Learning Style Inventory, or LSI, provided by Dunn et al. (1989), this bears no resemblance to the VAK-type found in schools. Indeed, the LSI actually attempts to match an individual's preferred learning style to the emotional, sociological, physical and psychological elements of the learning environment. Not only might those setting out to investigate using learning styles be daunted at the range of models, instruments and theoretical perspectives actually available, they might be equally daunted at the confusing terminology and definitions that also exist. Of course, there are mixed views about the nature of learning styles and there is no general agreement on a definition. Dunn and co-workers, for example, define learning styles as the ways students begin to concentrate on and process, internalise and remember new and difficult academic information. Riding and Rayner (1998) have added that a learning style might equally be defined as the process used by an individual to respond to the demands of a learning activity. The VAK instruments found in schools measure none of these things rigorously.

## Validity, reliability and dimensionality

The development, design and range of applicability of all sophisticated learning styles instruments from within psychology, such as LSI, have been rigorously used and tested. Even then, the validity and reliability of some instruments remain the subject of controversy, the seriousness of which is closely related to the importance of the claims they make. From the most cursory glance at the VAK instrumentation used in schools, some questions asked of individuals would appear to probe attitudes towards learning, learning habits, learning preferences, personality traits and sociability. These are very different things. Some questions also appear to be so generally expressed as to be of little relevance to education or learning style at all. In addition to undermining validity, these features also raise doubts over dimensionality and whether or not VAK instrumentation measures one or a number of different learning attributes. The difficulty of establishing whether an individual's preferred learning style affects performance or an individual's performance affects learning style should not be overlooked.

## Universality

VAK instrumentation in schools adopts a 'one size fits all' stance. Schools and classrooms are, however, diverse learning environments filled with individuals with diverse learning needs taught by teachers with their own ideologies and philosophies of education. The demands imposed by each curriculum area are also diverse. Children in schools rarely work in isolation but in groups, and develop rapidly throughout the primary and secondary years. Most teachers and other educators agree that the choice an individual makes regarding how they approach a task is largely automatic and derived from prior experience and may vary according to each and every learning situation or context. What is less clear is whether or not such a preferred learning style remains constant over time. It would seem unreasonable, therefore, to claim that any preferred learning style made available by a single VAK questionnaire would provide any meaningful insight into any individual's needs on a day-to-day or even longer-term basis.

---

***Pause for thought*** | determine your own preferred learning style

The following questionnaire in three parts has been adapted from the work of Clark (1998). Its inclusion here is for illustration and discussion only. It should not be taken and used out of context.

Read each statement carefully and use the following Likert-type scale to score your response. Add all of the scores in each part together and record them as indicated (each part has a minimum score of 6 and a maximum score of 30). Are you a visual, auditory or kinaesthetic learner?

Score 1 – almost never applies
Score 2 – applies once in a while
Score 3 – sometimes applies

Score 4 – often applies

Score 5 – almost always applies

Part 1: visual

(a) I take lots of notes and like to doodle.

(b) When talking to someone else I have the hardest time handling those who do not make good eye contact with me.

(c) I make lists and notes because I remember things better if I write them down.

(d) I need to write down directions so that I may remember them.

(e) When recalling information I can see it in my mind and remember where I saw it.

(f) If I had to explain a new procedure or technique I would prefer to write it out.

Total score:

Part 2: auditory

(a) When I read I read out loud or move my lips to hear the words in my head.

(b) When talking to someone else I have the hardest time handling those who do not talk back with me.

(c) I do not take lots of notes but I still remember what was said – taking notes distracts me from the speaker.

(d) I like to talk to myself when solving a problem or writing.

(e) I remember things more easily by repeating them again and again.

(f) If I had to explain a new procedure or technique I would prefer telling about it.

Total score:

Part 3: kinaesthetic

(a) I prefer to start working on tasks without listening to instructions first.

(b) I take notes and doodle but rarely go back and look at them.

(c) My working space appears disorganised to others.

(d) I like to move around – I feel uncomfortable sitting for too long.

(e) If I had to explain a new procedure or technique I would prefer to demonstrate it.

(f) With free time I am most likely to exercise.

Total score:

Look at the statements again carefully. Do you think they measure learning styles or something else? Do you really think your preferred learning style can be determined so easily? Even if it could, what does your profile mean? What if it's mixed? At what point does an apparent preference actually become significant?

In learning styles research, most authors, recognising the significance of their work, do advocate a balanced and sensible approach that involves using a carefully chosen variety of teaching strategies which consider a variety of styles with the aim of providing all individuals with the opportunity to learn in different ways. But is this not just good practice? Even the most 'traditional' primary classroom provides an active learning environment with children's senses stimulated in all kinds of different ways and even the most 'traditional' lecture is more likely to be a multimedia event than a recital. At best, and within certain academic journals, some published studies involving rigorously tested psychological learning styles instruments do report improved understanding and self-reflection of individuals as learners themselves.

But the majority of such studies involve adults not children. Cassidy (2004) reminds us, *for those working within an educational setting wishing to utilise learning style to promote more effective learning, whether through individual or group profiling, design of instructional methods, or identifying learner preferences, operationalising learning style is a necessary but highly problematic endeavour.* VAK in schools, if it is ever to be taken seriously and beyond generalisation at an intuitive level, has a long way to go.

## Summary and conclusions

Learning is hard work and far from straightforward. Developments from within the fields of neuroscience, cognitive psychology and education have shed a great deal of light on how we learn and how we come to know what we know, yet at the same time confirming that learning is a profoundly complex process. While tempting, making close links between all three fields is a hazardous activity. Even when neuroscientists, cognitive psychologists and educators appear to explore similar things, they usually do so in very different ways and at very different levels of abstraction. The harsh truth is that even relevant findings from within each field are all too often ambiguous and hotly debated. Occasionally, and in our search to unlock the mysteries of learning and how best to maximise our own learning potential and that of others, we all have to be reminded at times not to simply believe, rely upon or readily accept without question what we are told. This in itself is a part of learning. Of course, what we learn and learn to do throughout a lifetime is vast, extending well beyond the simple acquisition of knowledge. Some of the many factors that contribute to this can be identified but a great many others elude us still. Even in formal learning environments such as schools, colleges, universities and the workplace, the extent to which we reach our full potential as learners is often about opportunity rather than ability, and knowing when and how to seize it. To achieve our full potential we also have to learn how to learn, to acquire good learning habits and to take or share responsibility for our own learning as well as the learning of others. There are no short cuts, no quick fixes and no magic bullets.

## References

Anderson, OR (1997) A neurocognitive perspective on current learning theory and science instructional strategies. *Science Education*, 81: 67–89.

Blakemore, SJ and Frith, U (2002) The implications of recent developments in neuroscience for research on teaching and learning. Available at **www.icn.ucl.ac.uk/sblakemore/SJ_papers/ESRCmainreport.pdf** (accessed 12 May 2006).

Bloom, BS, Englehart, MD, Furst, EJ, Hill, WH and Krathwohl, DR (1956) *Taxonomy of Educational Objectives. Handbook I: Cognitive domain*. New York: McKay.

Bruer, JT (1997) Education and the brain: a bridge too far. *Educational Researcher,* 26(8): 4–16.

Byrnes, JP and Fox, NA (1998) The emotional relevance of research in cognitive neuroscience. *Educational Psychology Review,* 10(3): 297–341.

Cassidy, S (2004) Learning styles: an overview of theories, models and measures. *Educational Psychology*, 24(4): 419–44.

Clark, D (1998) Visual, auditory and kinaesthetic survey. Available at **www.nwlink. com/~donclark/ hrd/vak.html** (accessed 1 December 2005).

Coffield, F, Moseley, D, Hall, E and Ecclestone, K (2004) *Should we be Using Learning Styles? What research has to say to practice*. London: Learning and Skills Research Centre.

DEMOS (2004) *About Learning: Report of the Learning Working Group*. London: DEMOS. Available at **www.demos.co.uk** (accessed 1 May 2013).

Driscoll, MP (2000) *Psychology of Learning for Instruction*. Boston, MA: Allyn and Bacon.

Driver, R, Asoko, H, Leach, J, Mortimer, E and Scott, P (1994) Constructing scientific knowledge in the classroom. *Educational Researcher*, 23(7): 5–12.

Duit, R and Treagust, DF (2003) Conceptual change: a powerful framework for improving science teaching and learning. *International Journal of Science Education*, 25(6): 671–88.

Dunn, R, Dunn, K and Price, GE (1989) *Learning Styles Inventory*. Lawrence, KS: Price Systems.

Eysenck, MW and Keane, MT (2010) *Cognitive Psychology*. Hove: Psychology Press.

Franklin, S (2006) VAKing out learning styles – why the notion of 'Learning styles' is unhelpful to teachers. *Education 3–13*, 34(1): 81–7.

Gagné, RM (1985) *The Conditions of Learning*. New York: Holt, Rinehart and Winston.

Gagné, RM and Driscoll, MP (1988) *Essentials of Learning for Instruction*. Englewood Cliffs, NJ: Prentice Hall.

Geake, JG (2009) *The Brain at School: educational neuroscience in the classroom*. Maidenhead: McGraw Hill.

Geake, J and Cooper, P (2003) Cognitive neuroscience: implications for education. *Westminster Studies in Education*, 26(1): 7–20.

Goswami, U (2004) Neuroscience and education. *British Journal of Educational Psychology*, 74: 1–14.

Goswami, U. (2008) *Cognitive Development: the learning brain*. Hove: Psychology Press.

Goswami, U. (2011) What cognitive neuroscience really tells educators about learning and development, in Moyles, J, Georgeson, J and Payler, J (eds) *Beginning Teaching, Beginning Learning in Early Years and Primary Education*. Maidenhead: Open University Press.

Greenfield, S (1997) *The Human Brain*. London: Phoenix.

Hodson, D (1998) *Teaching and Learning Science: towards a personalized approach*. Milton Keynes: Open University Press.

Linder, CJ (1993) A challenge to conceptual change. *Science Education*, 77(3): 293–300.

Luffiego, M, Bastida, MF, Ramos, F and Soto, J (1994) Systemic model of conceptual evolution. *International Journal of Science Education*, 16(3): 305–13.

Mayer, RE (2002) Understanding conceptual change: a commentary, in Limón, M and Mason, L (eds) *Reconsidering Conceptual Change: issues in theory and practice*. Dordrecht: Kluwer.

Millar, R and Osborne, J (1998) *Beyond 2000: science education for the future – a report with ten recommendations*. London: King's College.

O'Shea, M (2005) *The Brain: a very short introduction*. Oxford: Oxford University Press.

Perks, D (2004) The shattered mirror: a critique of multiple intelligences theory, in Hayes, D (ed) *The RoutledgeFalmer Guide to Key Debates in Education*. London: Routledge Falmer.

Riding, RJ and Rayner, S (eds) (1998) *Cognitive Styles and Learning Strategies*. London: Fulton.

Sharp, JG and Grace, M (2004) Anecdote, opinion and whim: lessons in curriculum development from primary science education in England and Wales. *Research Papers in Education*, 19(3): 293–321.

Sharp, JG, Bowker, R and Byrne, J (2008) VAK or VAK-uous? Towards the trivialisation of learning and the death of scholarship. *Research Papers in Education*, 23(3): 293–314.

Smith, A (2002) *The Brain's Behind it: new knowledge about the brain and learning*. Stafford: Network Educational Press.

Weinberger, NM (2005) Music and the brain. *Scientific American*, 291(5): 66–73.

# Chapter 3

# Approaches in the early years: issues and reflections

## Pat Beckley

### Introduction

The chapter explores key aspects of early years pedagogy and the research that informs it. Early years provision in England is undergoing significant change through the introduction of the government's Early Years Foundation Stage framework (DfE, 2012) and its accompanying EYFS profile. These aspects are considered in this chapter, which opens with a discussion of research that has impacted on views of child development and possible approaches when devising educational provision for young children.

### Research box

### children's early development

Read Keenan and Evans (2009), Chapter 5, pages 107–16. Children's development can be affected by a range of happenings. Development, while occurring throughout a person's life-span, can progress at differing rates depending on the contextual circumstances. Exciting research findings suggest babies can be affected by their surroundings soon after birth. *At six-months-old infants will be aware of and will take interest in other infants, indicated by the increased smiles, vocalizations, and gaze in the presence of other infants* (Rubin and Coplan, 1992, cited in Keenan and Evans, 2009, p.274). Children begin learning, becoming aware of familiar sounds and emotions at the earliest age. Why are the early years such a crucial period for brain development? What could happen if children are not given the stimuli they need? What implications could this have for the *School Readiness* debate, where children are required to be ready and prepared to access a school organisation?

*Pause for thought* | strategies to develop children's awareness

What strategies can be used to develop children's awareness of their world and their knowledge and understanding of it? Is it through specific tasks, the environment created, interactions with peers and adults, or a combination of these? How is the environment for learning organised? How is supervision of the areas organised? Is there free access to outdoor learning as well as indoors?

# Approaches to early years provision

Approaches to early years provision are wide and varied and are influenced by the philosophy which underpins the pedagogy and organisation of the setting. Many theorists and philosophers have considered children's learning and development, for example, Rousseau (1712–1778), Dewey (1859–1952), Montessori (1870–1952), Piaget (1896–1980), Vygotsky (1896–1934), Bruner (1915–) and Bronfenbrenner (1917–2005).

Rousseau believed that children were born good and were tainted by the influence of those around them and the experiences they have. *His ideas are based on the philosophy that humans are born free and good, but influenced by society, its conventions and through the process of socialization, and that children have a different way of thinking to adults* (Johnston and Nahmad-Williams, 2009, p.17).

Dewey felt children should be guided to help them participate in a democratic way of living. They should consider their actions and their learning. This reflected Rousseau's ideas in that he recommended the child-centred approach rather than an instructive model of learning.

Montessori suggested the approach should be child-centred but not child-led. Children progress in their learning through periods as they grow older. Children begin at a sensorial phase, through to cultural and language skills, later developing skills such as mathematics.

Piaget identified stages of development that children pass through in their cognitive development. At the *pre-operational stage* a child responds to stimuli. At the *sensori-motor* stage children develop their early ideas and begin to develop their language. The *concrete operational* stage shows a development of children's understandings of their world and the beginnings of making sense of their surroundings, linked to an ability to have concrete resources to support thinking. At the *formal operational* stage children are able to problem solve in an abstract way, mentally working out solutions.

Vygotsky identified the *Zone of Proximal Development* (ZPD), which demonstrated the potential development of children when they had access to interaction with adults. He believed language supported children's thinking and understanding and emphasised the importance of children's interactions, for example through play, to encourage their thought processes.

Bruner considered the importance of *scaffolding* children's language by pitching language at a slightly higher level than the child has to encourage further language development. *With support from the parent, scaffolding can lead the child to acquire complex language more quickly than they could on their own* (Keenan et al., 2009, p.210).

Bronfenbrenner (1979) emphasised the importance of considering the child in context. A child might be influenced by the home or other situational settings but also by those who are not in direct contact. For example, a father's workplace could have a positive impact if he enjoyed his work and responded happily at home. Cultural expectations influence what is considered important when planning how and what is an appropriate environment for children.

The context of the provision plays a part in a child's development, with approaches evolving both within the community they serve and through a growing awareness of differing pedagogies and practices which can be shared and reflected upon. Early childhood may be viewed as a time in its own right or, as a time of preparation for the future in school or, for paid work the child may enter in later life. How the adult views the child can have a significant impact on how the child learns, for example whether the adult's role is as a facilitator or instructor.

# Different models of early years provision

Among the more interesting models of early years provision are Reggio Emilia, Te Whariki and Forest Skoles.

## The Reggio Emilia approach

The Reggio Emilia approach in Northern Italy grew out of a desire to recover after the Second World War and to build a provision that would help children and families. The approach values the child as an individual and supports children's creativity and learning. Nutbrown et al. (2005, p.6) suggest: *All the adults involved in Reggio preschools and centres seem to work within and live out the same belief in children as strong, powerful and competent members of their community of living and learning together.* Children and adults work together co-operatively to undertake projects. A resident artist works with different teams to support their creative learning. Children have access to materials to enable them to work together to create their designs, art work or sculptures for their projects. The importance of interacting and sharing ideas, being prepared to explore ideas, is highlighted: *Working together, indeed, being together, is deeply rooted in everything that is Reggio* (Nutbrown et al., 2005, p.6).

## Te Whäriki

Pugh and Duffy (2010, p.42) comment on the early years framework in New Zealand where they describe the *'sensitive and relevant curriculum' that can serve the interests of children from any country or culture – a curriculum not based on subject knowledge and particular skills, but on rich, complex experiential processes involving the co-construction of social reality with people they love, who love them.* Te Whäriki is based on four principles: the holistic view of the child; the perspective of children's empowerment to learn and grow; the relationships around the child; and the importance to the child of the family and community in which the child lives.

Elements of practice from other countries can be incorporated while consideration of different ways of working can provide a means of giving objective reflections of personal practice. In this way, what is deemed appropriate continues to evolve and change in response to societal demands and reflections of practice.

## Forest Skoles

The Forest Skoles approach demonstrates the fostering of an understanding and care for the natural environment while also developing strengths in other areas, for example social abilities. Many early years settings in the UK are incorporating the philosophy of outdoor 'Forest' learning into their practice, for example through changing an existing learning environment to accommodate this aspect or visiting a neighbouring woodland area as part of the planned activities. Miller and Pound (2011, p.140) suggest: *The approach rests on the belief that the natural woodland environment provides so much that is different to the indoor environment.* It is a child-centred, child-led approach where children can explore their surroundings, their skills and abilities including engaging in imaginative play. Suitable clothing is available to enable children to access the outdoors whatever the weather.

Research box

## Forest School ethos in the UK?

Networks of practitioners and those interested in early years provision can use meetings in the locality, national or international conferences or articles and the internet to share views of practice and approaches used. Knight (2009, Chapter 7) describes incorporating a Forest School ethos into a setting in the UK. How could this be achieved? What changes to the existing environment or organisation would need to be made? Would you predict any difficulties? Would it be the same as a Scandinavian model or might there be differences?

Historically, English settings were influenced by governmental initiatives such as 'Starting with Quality' (1990) and 'Desirable Outcomes for Young Children' (1996). Directives provided a more widespread underpinning of practice through the Curriculum Guidelines for the Foundation Stage (2000) and the statutory Early Years Foundation Stage framework (2008) followed by the documentation of the revised Early Years Foundation Stage (2012).

# The revised Early Years Foundation Stage (2012)

The Early Years Foundation Stage framework (2012) combines features of Birth to Three Matters (2003) and the Foundation Stage framework (2008). The framework has responded to reviews of the Foundation Stage, such as those undertaken by Tickell (2011) to provide a basis of provision for children from birth to five. Provision has also been influenced by reviews such as the Cambridge Primary Review (Alexander, 2010, p.510), which outlined recommendations for early years including *to strengthen and extend early learning provision*. It is underpinned by discussion of what is deemed to be an appropriate approach for young children's learning and development and to form characteristics of effective learning. These have three main categories:

- Playing and exploring – engagement

  This characteristic builds on children's understandings in their exploration of the world around them. They engage with their surroundings, finding out and using an inquisitive interest to deepen their knowledge of such aspects as living things and materials that make up their world. This exploration enables them to gain an understanding of happenings and how they interact with other creatures and items. They gain an awareness of their abilities and can build on this to take risks in their play, based on a growing knowledge of their capabilities and what is happening around them.

- Active learning – motivation

  Children are intrinsically interested in the tasks they set themselves. This promotes their motivation to achieve the goals they set and resilience when faced with a problem that could challenge this. This schedule can become an important learning process where children can learn to adapt, be flexible, face setbacks and change their goals in light of their experience and findings. It can lead to a sense of fulfilment in overcoming personal challenges and resolving problems.

- Creating and thinking critically – thinking

  This characteristic draws on children's own views, ideas and plans to devise, design and organise happenings in their play. It enables them to make choices when playing with materials or ways of working which build on their previous knowledge. This knowledge can be used to develop further experiments, observing links and results.

The framework also highlights the principles for working with young children and the importance of viewing each child as unique – providing an enabling environment, positive relationships and securing access to areas of learning and development. The importance of the 'Key Person' in the young child's life, as well as the promotion of wellbeing and safeguarding, has been further highlighted in the revised documentation.

The Learning and Development section consists of Prime areas: Personal, Social and Emotional Development; Physical Development; and Communication and Language. These areas are highlighted as Prime as they are age specific. Children require access to these areas as part of their development. Difficulties would arise if children were not exposed to these areas at this early stage. In the brain, neurons send and receive electrical signals. This information is sent across the synapse. At a very early age there is an overproduction of the neurons and synapses. Keenan and Evans (2009, p.110) claim this *allows experience to dictate which connections between neurons are kept and which connections are lost, thereby ensuring that the child acquires all of the skills and information required to enable development to take place.* However, if the neurons and synapses are not used, there is thinning in which the brain disposes of those not used. The brain has *plasticity,* which to some extent may compensate for early difficulties. *Development is often comprised of multiple abilities which take different types of change or constancy* (ibid, p.8). Hence the crucial nature of ensuring a child has access to the Prime Areas of Learning and Development at this early age.

The Specific Areas of Learning and Development consist of Literacy, Mathematics, Understanding the World and Expressive Arts and Design. Although these are highly relevant to a child's development, wellbeing and progress, they are not so dependent on being age-related. If they are not addressed sufficiently in the early years they can continue to be developed later. The Areas of Learning and Development are covered from birth to 60 months in Development Matters, culminating in the Early Learning Goals (ELGs). They are implemented through a play-based approach.

---

***Pause for thought*** | EYFS

Read the outline of the Early Years Foundation Stage framework (DfE, 2012a) and Early Years Foundation Stage Profile (DfE, 2012b) through accessing the Department of Education website: **www.education.gov.uk/publications**. Access to the non-statutory guidance material which supports practitioners in implementing the statutory requirements of the EYFS can be found at the Foundation Years website (**www.foundationyears.org.uk**). Information can also be accessed through the British Association for Early Childhood Education at **www.early-education.org.uk**

---

## ICT in the early years

ICT is becoming an increasingly important aspect of everyday life. Alongside direct experiences, children can access a variety of information through the internet. Increasingly, the internet has become part of children's everyday lives via accessible hardware like tablets, PCs and mobile phones. Children become familiar with their use as they have ready access to devices and can incorporate them into their repertoire of skills. New technological equipment can enable children to develop their IT skills, for example with the use of child-friendly camera equipment or Beebots. Sites can be accessed to provide support for ideas for children, such as RM Colourmagic, Mouse Music or Natural Art. Specific products like *'Flying Colours'* or *'Izzy's Numbers, Izzy's Island'* can be purchased and products appropriate for small fingers obtained, such as a small-sized mouse. Further safeguards have been put in place in the revised framework to ensure children are safeguarded from what they might access inadvertently. (See Chapter 18.)

# A play-based approach to learning

Classical theories of play include the *recapitulation* theory where children rehearse the activities of our ancestors, for example 'play' fighting; the *surplus energy* theory where children can experience a release of energy as they run and exercise; the *relaxation* theory where children can relax and recharge their energy levels; the *practice* theory where children can rehearse roles they may take in later life, for example the role of a parent caring for a child or a nurse caring for a patient.

Play-based learning enables children to experience different roles and situations. The experiences children have enable them to form 'schemas'. Nutbrown (2011, p.15) emphasises the importance of schemas: *Schemas, or repeatable patterns of behaviour, speech, representation and thought, can extend learning as they become fitted into children's patterns of thought. Early schemas provide the basis for later learning.* In the early years, play is used as the means of learning.

The adult role can vary depending on the culture within the setting, for example it might be adult-led, adult-initiated, child-initiated or a combination of different ways of working depending on the context. For example, a combination of interactions may be incorporated in activities such as making a house from construction materials or clothing for teddy, and child-initiated to follow up their ideas and build on their learning. In Norway, child-initiated play was observed in the natural forest environment. Children explored the branches and woodland fixing together natural materials, making such articles as dens, shelters, homes or resources for a story. Adults did not take a lead role in the settings observed. They waited for children to attempt to make their creations only supporting when asked or when it was felt advisable. They let children make their own mistakes and learn from them, whether it was climbing a tree or putting the roof on a 'house'. In this way they learned about their own skills and what they could achieve so far.

While children are playing they are developing a range of skills through their interactions with others and their own reflections. They can consider their experiences in the home or their world, consolidating their understanding of cultural happenings around them. They learn to interact socially–giving way, taking turns, becoming a leader or follower with their friends. They can practise their physical skills from fine motor skills when mark making or cutting to gross motor skills when balancing or climbing. Adults can lead the play, model a role-play part, assess the learning taking place or interact with the children being part of the play.

Play can be a motivating and stimulating way of working, providing opportunities for children to develop their schemas and their understanding of the world around them. For example, a group of children discussed their visit to a farm the previous day. They developed their play into the small world area, designing a farm using small blocks and populating the farm with the small farm animals available. The children discussed the positions of the separate pens, huts and fields, how many animals were in each area and which animals should be placed in them. Were the areas big enough for the animals? What would they need? They used their actions in their play to practise and rehearse their thoughts and considerations about what they had seen.

# Transitions

Transitions between settings, such as the home, a child-minder, a private nursery, Children's Centre, school early years setting or Key Stage 1 in school should be managed to maintain children's self-esteem and confidence and to enable a smooth transition to occur. *Being aware of, and managing appropriately, the effect that transition events may have on the feelings of the children in our settings is central to supporting them* (Allingham, 2012, p.4). Key elements of the Early Years Foundation Stage framework highlight aspects necessary for these adjustments. Aspects such as the role of the Key Person can support children's development to foster smooth transitions for children.

The assessment for two year olds, introduced in 2012, ensures children are given any support they may need for their wellbeing and development and provides useful information for those involved in the welfare of the child. It provides a useful check and feeds into an awareness of each child's development. It can be used to assess any intervention strategies that may be required.

The Early Years Foundation Stage Profile (DfE, 2012b) forms a summative assessment at the end of the Reception year. It comprises 17 aspects based on the Early Learning Goals of the EYFS in which a child's level of attainment might be met, working towards or exceeded. This results in a judgement of 'expected', 'emerging' or 'exceeding'. They were revised following Dame Tickell's recommendations as chair for an independent review of the EYFS in March 2011.

*The earliest years in a child's life are absolutely critical, providing the essential foundations for healthy development. If these foundations are not secure, children can experience long-term problems which often present wider social consequences. Children's attainment, wellbeing, happiness and resilience are profoundly affected by the quality of the guidance, love and care they receive during the first years of their lives.*

(Tickell, 2011, p.2)

The revised Early Years Foundation Stage Profile (DfE, 2012b) gives practitioners the opportunity to use their professional expertise to form a judgement about a child, backed by relevant evidence. The two-year assessment and EYFSP provide summative assessments based on on-going formative assessment used to support the child throughout their early years and to gain a picture of the unique child, their interests, strengths and areas they find challenging.

## Research box

### some questions about schemas

Nutbrown (2011, p.13) consider schemas as patterns of behaviour and thinking in children and as *babies suck and grasp, they rehearse the early schematic behaviours which foster their earliest learning. Early patterns of behaviour seen in babies become more complex and more numerous, eventually becoming grouped together so that babies and young children do not perform single isolated behaviours but coordinate their actions.* These actions become *established foundations of learning.* Read Nutbrown (2011), Chapter 2: 'Some questions about schemas'. Consider how schemas young children are learning can be identified. How could the schemas be recorded to gain a deeper perspective of the child as unique?

**Pause for thought** | approach to learning

Consider an approach to learning for young children that you have observed. Is the adult the facilitator, instructor or do children and adults learn together? What strategies were used to keep track of children's development? Are the findings readily available to discuss with others involved with the child?

# Issues concerning early years

Changes in early years provision reflect many factors such as financial constraints, differing views concerning appropriate learning environments, how children learn and practicalities of implementing frameworks within a variety of settings. These issues impact on practitioners who may need to juggle responsibilities for such items as cost of space with an awareness of providing a high-quality learning environment for their children. Funding for Children's Centres or for additional space in a nursery class can be additional considerations when planning for provision. New initiatives, such as the incorporation of a natural woodland area in the outdoor area require carefully organised action plans. Staffing of the facility requires consideration, including extra budgets for professional development. The Nutbrown Review, Foundations of Quality (2012), gave 19 recommendations on early education and childcare qualifications. These aimed to improve the quality of the early years sector and ensure all children receive an appropriately high standard of education and care. The minimum requirements for qualifications for those working with young children were proposed. A framework for progression in early years towards leadership was proposed and the importance of a high-quality environment emphasised.

# Qualifications for staff

Those working with children in their early years will know what a demanding but rewarding task it is. It requires a professional outlook where adults seek the best interests of their children and use their judgements and experience to enable them to do this for each child as a unique person. The Oxford English Dictionary (2013) states professionalism denotes a person who is *worthy of or appropriate to a professional person; competent, skilful, or assured...* This professionalism underpins a variety of qualifications enabling practitioners to work with young children. It combines academic qualifications with a practical ability to implement policies within a code of care.

*Change, complexity and uncertainty are part of life in the 21st century and practitioners and those leading and managing practice need to be able to reflect on and respond to what this means for the children and families they work with and the environments in which they work, both at micro and macro level.*

(Miller and Pound, 2011, p.149)

Early years professionals are equipping children with the foundations of enabling children to make their own way in the changing world. Curtis and Pettigrew (2009, p.39) state: *The combined impact of plurality, fluidity, fragmentation, uncertainty and complexity is the erosion of taken-for-granted authority.* Professionals working with young children need to help them to make sense of the child's world and to be able to have sufficient resilience to face the challenges they may encounter.

To be able to do this challenging work, practitioners need to be able to access professional development to maintain their skills and keep up-to-date with new initiatives and how to implement them. Nutbrown and Page suggest:

*Young children need professional educators who take advantage of opportunities to stretch their own minds – who engage in critical reflection on their own practice and participate in professional development programmes. The younger the children, the more crucial it is that their close adults are informed, alert, attentive and informed, as well as loving, caring, sensitive and reflexive.*

(Nutbrown and Page, 2008, p.176)

A variety of qualifications are used within the early years sector – aimed at a variety of stakeholders within relevant settings. Proposals are in place for an Early Years Teacher, who would be trained specifically for this age phase.

---

### *Pause for thought* | adult:child ratios

In 2013, the government proposed to increase the number of children supervised by one adult. However, following representations from those involved with early years care and learning the proposal was dropped and existing ratios maintained. It was felt a higher number of children supervised by an adult would not help the quality of provision accessed by the children. Where a person with Qualified Teacher Status, Early Years Professional Status or another suitable Level 6 qualification is working directly with the children, the following requirements apply:

- There must be at least one member of staff for every 13 children.
- At least one other member of staff must hold a full and relevant Level 3 qualification.

England's current ratios consist of:

Under one and one-year-olds – 1:3;

Two-year-olds – 1:4;

Three-year-olds and above – 1:8 or 1:13 (teacher-led).

The proposed changes suggested a rise of 1:4 for under one and one-year-olds and 1:6 for two-year-olds.

What do you think are appropriate adult:child ratios? What leads you to these conclusions? How do you interact with the children? Do you allow them to take the lead in their thinking, guide them or instruct them?

### Summary and conclusions

This chapter provides an overview of some of the many issues facing practitioners in early years settings, the challenges they experience and the crucial nature of work with young

*(Continued)*

*(Continued)*

children. Being part of young children's lives requires among many qualities, patience and a desire to support young children's learning and development. Deliberations continue about the best ways forward for early years provision, including child-adult ratios, qualifications for staff and the age the Foundation Stage covers. Some educationalists, for example the Cambridge Primary Review (Alexander, 2010) and the Nutbrown Review (2012), suggest the age phase should be raised to six or seven years respectively. Whatever the outcome, the importance of these early years is indisputable. Provision for early years reflects society's aspirations and shapes our collective future.

## References

Abbott, L and Nutbrown, C (eds) (2005) *Experiencing Reggio Emilia: Implications for pre-school provision*. Maidenhead: Open University Press.

Alexander, R (ed.) (2010) *Children, Their World, Their Education*. Abingdon: Routledge.

Allingham, S (2012) *Transitions in the Early Years: A practical guide to supporting transitions between early years settings and into Key Stage 1*. London: Practical Pre-School Books.

Beckley, P (ed.) (2012) *Learning in Early Childhood: A whole child approach from birth to eight*. London: Sage.

Bronfenbrenner, U (1979) *The Ecology of Human Development*. Cambridge: Harvard University Press.

Curtis, W and Pettigrew, A (2009) *Learning in Contemporary Culture*. Exeter: Learning Matters Ltd.

DfE (2012a) *Statutory Framework for the Early Years Foundation Stage: Setting the standards for learning, development and care for children from birth to five*. Available online **www.education.gov.uk/publications/standard/AllPublications?Page1/DFE-00023-2012**

DfE (2012b) *EYFS National Curriculum Assessments: Early Years Foundation Stage Profile Handbook*. Available online **www.education.gov.uk/eyfsp**

Johnston, J and Nahmad-Williams, L (2009) *Early Childhood Studies*. London: Pearson Longman.

Keenan, T and Evans, S (2009) *An Introduction to Child Development*. London: Sage.

Knight, S (2009) *Forest Schools and Outdoor Learning in the Early Years*. London: Sage.

Miller, L and Pound, L (eds) (2011) *Theories and Approaches to Learning in the Early Years*. London: Sage.

Ministry of Education and Research (2006) *Framework Plan for the Content and Tasks in Kindergartens*. Norway: Ministry of Education and Research.

Moyles, J (ed) (2010) *Thinking About Play*. Maidenhead: Open University Press.

Moylett, H and Stewart, N (2012) *Development Matters in the Early Years Foundation Stage: Non-statutory guidance*. London: Early Education

Nutbrown, C (2011) *Threads of Thinking: Schemas and young children's learning*. London: Sage.

Nutbrown, C and Page, J (2008) *Working with Babies and Children; From birth to three*. London: Sage.

Nutbrown, C, Hannon, P and Morgan, A (2005) *Early Literacy Work with Families: Policy, practice and research*. London: Sage.

Oxford English Dictionary (OED) (2013) **http://dictionary.oed.com** (accessed June 2013).

Pugh, G and Duffy, B (eds) (2010) *Contemporary Issues in the Early Years* 5th edition, London: Sage.

Tickell, C (2011) *The Early Years: Foundations for life, health and learning: An independent report on the Early Years Foundation Stage to Her Majesty's Government.* London: Her Majesty's Stationery Office (HMSO).

# Chapter 4

## Schools and classrooms

### Denis Hayes

**Introduction**

We take the existence of schools and classrooms for granted, but those of today bear little resemblance to the earliest types of education provision. The present system, in which a group of pupils works with a qualified teacher and, perhaps, a teaching assistant, has evolved down the years and is now seen as the best way to educate large numbers of children and students at manageable cost to the taxpayer. The curriculum has also changed markedly from a concentration on a narrow range of subjects to a more expansive one, in which pupils are not only encouraged to learn facts but also to understand and think for themselves. Tests and examinations have always been used as a means of monitoring progress; they have assumed great significance recently, not only in assessing how each individual is faring but, more controversially, as a measure of how well teachers are teaching. In the present day, the debate centres around four key areas: (1) the introduction of different types of 'free' schools and academies; (2) so-called 'marketisation', in which education is viewed as a commodity; (3) narrowing of the curriculum, especially in the primary 5–11 years phase; and (4) increased emphasis upon testing of pupils and assessing of teacher competence. In this chapter, we explore the trends and features of previous forms of education to learn the lessons of the past and thereby gaining a better understanding of what is happening in schools today.

## The growth of formal education

### Educating 'the masses'

The formal education of pupils in Britain has its roots deep in history and is inextricably linked to the growth and mission of the Christian Church. For a long time, there were very few schools, colleges, universities or centres for academic learning available to the general public, or 'the masses' as they were sometimes described. For the small number of children from wealthy backgrounds who had access to schooling, many received an education rooted in Latin. This form of schooling became known as 'grammar' education, from which the term 'grammar school' emerged.

During the industrial revolution, the plight of children working in factories and mines became a serious political and social issue. Pioneers such as Robert Raikes, who founded the Sunday School movement in 1780, Charles Gordon, who built 'ragged schools' to educate and provide sustenance for the destitute, and Charles of Bala in Wales were determined to provide a basic education for these child labourers. The Quaker, Joseph Lancaster, and, some time later, the priest Andrew Bell, promoted a system of elementary schooling in which more experienced and capable pupils ('monitors') would help to teach the younger and less able scholars. This 'monitorial' system required a small number of teachers and became a means of providing mass education for working-class children, though some of the teachers were only marginally better educated than the pupils.

## Publicly-funded education

The first publicly-funded schools were established in the mid-1800s to give a basic education to children from poor families. Throughout this time, control of education gradually switched from the Church to the state, though provision was uneven and there was acrimonious debate about which of the two bodies should have the greater influence over its organisation and curriculum (Chadwick, 1997).

One of the key political figures determined to extend state provision of education in the first half of the nineteenth century was James Kay-Shuttleworth. He not only founded training colleges for teachers but also encouraged newly founded Board Schools (funded from taxation) and voluntary schools to widen the curriculum beyond reading, writing and arithmetic (the so-called three Rs).

As the nineteenth century progressed it became increasingly clear that government intervention would be needed if education were to become universally available. However, there was genuine anxiety expressed by many sections of society about the adverse impact on the economy of removing children from the workplace and sending them to school each day. Employers were concerned about labour shortage, and poor parents, often with large families to feed, were worried about the loss of earnings, a tension that continues in impoverished nations today.

A feature of schooling during the mid- to late-nineteenth century was the 'payment by results' system that was introduced in 1861 and persisted until its abolition in 1895, by which the government gave a grant to a school based on the assessment of each child's academic ability and attendance. Teachers felt obliged to introduce rote learning and drill the pupils to absorb factual knowledge. After the abolition of 'payment by results', the curriculum was extended in many schools to include a wider range of subjects and teaching approaches. It is interesting to note the similarity with schools today, where teachers are expected to ensure that pupils meet pre-specified 'standards', the same term that was used in the 1800s. It is also noteworthy that an emphasis upon mastery of facts and regular testing remains a contentious issue, not least in respect of the development of early reading skills.

Between 1846 and 1848, the Welsh Education Committee and the Cambrian Society were formed, which evolved into national schools in Wales. The 1867 report of the Royal Commission on Education led to the Education Act of 1872 that resulted in improvements in education for every child in Scotland. In the period preceding the setting up of the state of Northern Ireland in 1920, education became one of the areas of tension between Ulster unionism and Irish nationalism. Before partition, the overwhelming majority of Irish schools were under denominational control, even though they were financed chiefly from public funds (Harris, 1993).

Meanwhile, in the face of considerable opposition, and as a means of guaranteeing education free of charge for all pupils, WE Forster introduced the important 1870 Elementary Education Act in England. At that time, the government's obligation was principally to 'fill the gaps' where voluntary provision did not exist. Reforms were slow in being implemented and even at the commencement of the twentieth century schooling was inconsistent and attendance spasmodic. Paradoxically, however, there were more three- and four-year-old children attending school at the end of the 1800s than there were about 100 years later. With singing, hand-work, games and dancing, the infant curriculum around the start of the twentieth century was surprisingly innovative.

## Secondary and further education

Secondary and further education also has its roots in the mid-1800s. Politicians were increasingly concerned that Britain's lack of competitiveness in the world was due to a skills shortage, this resulted in an increasing emphasis on vocational education and training – an issue that has re-emerged during the twenty-first century. At the same time, the Education Act of 1902 ushered in three key changes.

1. Education came under county council control.
2. Money from local rates was made available to voluntary schools.
3. Councils were empowered to fund secondary education.

These changes were revolutionary for two reasons: (a) public funds were made available for education for the first time; and (b) secondary education was formally established. Indeed, the year 1902 can rightly be described as the birthday of secondary education. Important, too, was the fact that voluntary schooling that had dominated the nineteenth century was struggling to cope with the increasing demand for education. Without state financial intervention the school system would have collapsed.

In 1918 the school leaving age was raised to 14 years. A few years later, the influential Hadow Report (1926) gave official sanction to the principle that the elementary phase of education in England should formally conclude for all children at age 11 (to be known as the 'primary' phase), followed by separate provision of secondary schooling. There were many important Education Acts over the following years, most notably the highly influential Butler Act of 1944, which introduced the following statutory requirements that have, with minor changes, remained in force to the present day.

- The appointment of a Minister for Education in England and Wales.
- Local authority funding for secondary as well as primary schools.
- Raising the school leaving age in stages from 14 years to 15 years to 16 years.
- The requirement for schools to hold an act of worship.
- Free medical (including dental) care for all pupils.
- Education provision for pupils with special learning needs.
- Payment for all teachers according to a nationally agreed scale.
- The prevention of schools from debarring or dismissing a female teacher when she gets married.

*Pause for thought* | contrasting 'then' and 'now'

Look again at the summary of reforms drawn from the Education Act of 1944. Consider the similarities and differences between the conditions for teachers in 1944 and today. Are there any surprises? Note that female teachers did not receive equal pay until 1955 and, until the 1970s teachers' salaries were similar to those received by manual workers. Was the post-war period really the 'golden age' in the way that it is sometimes described?

## Curriculum developments

Between 1944 and the early 1980s there was a series of curriculum developments, including a major extension of so-called 'sandwich' courses (periods of study in the middle of regular employment), and the establishment of a Schools Council. A major school-rebuilding programme was undertaken and the comprehensive (all-ability, non-selective) secondary schools made their appearance. A limited number of more academic pupils was able to gain free places in a grammar school if they passed an examination at the age of 11 years (the so-called 'eleven-plus'). This policy led to divisions of pupils across the country on the basis of ability, and was the subject of intense political debate that has continued to the present time. Pupils who did not sit or failed the examination could only gain access to a secondary modern school or to the newly founded technical schools for children of average ability who were considered more suited to practical rather than academic work.

In 1965, an additional external examination (the Certificate of Secondary Education or CSE) was introduced for pupils in the middle ability range for whom the traditional Ordinary level examination (O level, introduced in 1953) was too demanding. The O level and CSE examinations were combined in 1986 to create a new national secondary examination known as the General Certificate of Secondary Education (GCSE) in England (equivalent to the TGAU or Tystysgrif Gyffredin Addysg Uwchradd in Wales and the Standard Grade in Scotland). The GCSE is usually taken by secondary school pupils at age 16, though more able children may sit the examination earlier.

### Research box

### gender issues in schooling

On the basis of their research, Miller and Davey (2005) argue that too little emphasis was placed on the role of women and girls in the past and that debates about citizenship and liberal democracies underpinning education theories about schools were too patriarchal ('male-dominated'). To what extent is the modern-day secondary school operated from what may be broadly described as a male perspective? How is the situation different in primary schools where a large majority of staff is female? What are the possible implications for pupils and their learning of male or female dominance on the staff?

# Introduction of a National Curriculum

In the mid- to late-twentieth century, primary teachers had great liberty in making decisions about what to teach and how to teach it. Secondary teachers were governed more strictly by syllabuses and national examinations but were not normally under pressure to adopt specific teaching approaches. The freedom that teachers enjoyed to organise learning in a way that suited classroom circumstances was considered to be an essential element of their professional autonomy (Harrison et al., 2005; Hurst and Reding, 2006).

By the mid-1970s there had been very few studies about the aims of education from the teacher perspective, a notable exception being Ashton et al. (1975). There was also a dearth of research about 'school effectiveness' and 'school improvement' (see Harris and Hargreaves, 2013, and articles published in the journal *School Effectiveness and School Improvement*).

The famous (some would say, infamous) Ruskin College speech by the then Prime Minister, James Callaghan, in 1976 was yet to unleash what was grandly titled 'The Great Debate' about the future of education. There was an increasing political awareness, however, about the large amount of public money that was being spent on education and the need for rigorous accountability.

One of the most significant events that emerged out of this wide-ranging review of educational provision was the 1988 Education Reform Act (ERA) and a National Curriculum (NC) that would operate in all state-maintained schools and many private ones in England, Wales and Northern Ireland (through the Department of Education in Northern Ireland or DENI). The NC was designed to provide a minimum educational entitlement for pupils of compulsory school age, to ensure that the curriculum of each school was balanced and broadly based, and to promote the spiritual, moral, cultural, mental and physical opportunities, responsibilities and experiences of adult life.

Though broadly welcomed by teachers, some educators were anxious about the 'one size fits all' aspect of a national curriculum and its likely impact on teachers' independence. As the first NC became statutory, it soon became clear that the content was unmanageable, especially for primary teachers, and the imposition of associated reforms led to the coining of a new expression to describe the experience of teachers attempting to implement these rapidly changing political priorities: *innovation fatigue*.

Prior to 1988, schools had been able to make their own decisions about curriculum provision at a local rather than a national level, but the NC curtailed this freedom. In addition, education provision was divided into four key stages:

Key Stage 1 (KS1) for pupils aged 5 to 7 years;
Key Stage 2 (KS2) for pupils aged 7 to 11 years;
Key Stage 3 (KS3) for pupils aged 11 to 14 years;
Key Stage 4 (KS4) for pupils aged 14 to 16 years.

Another significant dimension of the NC was the introduction of pupil assessments by means of national tests at the end of each key stage, with KS4 work assessed by levels of pupil achievement through the GCSE examination. Having completed GCSEs, pupils have a choice of whether to continue with further education at school or college or to seek a job, though the government has used a variety of incentives to encourage students to remain in full-time education after the age of 16.

Since its introduction in 1989 there has been a number of versions of the NC with considerable emphasis placed on the teaching of English (literacy) and mathematics (numeracy) at primary level, and the development of information technology (IT) at both primary and secondary levels. In 1999, a *Foundation Stage* curriculum was published for children aged 4 and 5 in nursery and reception classes. Pupils with special educational needs received particular attention and additional resources.

## Changes to Key Stage 3

In the early years of the twenty-first century, the lower end of secondary education (KS3) became the focus of increased attention, as it was perceived that standards of attainment levelled out once pupils left primary school. The KS3 curriculum now consists of English, mathematics, design and technology, ICT, history, geography, modern foreign languages, art and design, music, PE and citizenship. Other areas of the curriculum that must be taught are religious education (RE), sex and relationships, and careers' education (from Year 9). All schools must teach RE according to the locally agreed syllabus, unless they are designated as voluntary-aided or faith schools.

A detailed critique of KS3 in the *14–19 Education and Skills* White Paper (DfES, 2005) had noted that some programmes of study were incoherent and content was repeated in different subjects. The heavily prescribed curriculum left schools with little space to assist struggling pupils or to extend gifted students. Consequently, science, history, geography and design and technology now receive extra attention, with an emphasis on real-life issues. The KS3 strategy is properly referred to as the *Secondary National Strategy* as some of its work extends to KS4.

# Increased political intervention

## Government involvement

A feature of the education system in recent years has been what is seen by some educationalists as an over-simplification of complex educational issues in political debate (e.g. Alexander, 2004; Walford, 2008; Richards, 2013). Education priorities have moved a considerable way from the time of the Taylor Report in the mid-1970s when a key characteristic of teachers' professionalism was deemed to be their freedom to design and teach unhindered by external pressures (Taylor et al., 1974). Astonishingly, at the time, surveys of teachers concluded that they believed that politicians were the least influential people in school life. By contrast today, political priorities are now imposed, promoted, scrutinised, implemented and closely monitored.

The government's insistence that schools and teacher training institutions follow its educational agenda has resulted in a situation where failure to comply with its demands invites sanctions for the schools and colleges concerned. At the same time, the amount of school-based training, as opposed to college-based, has gradually increased in recent years, with the trend likely to accelerate (White and Jarvis, 2013).

Every institution, from those providing childcare for the under-fives to the largest higher education establishment, has its education provision closely monitored. A poor inspection outcome can result in closure. Success in reaching the required targets for examination success, on the other hand, results in increased resources, public accolades and the possibility of salary enhancements for staff.

## From autonomy to compliance

The government's desire to exercise tight control has created a situation in which teacher professionalism has largely changed from autonomy to compliance (Hayes, 2001; Groundwater-Smith and Mockler, 2009). It is difficult for schools to avoid being sucked into an attitude of deference that threatens to stifle teachers' creativity. Frowe (2005) reasons that while the amount of money invested in education necessitates accountability and monitoring of practice, the over-regulation of the profession stifles initiative.

It quickly became evident that the attempt to telescope all teaching and learning situations into a single model relevant to every pupil in every class was not sensible or sustainable. Circumstances from school to school and class to class are so diverse that it is difficult to justify a policy that takes little account of the immediate choices and decisions that all teachers have to make every working day. As a result, successful schools are now permitted a degree of flexibility over the curriculum, though national tests and examinations remain the yardstick for evaluating school success, and adverse local circumstances (e.g. inner-city poverty or rural deprivation) cannot be used as an excuse for poor results.

---

***Pause for thought*** | the impact of 'value-added'

To combat the argument that schools in more affluent and socially stable areas are unreasonably advantaged over schools in so-called 'deprived' areas, a system of 'value-added' was introduced, by which a school had to demonstrate that pupils were not only meeting the required standards but also that its overall performance was improving year upon year. In other words, schools are not only broadly competing with one another but each school is, in effect, 'competing' with itself.

- What factors that are beyond a school's immediate control might jeopardise its year-on-year improvement?

---

### Research box

## teacher satisfaction

Data from the 2011 *Trends in International Mathematics and Science Study* (TIMSS) and *Progress in International Reading Literacy Study* (PIRLS) carried out by the NFER reveals teacher satisfaction in England is among the highest in the world, with teachers reporting levels of career satisfaction similar to, or higher than, those of teachers in the highest achieving countries and rating their working conditions positively.

- What aspects of teaching motivate you?
- What are the disincentives?

---

# Educational initiatives at the start of the twenty-first century

The late twentieth and early twenty-first centuries saw great changes take place in the way that education is organised and monitored. The KS2 primary curriculum has become more subject-focused with the introduction of fixed duration lessons. Secondary education has also undergone a transformation, including the founding of specialist and so-called 'beacon' schools, and more private involvement in the state sector.

A vocational GCSE was introduced in 2000 to encourage students to take a work-related route at school and includes courses such as engineering, applied business, and leisure and tourism. In September 2004, the word 'vocational' was dropped to show that the vocational side of learning was equivalent in status to the academic side. Some schools have encouraged their pupils to progress straight to A-level (disregarding GCSE) or to take the international baccalaureate diploma.

# Exams and testing

The appropriateness and relevance of testing and examinations continues to be actively debated among educationalists, in particular the suitability of formal tests for young children and the need for a public (national) examination for all pupils at the age of 16.

In the primary sector, there has been a rediscovery of the significance of play in the education of younger children (Broadhead et al., 2010; Briggs and Hansen, 2012) and creativity in learning (for primary perspectives see Desailly, 2012; Fumoto et al., 2012). A decision about using 'synthetic phonics' – a system based on teaching children letter sounds so that they recognise the different components within a word – see for example, Waugh and Jolliffe (2012) – together with regular testing of young children to ascertain mastery of key words as the core strategy in teaching reading and spelling to be employed in schools, has provoked a sceptical response from teachers, some of whom fear that reading will become mechanistic.

# Expansion of school types

Until the last few years, a variety of mainstream schools have been operating within the state education system in England and Wales:

- *Community schools*. The local authority (LA) employs staff, owns the school land and buildings, and determines the arrangements for admitting pupils.
- *Foundation schools*. The governing body employs staff and has primary responsibility for admissions. The school land and buildings are owned by the governing body or a charitable foundation.
- *Voluntary aided schools*. Most of these schools are church schools. The governing body employs staff and has responsibility for admissions. The school land and buildings are owned by a charitable foundation.
- *Voluntary controlled schools*. The same conditions apply as pertain in aided schools, except for the important provisos that the LA employs the staff and has responsibility for admissions.

During the second decade of the twenty-first century, the government introduced greater flexibility into the system by encouraging the growth of a larger number of schools that were independent of the local authority and autonomous with regard to teaching staffs, budgets and curriculum. See 'Current changes in education provision' later in this chapter.

# Primary reviews

In 2009 both the Primary Review (Alexander, 2009) – an independent study led by Robin Alexander – and the Primary Curriculum Review (Rose, 2009) – a government-sponsored report led by Jim Rose – reported their findings. The Primary Review (PR) identified the purpose the primary phase of education should serve; the values it should espouse; the curriculum and learning environment it should provide; and the conditions necessary to address the future needs of children and society. The Primary Curriculum Review (PCR) advised on how the primary curriculum should change to ensure all children gain a good grounding in reading, writing, speaking, literacy and numeracy; offer schools greater flexibility of choice about content and delivery; allow time for a foreign language; place greater emphasis on personal development; support a smoother transition from play-based learning to formal learning; and encourage creativity.

The Alexander Review provoked strong reactions in the education community, both in favour of, and sceptical about, its conclusions and recommendations – see, for instance, contrasting perspectives by Campbell (2011) and Armstrong (2011). In the event, however, neither the PR nor PCR were significantly influential in determining Coalition Government education policy after its establishment in April 2010.

---

Research box

## the EPPE 3–11 project

The Effective Pre-School and Primary Education (EPPE 3–11) project in the UK (2003 to 2008) was a major longitudinal investigation into the effects of pre-school education on children's developmental outcomes at the start of primary school (Siraj-Blatchford et al., 2008). The study tracked 3,000 children from the time they started pre-school until they reached 11 years of age. Four key questions were explored during the project:

1. Do the effects of pre-school continue into the upper stages of primary education?
2. What are the characteristics of effective primary classrooms and schools?
3. Who are the resilient and the vulnerable children in the EPPE sample?
4. What is the contribution of 'out-of-school learning' (homes, communities, internet) to children's development?

One important but predictable result was that the better the *home learning* environment, pre-school and primary school, the higher academic results children achieve.

---

Research box

## Secondary National Strategy

The Secondary National Strategy (SNS) for school improvement formed part of the government's major reform programme for transforming secondary education and was intended to encourage young people to attend and enjoy school, achieve personal and social development and raise educational standards in line with the *Every Child Matters* (ECM) agenda (DfES, 2004; see also Barker, 2009). The five outcomes of the ECM agenda are as follows: being healthy; staying safe; enjoying and achieving; making a positive contribution; and securing economic wellbeing. The aim of the SNS is to create a dynamic and diverse education system built on high expectations and a commitment to the needs of every learner.

---

Research box

## vocational learning for 14- to 16-year-olds

In their study of the effectiveness of the Increased Flexibility for 14- to 16-year-olds Programme (IFP) to provide vocational learning opportunities at Key Stage 4 for those young people who would benefit from them, Golden et al. (2005) found that around 90 per cent of young people who had been involved in the first cohort of IFP had continued into further education or training post-16. Some 42 per cent of young people said that their participation in vocational learning had influenced their decision about their post-16 education futures. Note that from September 2013, teenagers continue in training for at least 20 hours a week until they reach the age of 17, the figure rising to 18 in 2015.

# Current changes in education provision

A number of significant changes have taken place in education provision recently, not least increased autonomy for Wales and Scotland in allocating budgets and determining curriculum priorities, facilitated by their respective parliaments. However, many of the most profound changes have taken place in England.

## Academy schools

An academy school is directly funded by central government and, in England, is independent of direct control by the local authority. Most academies are in secondary education, but some cater for children from nursery age upwards. All academies have a curriculum specialism within the English Specialist Schools Programme (SSP). The number of schools with academy status has increased over recent years with a changed emphasis from the original plan of being a fresh start for so-called 'failing schools' to being a reward for schools deemed very successful.

As part of plans to diversify schools provision, *technical academies* are seen as a way of improving the quality of vocational education, including increased flexibility for 14–19-year-olds. *Studio schools* are small schools, typically with around 300 pupils, offering students a path to mainstream qualifications through project-based learning. Students work with local employers and a personal coach, and follow a tailored curriculum designed to give them the skills and qualifications they need for work or further education.

## Free schools

In September 2011, the first *free schools* opened. Free schools are non-profit making, independent, state-funded schools, established in response to demand within a local area. The schools are subject to the same Ofsted inspections as state schools and are expected to maintain the same standards. There has been considerable opposition from some quarters to the principle of free schools, which opponents have described as fragmenting education provision.

## Trust schools

*Trust schools* are defined as state-funded foundation schools that receive extra support (usually non-monetary) from a charitable trust made up of partners working together for the benefit of the school. Business corporations have been particularly active in providing such support.

## Federations

At primary and secondary levels there has been a move towards the creation of 'federations', a term used to describe different types of collaborative school groups, partnerships and clusters, including mergers and the creation of new schools. Clusters involve groups of schools with a formal agreement to work together to raise standards, promote inclusion, and find new ways of approaching teaching and learning. In many instances the aim is facilitated through a governing body having responsibility for two or more schools.

## Faith schools

Since 1944, faith communities of different types have been able to apply to set up schools in the state sector in response to demand from parents. Today, around a third of maintained schools have a religious character and are usually referred to as 'faith schools'. Faith schools are popular with parents and typically achieve high standards of behaviour and academic results.

### Research box

## teachers in faith schools

Research by Francis and Robbins (2010) found that different priorities are given to the aims of religious education by teachers in faith schools, depending on three key factors: (a) *personal factors*, such as age, sex and church attendance; (b) *professional factors*, such as years teaching, qualifications and continuing professional development; and (c) *contextual factors*, such as the type of school in which they work.

- How might the above factors influence teachers' priorities and teaching approach?
- To what extent are the three factors relevant to *every* school situation?

# The revised primary curriculum 2013

The latest version of the NC for primary schools (2013) provides for some flexibility in curriculum provision for schools deemed successful by Ofsted inspectors. However, concerns have been expressed about the dangers of 'teaching to the test' and thereby failing to explore areas of learning that are not subject to examination, in particular 'the arts', using the imagination, innovation, teamwork and study of the local environment.

The new Programmes of Study (PoS) for primary English, mathematics and science have been made more demanding in terms of subject knowledge and conceptual difficulty. Equally controversial was the decision to make PoS for subjects other than English, mathematics and science much shorter, in the belief that schools will have greater flexibility to set high expectations for these subjects and tailor the curriculum to best meet the needs of their pupils.

Learning a foreign language is now compulsory at Key Stage 2, based on the claim that there is evidence suggesting that children are better able to learn the sounds of new languages when they are younger. Schools can offer a classical language, such as Latin, as an alternative to a modern foreign language.

Other changes included removing the current system of levels and level descriptors. The new programmes for English, mathematics, science and physical education commence in September 2014.

### Summary and conclusions

Governments of every persuasion continue to take a deep interest in education provision. The positive consequence has been an improvement in its continuity and coherence across the country. The adverse consequence has been constraints on teachers' ability to exercise professional judgement about what is appropriate for their pupils. There is also some anxiety about the way in which the climate of testing and inspecting has developed at the expense of attending to the social needs of children and young people (Goodman and Burton, 2012).

Regardless of government edicts or externally imposed requirements, your personal framework of values is of crucial significance, as learning is powerfully influenced by the attitudes and behaviours fostered by teachers: *explicitly* through the curriculum, and *implicitly* through interactions and the quality of relationships (Mowat, 2010). Every survey about teachers that are most popular with pupils reports that in addition to maintaining discipline and enthusiasm, the list of desirable attributes invariably includes being approachable and personable, preferably with a good sense of humour.

Winning the hearts and minds of pupils has been the challenge and inspiration for every teacher since schooling began and will, hopefully, remain at the core of what happens in schools and classrooms for the foreseeable future (Aggleton et al., 2010; Starrat, 2012). It will be up to you, as one of the new generation of teachers, to make sure that it does.

## References

Aggleton, P, Dennison, C and Warwick, I (2010) *Promoting Health and Wellbeing Through Schools*. Abingdon: Routledge.

Alexander, RJ (2004) Still no pedagogy? Principle, pragmatism and compliance in primary education. *Cambridge Journal of Education*, 34(1): 7–33.

Alexander, RJ (2009) *Children, their world, their education: final report and recommendations of the Cambridge Primary Review*. Cambridge: University of Cambridge/Esmee Fairburn Trust.

Armstrong, M. (2011) Curriculum, pedagogy and the Cambridge Review: a response to RJ Campbell. *Education 3–13*, 39(4): 357–61.

Ashton, P, Davies, F and Kneen, P (1975) *Aims into Practice in the Primary School: A guide for teachers*. London: University of London Press.

Barker, R. (ed) (2009) *Making Sense of Every Child Matters: multi-professional practice guidance*. University of Bristol: Policy Press.

Briggs, M and Hansen, A (2012) *Play-based Learning in the Primary School*. London: Sage.

Broadhead, P, Howard, J and Wood, E (2010) *Play and Learning in the Early Years*. London: Sage.

Campbell, RJ (2011) State control, religious deference and cultural reproduction: some problems with theorising curriculum and pedagogy in the Cambridge Primary Review. *Education 3–13*, 39(4): 343–55.

Chadwick, P (1997) *Shifting Alliances: Church and state in English education*. London: Cassell.

DfES (2004) *Every Child Matters: Change for children*. London: Crown Copyright.

DfES (2005) *14–19 Education and Skills*. London: Department for Education and Skills.

Desailly, J (2012) *Creativity in the Primary Classroom*. London: Sage.

Francis, LJ and Robbins, M (2010) Teachers at faith schools in England and Wales: state of research. *Theo-Web*, 1(2): 141–59.

Frowe, I (2005) Professional trust. *British Journal of Educational Studies*, 53(1): 34–53.

Fumoto, H, Robson, S, Greenfield, S and Hargreaves, DJ (2012) *Young Children's Creative Thinking*. London: Sage.

Golden, S, O'Donnell, L, Benton, T and Rudd, P (2005) *Evaluation of increased flexibility for 14- to 16-year-olds programme: outcomes for the first cohort* (DfES Research Report 668). London: Department for Education and Skills.

Goodman, R and Burton, D (2012) What is the nature of the achievement gap, why does it persist, and are government goals sufficient to create social justice in the education system? *Education 3–13*, 40(5): 500–14.

Groundwater-Smith, S and Mockler, N (2009) *Teacher Professionalism in an Age of Compliance*. New York: Springer.

Harris, M (1993) *The Catholic Church and the Foundation of the Northern Irish State*. Cork: Cork University Press.

Harris, A and Hargreaves, A (2013) *Schools Performing Beyond Expectations*. London: David Fulton.

Harrison, JK, Lawson, T and Wortley, A (2005) Mentoring the beginning teacher: developing professional autonomy through critical reflection on practice. *Journal of Reflective Practice*, 6(3): 419–41.

Hayes, D (2001) Professional status and an emerging culture of conformity amongst teachers in England. *Education 3–13*, 29(1): 43–9.

Hurst, B and Reding, G (2006) *Professionalism in Teaching*. Upper Saddle River, NJ: Pearson.

Miller, P and Davey, I (2005) Family formation, schooling and the patriarchal state, in McCulloch, G (ed.) *The RoutledgeFalmer Reader in the History of Education*. Abingdon: Routledge.

Martin, MO, Mullis, IVS, Foy, P and Stanco, GM (2012) *TIMSS 2011 International results in science*, Chestnut Hill, MA: TIMSS. & PIRLS. Internation Study Centre, Boston College.

Mowat, JG (2010) He comes to talk to me about things. *Pastoral Care in Education*, 28(3): 163–80.

Mullis, IVS, Martin, MO, Foy, P and Arora; A (2012) *TIMSS 2011 International results in mathematics*, Chestnut Hill, MA: TIMSS. & PIRLS. International Study Centre, Boston College.

Richards, C (2013) Primary teaching: a personal perspective, in Arthur, J, Grainger, T and Wray, D (eds) *Learning to Teach in the Primary School*, 3rd edn. Abingdon: Routledge.

Rose, J (2009) *Primary Curriculum Review*. London: HMSO.

Siraj-Blatchford, I, Taggart, B, Sylva, K, Sammons, P and Melhuish, E (2008) Towards the transformation of practice in early childhood education: the effective provision of pre-school education project. *Cambridge Journal of Education,* 38(1): 23–36.

Starrat, RJ (2012) *Cultivating an Ethical School*. Abingdon: Routledge.

Taylor, PH, Reid, WA, Holley, BJ and Exon, G (1974) *Purpose, Power and Constraint in the Primary School Curriculum*. Basingstoke: Macmillan Education/Schools Council.

Twist, L, Sigmur, J. Bartlett, S and Lyn, L. (2012) PIRLS 2011, *Reading achievement in England*, Slough: NFER.

Walford, G (ed) (2008) *Education and the Labour Government*. Abingdon: Routledge.

Waugh, D and Jolliffe, W (2012) *Teaching Systematic Synthetic Phonics in Primary Schools*. Exeter: Learning Matters.

White, E and Jarvis, J (2013) *School-based Teacher Training*. London: Sage.

# Chapter 5

# The curriculum

# Clive Hedges

## Introduction

The boundaries of the term 'curriculum' are notoriously difficult to define and it sometimes seems that everyone, from academics to politicians, have sought to police them. Current discussions in England about the place of climate change in the national geography curriculum, for example, illustrate the political nature of the subject. In areas of the world such as Spain or Ireland, where political identity has been a source of intense, and sometimes violent, political clashes, the place of minority languages in the curriculum, or the content of history teaching, can become proxies for long-standing social divisions. Curriculum is a potentially complex and politically charged topic, even in its narrow sense of 'what children should be taught'.

Curriculum as a term, however, can mean more than the topics of study. As the often heated debate about literacy teaching and the benefits of synthetic phonics in Britain illustrates, it can include a centrally directed approach to aspects of pedagogy. It can encompass means of formative and summative assessment and suggest explicitly or implicitly, particular models of learners and the cognitive process of learning. In this wider sense, curricula become very important documents for the educator. If they are followed slavishly, as a method, they potentially stifle and distort the educational experience by taking away some of the professional autonomy of the teacher. However, if they are treated as a code to be deconstructed, they might be a framework for revealing the way in which knowledge is constructed. With this awareness, curriculum can be planned as a framework for students to construct knowledge for themselves, with the aid of the teacher.

How can we understand some of the contemporary pressures on our curricula and what the effect might be on us as teachers to help us use a curriculum in a creative fashion? This chapter will examine some of the current issues facing educators, relating them to long-standing areas of educational debate in an attempt to understand the current state of 'the curriculum'.

There are a number of tasks to help you deconstruct a curriculum, understand its underlying assumptions and the influences that have shaped it. Then we can recognise the cultural and political history that has shaped content and the educational thinkers that have helped inform approaches to delivery and assessment.

*Pause for thought* | a closer look at the curriculum

While reading the chapter it would be useful to have a copy of an example curriculum to consider in the light of some of the questions being posed and research being looked at. For the purposes of this activity consider curriculum to be composed of:

- the full guidance for a programme of study, including the purpose of study;
- the attainment targets;
- the content of study;
- the skills and abilities to be learnt and tested and the means of testing, such as a copy of a test paper, for example.

Copies of these, if they are not readily to hand, are easily available on government and other websites such as: **www.education.gov.uk/schools/teachingandlearning/curriculum** for the English National Curriculum, or **www.australiancurriculum.edu.au** for Australia, **www.ncca.ie/en** for the Republic of Ireland or **www.scotland.gov.uk/Topics/Education/ Schools/curriculum**, for Scotland.

Have a look at the curriculum pages on such a website and download a copy of the programme of study. Assessment papers for the programme of study, if they are not included in the curriculum, should also be readily available on websites such as **www.sats-papers. co.uk** or the equivalent.

Study the different components of the curriculum and consider how it is structured and the links between the different component parts.

- Do you think the subject content reflects the aims clearly?
- What social and political values are reflected in these aims and are they obvious in the content?
- Can you think of other areas of content that could have been included and, if so, why might they not be?
- Do the assessments test all of the attainment targets or do they appear to prioritise some over others?
- Are the attainment targets, or learning outcomes, concerned with skills and abilities or attributes? Or both?
- Are the attainment targets specific to that subject or might some of them cut across subject areas?
- How clear is the curriculum about the previous learning students will be expected to have done or about what the next steps of learning might be afterwards?

# What is a curriculum for?

It should become clear as you read this chapter that the various aspects of the curriculum cannot be understood in isolation from one another, that it is not enough to see your chosen curriculum as merely a syllabus or selection of topics. If this were the case, how could this selection be justified to others and what would the clear purpose of learning this syllabus be?

The concept of a curriculum only makes sense, and it can only be planned, if it is recognised as part of wider debates about the purpose of education. It is this contextualisation that enables us to understand, and possibly contest, as Basil Bernstein (1971, p.47) put it, *what counts as valid knowledge*.

## Curriculum as a transmitter of culture

The issues above come very much into focus when government and educational bodies undertake a curriculum review, but they have always been a central concern of curriculum theory. Early modern attempts to define and systemise concepts of curriculum were very much concerned to give it a function in modern society. Medieval ideas of what and how to teach were replaced in some countries with a 'scientific' view of the purpose of curriculum, partly based on an analysis of what suited children for the world of work, of which more later, and partly on what was considered to be suitable for developing social consensus. A purpose of education was to, as Franklin Bobbitt (1876–1956), an early and influential American curriculum thinker, put it, develop *certain social attitudes, valuations, criteria of judgement* (1918, p.131). This suggests the role of curriculum to be a form of 'socialisation', in line with the views of functionalist sociologists, such as Emile Durkheim.

More influential in Britain was the thinking of Victorian reformers, such as Matthew Arnold (1822–1888), who believed the curriculum should transmit what is 'best' about a culture, which is to say, its pre-eminent thinkers, artists and major achievements. Perhaps partly as a result of this, Britain has been something of a late, and slightly unenthusiastic, convert to ideas of citizenship education.

Both of these positions, of course, assume a consensus about what social values and attitudes should be, or something close to a consensus, such as a foundational set of values, and, of course, this is not necessarily the case. Society and culture are heterogeneous and dynamic entities – that is, they have a dizzying number of sub-groups and are constantly changing. Culture is the site of power relationships put into forms of representation, in images and narratives, which portray social types seen as representative of wider elements of society. Any selection of historical figures or literary texts for study becomes a form of enacting these wider power relationships. Culturally insensitive selection can become a means of further alienating the already marginalised, by failing to include representations meaningful to them or, even worse, propagating negative stereotypes of them. The teaching of, for example, the history of colonialism as the 'discovery' by Europeans of other 'primitive' societies; or the uncritical use of texts in the study of English literature, such as Joyce Carry's *Mister Johnson* or Joseph Conrad's *Heart of Darkness*; or the use of 'Third World' examples to foster a sense of charity and global awareness.

Michael Apple (2004), among others, has argued convincingly that curriculum is actually a site of fairly obvious ideological struggle. A quick glance at a contemporary curriculum can give us a snapshot of what can be seen as the evidence of struggles over 'valid knowledge' and the ways in which this represents changing balances of power in society.

The currently proposed English programme of study for Key Stages 1 to 3 History (DfE, 2013) is a good example of how conceptions of 'national' culture and identity in a modern, self-consciously, multi-cultural society reflect political and social change. The aims of the programme repeat, apparently uncritically, the idea that there is a 'British people', indeed a 'coherent, chronological narrative' of 'Britishness', built around ideas of progress, parliamentary democracy and empire. The subject content, however, shows a much more contested and varied notion of identity. The subject content covers the role of the socially marginalised in shaping historical change within the UK, from abolitionist Olaudah Equiano and Victorian nurse Mary Seacole to the social activist Annie Besant, for example. It then highlights leaders of national liberation movements, such as Nehru in India and Kenyatta in Kenya, perhaps illustrating a curriculum anxious to mention the 'best' and 'most eminent' figures of communities from outside the ethnic majority.

*Pause for thought* | wider purposes

As well as choosing a curriculum from a government website or an educational setting, make a short list of your own priorities for teaching a particular subject at a particular level. Beginning with a sentence or two, or a number of phrases, sum up what the wider purpose(s) of studying the subject at that age might be; is it a stepping stone to another curriculum or does it have aims and values that are valid by themselves? Then make a quick list of the most important topics to be covered, the main types of activity you would use and think about an appropriate way for a teacher to decide whether or not the child has learnt what you would want them to learn.

## Research box

### where should children be citizens of?

Education 'reform' is often Janus-faced in its desire to uphold past cultural traditions while reacting to clamour for 'modernisation'. Contemporary education reviews generally propose to both inculcate an understanding of 'national identity' and prepare future generations to be members of a globalised world. Is there a contradiction here?

Research has suggested that curriculum reform worldwide does tend to follow common patterns. This can be the case in terms of content, where ideas of globalisation have led to more focus on notions of wider human cultures and society and issues of politics and science affecting the globe as a whole, not just the nation state (Meyer, 2006). It can also be the case in terms of organisational principles, becoming less content driven and more focussed on learning outcomes, driving forwards conceptions of an individualised learning and teaching experience (Rosenmund, 2006).

Governments are also now profoundly aware of international comparisons of the relative 'performance' of educational systems made by organisations like the European Union and the Organisation for Economic Cooperation and Development, although many question the validity of such performance tables (Dunn and Goddard, 2002). Is the inclusion in curricula of global issues and a promotion of awareness of others across the world then a sign of fostering genuine 'global citizenship' or is it more to do with preparing children to be part of an international workforce? (Schattle, 2006).

## Curriculum as a stepping stone

If curriculum planning does not start with content where else might it begin? While Bobbit, and other later thinkers, such as Ralph Tyler (1949), saw cultural transmission as an important aspect of curriculum planning, this wasn't their starting point. If education was to be approached 'scientifically', it was argued, then this meant there had to be valid and reliable testing and this is only possible if there are a set of testable learning outcomes/objectives/

attainment targets (the jargon may change but the meaning is essentially the same) set out as the curriculum aims. Otherwise, they argued, testing would be unfair and evaluation of the curriculum impossible.

In contemporary education it may be seen as a truism by many that programmes of education must have some idea of pre-set outcomes, something to test the understanding of the learner against, to see if their learning can be accredited and, if so, at what level. However, beginning planning your curriculum with the outcomes has been criticised for a number of reasons. It could suggest that the predispositions, the feelings and interests of the learner are irrelevant. What counts are the learning outcomes and the need to, cognitively or behaviourally, 'mould' passive learners. This is perhaps too simplistic a criticism but it does point us towards two other major problems with this idea of curriculum planning.

First, it suggests that curriculum is experienced in a fairly straightforward linear fashion, moving through a set of tasks that build in some kind of stacking system, towards a final test in which the achievement of the whole will be demonstrated. This further suggests that knowledge simply progresses from the basic to the complex and questions of the basis of that knowledge are essentially technical ones. It is no surprise, perhaps, that this placing of discrete blocks of knowledge in a hierarchy, to be learnt in a linear process, arose at a time when the Fordist production-line model had come to be seen as the most efficient means of organising labour in both manufacturing and office work.

Second, it suggests that the purpose of the curriculum is a purely instrumental one, either the gaining of a certificate or a progression on to the next level of learning. Education, in this scenario, is not about learning for its own sake or the creation of knowledge for oneself. It does not enable us to discover, by focussing on the means and activities used to learn, but shackles us to a predestined outcome, ensuring we are focussed on the summative test that will ensure success.

## Research box

### at what age should children start school?

One area of curriculum planning where there has been debate about the influence of learning outcomes has been in early years education, for example, in the English Early Years Foundation Stage (EYFS). There have been concerns that a focus on school readiness can be at odds with a curriculum that should be focussed on learning through play. The use of convergent learning outcomes emphasises target achievement, potentially marginalising some and positioning assessment more as an evaluative tool, than as an aid to learning. Many early years educators have suggested that a child-centred approach needs to include a divergent model of assessment, based on learning potential and teachers assessing with, rather than on, children (Nutbrown, 1998; Claxton and Carr, 2004; Broadhead, 2006).

The movement towards a formalised curriculum for early years in Britain was characterised by an interest in grounding policy in research evidence, notably the Effective Provision of Pre-School Education (EPPE) study (Sylva et al., 2010) and Researching Effective Pedagogy in the Early Years (Siraj-Blatchford et al., 2002). Transition between early years and formal education, with the move from play-based learning to more adult-directed, structured and regulated teaching environments, was seen as assisted by a gradual phasing-out of one and phasing-in of the other at an appropriate age. However, some have suggested that this is

*(Continued)*

*(Continued)*

based on a misreading of what is an appropriate age and that in other countries children are given a further two years to adapt to formal teaching (Wood, 2013, pp.53–4).

Concerns about transition and the use of such summative assessments on children at such a young age may well be fed by recent research suggesting that there are large differences in educational attainment between children born at different stages of the academic year and that these differences are most marked at an early age (Crawford et al., 2013). If this is the case, how useful are standard summative assessments as evaluations of learning or of the curriculum?

Transitions from one stage of education to another may be less stark as children develop but there are common issues. In Spain, for example, Ramesal (2007) has suggested that education reforms have led to different conceptions of assessment dominating in primary and secondary education, although not in a simple, even fashion, but nevertheless with structuring influences on pedagogy.

If a curriculum is to make sense to a learner, not just the teacher, then it would seem logical that it needs to be seen as part of a bigger sequence covering children's development as learners.

**Pause for thought** | curriculum's place in the wider system of education

Look back at your curriculum of choice and its place in the wider educational system. How much explicit referral to previous stages of learning and teaching are there in your curriculum and do these relate to content, skills or abilities? Will students arriving to undertake this course of study have experienced the same types of pedagogy, assessment and level of depth of the subject? What needs to be built into your curriculum to make sure all students have the ability to interact with the knowledge and skills being taught and are there assumptions being made about learners?

In countries where there is a national curriculum one might assume a 'natural fit' between stages of education but what if, for example, a student body arrives to take a specialist science programme with some of them having previously completed a specialist course in the subject and others having done a broad-based science course, covering subjects by themes? Alternatively, what if they arrive at your secondary school to study a foreign language and the children's experience ranges from relatively deep to almost no experience of foreign language teaching at all, or to a solid foundation of learning but in another language altogether?

How much control should government have over curriculum and how much should be left to the teacher? Relaxing centralised control of education and having a less prescribed curriculum in England was one of the early promises of the Conservative-led Coalition government. In your own idea of a curriculum how rigid was it and what were the pointers to its own place in a wider sequence?

# Curriculum and employment

The final stage of development for formal curricula is usually now seen as preparing the learner for employment. In secondary, further and many parts of higher education, a key word for evaluating the suitability of curriculum is increasingly 'employability', that is, how much does the world of learning prefigure the world of work?

In the last 20 to 30 years, education policy in the UK, and many other countries, has been dominated by ideas of curriculum design led by 'aims' – aims that encapsulate skills and aptitudes and suggest particular types of content, delivery and assessment (Whitty, 2010). This arose from concerns with global economic competitiveness and the need for 'flexible' and 'lifelong' learners to take part in a global 'knowledge-based economy' (DfEE, 2001). In the UK this was evidenced by government papers proclaiming knowledge to be 'the predominant part in the creation of wealth', a line of thinking that eventually led to the notion of 'personalised learning' (Robertson, 2005). This, in theory at least, downgraded the old Fordist model of institution first, and learner second, and put in its place an idea of independent learners, with tailor-made programmes of study and assessment. This discourse of education has been criticised for its hyperbolic language, over-inflated claims and lack of attention to detail about what a school system or national curriculum would look like in such a situation (Peters, 2001). Some suggest as well that it lacks much resemblance to the actual world of work for most people, where being 'flexible' often means accepting contractual precariousness and fluctuating wages, rather than being given the chance to be intellectually challenged.

What does it mean for curriculum and teaching? One research project in Australia found that a growing emphasis on vocational skills contributed to the parallel existence of different concepts of education, especially evident in the curriculum through models of assessment (Yates, 2009). In vocational education assessment is often based on the idea of competency, and learners are assessed according to whether they fulfil a standardised idea, by those who already possess this competency, as evidenced by their professional status. In traditional schooling accreditation is gained through numeracy and literacy, accredited, in a clearly graded fashion, through examinations. The result, according to this research, was a tendency to a lack of coherence in pedagogical approaches, unsurprisingly, given:

*the unmanageable array of different kinds of agendas about knowledge, change and the purposes of schools without providing a new way of conceptualising pedagogy or curriculum.*

(Yates, 2009, p.26)

The British government recently announced the commencement in September 2014 of a *technical baccalaureate*, supposedly placing vocational education in England on an equal footing with traditional 'academic' qualifications (Adams, 2013). This is a portfolio of qualifications, rather than a coherent single curriculum, professing to tackle the long-standing issue of the low status of vocational education in the country. This, it is suggested, is to be done through completion of a three-part portfolio. Alongside qualifying in one of an approved range of vocational qualifications, there is to be a post-16 mathematics qualification, not necessarily at the traditional level needed for entry to specialised science courses in higher education, and 'an extended project'. This last part of the qualification echoes elements of past national vocational qualifications in the way it talks of 'skills in extended writing, communication and research' linked to education for employment purposes, notably through some kind of accreditation of 'self-motivation' and 'self-discipline'. This is in line with the way some employers now seek to ensure not just compliance in the workplace, but willing compliance, evidenced and monitored through the employee's performance of a corporate identity (Southwood, 2011).

# Curriculum as a process

The EYFS can be seen as an example of a centralised curriculum very much concerned with the child that lies beyond its own boundaries, in this case when they enter formal schooling. Even in the recently revised version, this is reflected in a structure influenced by traditional subject boundaries and a clear focus on testable, convergent outcomes, in a hierarchical organisation of knowledge, skills and understanding. This is perhaps the result of planning through a learning outcomes first approach. However, it is useful to note that there will always be other ways of planning easily found in other parts of the world and this is certainly the case in the early years. In New Zealand the national curriculum from birth to 5 is called Te Whäriki (available at **www.educate.ece.govt.nz/learning/curriculum AndLearning/TeWhariki.aspx**), Maori for a woven mat, so called because the curriculum is supposed to be a holistic interweaving, or web, of principles and goals, expressing also the complex interweaving of individual and society. This is a way of seeing the curriculum not as a linear, stepped process but as organised more by themes and on the basis of child-centred learning.

This leads to the consideration of a central tension in curriculum planning: balancing a central framework with learner-centred knowledge and skill-building experiences. In New Zealand the compromise is evident in the way the curriculum enables local and culturally diverse approaches to meet children's interests and needs, but does this within a clear developmental sequence (Soler and Miller, 2003). Some have seen this as an inherent tension when curricula are planned on socio-constructivist models of learning, as developed by theorists such as Vygotsky.

Te Whäriki is a good example of the attempt to, at least partly, design curriculum as a process. Rather than starting with a prescribed idea of content or a set of learning outcomes, or some combination of the two, it aims to place the nature of the individual child and their development at the heart of planning. The activity of learning, rather than the programme content, dictates the nature of learning and teaching. What does this mean for the planning of the curriculum? The idea of curriculum reflecting the process of learning, that is, being a process based on the learner being involved in the construction of ideas, not just as their recipient, owes much to Dewey's (1997) ideas of learning through experience, and concepts of socio-constructivism, embodied in the work of thinkers like Vygotsky and Bruner (Pritchard and Woollard, 2010). The notion of curriculum as able to embody this was most fully developed by Lawrence Stenhouse (1975).

Stenhouse suggested that curriculum planning needed to be explicit about the underlying principles that shaped it, the principles behind the content, sequencing, models of learners and learning and the principles for evaluating it. Furthermore, all these principles should be concerned with the development of the learner. This focus on the learner also places a focus on the teacher as it necessitates an interpretation of the learner's needs as they are presented, rather than a pre-set idea of their disposition or a disregard for the learner's co-creation of knowledge. Curriculum, in this conception of it, is inevitably a loose set of guidelines, allowing considerable room for interpretation of both content and assessment. However, a loosely detailed curriculum is not, in itself, a sign of planning based around the gradual development of the learner.

Research box

## how can information technology change the curriculum?

There are few topics that have generated as much research and as many academic articles in the recent past as the role of new technology in the curriculum. ICT, we have been told, will transform pedagogy, or even change the way children learn. There are obviously transformational possibilities in new technology, software can offer the chance of combining different types of conceptual and sensory data and provide new methods of peer learning and interaction, for example. It can also, potentially, some say, be a tool for thematic learning and integration of the curriculum; basing knowledge building on problems and issues identified by the child and the educator (Toren et al., 2008). Others have suggested that focusing on pedagogy when increasing the use of ICT in the classroom can mean new technology acts as a support for developing a process-driven curriculum (Jones, 2007).

So, is a process-driven model common to curricula approaches to ICT? The current draft guidelines for the computing programme of study in England are, in line with other draft programmes, primarily structured by a combination of content and learning outcomes. Some may point to the provision for choice around problem solving, or the provision of tasks designed to display individual creativity, as signs of growing central awareness of the need to be less prescriptive on the part of government. Others may see this as a continuation of what Kelly (1999, p.71) described as curriculum based on *a view of teaching as the transmission of knowledge*, still dictated by an essentially ideological discourse about the role of ICT in education, driven by wider economic, rather than educational, concerns (Selwyn, 2008).

---

*Pause for thought* | curriculum issues

Consider the curriculum you have been using. What is the model of the learner embedded in it? Does the curriculum suggest a pre-set, hierarchical structure of outcomes and content or is it more exploratory? Will formative assessment be led by the curriculum, the teacher, or carried out through a partnership between the teacher and the student? Is the curriculum clear in its principles of planning and evaluation?

Considering these issues should enable you to think about how much room there is for the teacher to be creative in their approach to the curriculum and how much of their pedagogy is going to be structured by the curriculum from the start. It also enables you to think about what the curriculum's attitude to the learner is and thus read off what its underlying theory of learning is. Does the curriculum give room for co-construction of knowledge through negotiation of problem-solving tasks and assessment criteria for the success of these tasks? Does it place content in a wider context of understanding the subject's development and the means of creating knowledge in that subject area? Would you see it as essentially behaviourist or constructivist in its approach?

Compare and contrast this with your own ideas about content, activities and assessment that you drew up at the beginning of the chapter and the underlying theory of learning you prefer.

# Curriculum and school governance

Alongside the creation of national curricula in many countries there has been a supposed loosening of centralised control through the creation of financial independence for schools, such as the creation of 'academies' and 'free schools' in England. Some have argued that this causes problems for the whole idea of a national curriculum, as more and more schools are given the 'freedom' to opt out of these provisions (McCormick and Burn, 2011). In fact, not surprisingly, given the 'high-stakes testing' regime of Ofsted, in England few take this opportunity and, even among those that do, a radical approach to curriculum is rare.

How is curriculum evaluated in this type of education system? It is not generally evaluated by the teacher, or the learner, but by a centralised process according to standard criteria. This enables comparisons between institutions in league tables, published reports and achievement statistics – a model more obviously used to hold schools and teachers to account, rather than develop the curriculum. This is a type of control of education not restricted to Britain but related to dominant models of 'neo-liberal' regimes across the globe (Lingard, 2010).

It should be acknowledged that more learner-centred approaches to curricula evaluation are far from problem free, after all a ready-made model of outcome achievement is not available in this model. Stenhouse suggested that the answer lay in evaluation through research leading to curriculum development, so that there is a continuous cycle of evaluation involving both learner and teacher. Kelly (1999) suggests this form of evaluation as the democratic polar opposite of the autocratic regimes of compliance and ranking organised through centralised government regulation systems, such as Ofsted. Letting go of the purse strings does not, it would appear, necessarily mean letting go of the power to define 'valid knowledge'.

*Pause for thought* | evaluation

How would you evaluate your curriculum and what role, if any, would you give the learner in this? Should evaluation be focussed on achievement of outcomes, and success at accreditation, or should it have purposes beyond the ranking of learners, institutions and teachers? Can evaluation be an educational activity in itself, enabling teachers and students to (re)consider their approaches to learning and teaching and take a further step towards personal and social development?

One form of evaluation is through a process of negotiating the curriculum, involving the student in, for example, decisions on assessment practice. In this model the curriculum includes student evaluation of performance and the learner has an invaluable and inherent place in its development (Hart et al., 2004).

## Summary and conclusions

This chapter has focused on current areas of educational concern through the prism of the curriculum. Many of these issues arise from a consideration of the starting point for curriculum planning and whether this should be content, outcomes or the development of the learner. In reality, most curricula include elements of all three, but in most models one of these, or a combination of the first and second, is dominant and can be seen to structure the overall approach. This dominant influence will be spread throughout the whole approach to curriculum, including assessment, approaches to pedagogy and evaluation. Understanding this illustrates the inevitably political nature of the topic, which is to say that a study of any given curriculum has to include an understanding of the wider social context that has shaped it.

## *References*

Adams, R (2013) Michael Gove to unveil A-level alternative – the 'tech bacc'. *The Guardian*, Monday 22 April, [Online] Available at: **www.guardian.co.uk/education/2013/apr/22/ michael-gove-unveils-tech-bacc** (Accessed at: 10.05.2013)

Apple, M (2004) *Ideology and Education*, 3rd edn. London: Routledge.

Bernstein, B (1971) On the classification and framing of educational knowledge, in Young, MFD (ed) *Knowledge and Control: New directions for the sociology of knowledge*. London: Collier-MacMillan.

Bobbitt, F (1918) *The Curriculum*. Cambridge, MA: The Riverside Press.

Broadhead, P (2006) Developing an understanding of young children's learning through play: the place of observation, interaction and reflection. *British Educational Research Journal*, 32(2): 191–207.

Claxton, G and Carr, C (2004) A framework for teaching learning: the dynamics of disposition. *Early Years*, 24(1): 87–97.

Crawford, C, Dearden, L and Greaves, E (2013) *When you are born matters: evidence for England*, IFS Report 80 London: Institute for Fiscal Studies.

DEE (2001) *Schools: Building on Success – raising standards, promoting diversity, achieving results*. Norwich: The Stationery Office.

DfE (2013) *History: Programme of study for Key Stages 1–3* London: DfE.

Dewey, J (1997) *Experience and Education*. New York: Touchstone.

Dunn, M and Goddard, E (2002) *Student Achievement in England: Results in reading, mathematical and scientific literacy among 15-year-olds from OECD PISA 2000 study*. London: The Stationery Office.

Hart, S, Dixon, A, Drummond, MJ and McIntyre, M (2004) *Learning Without Limits*. Buckingham: Open University.

Jones, A (2007) Reflecting on the development of a new school subject: the development of technology education in New Zealand. *Waikato Journal of Education*, 13, 273–94.

Kelly, AV (1999) *The Curriculum: Theory and practice*, 4th edn. London: Paul Chapman Publishing.

Lingard, B (2010) Policy borrowing, policy learning: testing times in Australian schooling. *Critical Studies in Education*, 51(2): 129–47.

McCormick, B And Burn, K (2011) Editorial: reviewing the National Curriculum 5–19 two decades on. *The Curriculum Journal*, 22(2): 109–15.

Meyer, J (2006) World models, national curricula, and the centrality of the individual, in Benavot, A and Braslavsky, C (eds) *School Knowledge in Comparative and Historical Perspective: Changing curricula in primary and secondary education*. Hong Kong: Springer.

Nutbrown, C (1998) Early assessment, examining the baselines. *Early Years*, 19(1): 50–6.

Peters, M (2001) National education policy constructions of the 'knowledge economy': towards a critique. *Journal of Educational Enquiry*, 2(1): 1–22.

Pritchard, A and Woollard, J (2010) *Psychology for the Classroom: Constructivism and social learning*. Abingdon: Routledge.

Ramesal, A (2007) Educational reform and primary and secondary teachers' conceptions of assessment: the Spanish instance, building upon Black and Wiliam (2005). *The Curriculum Journal*, 18(1): 27–38.

Robertson, S (2005) Re-imagining and rescripting the future of education: global knowledge economy discourses and the challenge to education systems. *Comparative Education*, 41(2): 151–70.

Rosenmund, M (2006) The current discourse on curriculum change: a comparative analysis of National Reports on Education, in Benavot, A and Braslavsky, C (eds) *School Knowledge in Comparative and Historical Perspective: Changing curricula in primary and secondary education*. Hong Kong: Springer.

Schattle, H (2006) Communicating global citizenship: multiple discourses beyond the academy. *Citizenship Studies*, 9(2): 119–33.

Selwyn, N (2008) Realising the potential of new technology? Assessing the legacy of New Labour's ICT agenda 1997–2007. *Oxford Review of Education*, 34(6): 701–12.

Siraj-Blatchford, I, Sylva, K, Muttock, S, Gildren, R and Bell, D (2002) *Researching Effective Pedagogy in the Early Years*, Department for Education and Skills Research Report No. 356, London: DfES.

Soler, J and Miller, L (2003) The struggle for early childhood curricula: a comparison of the English Foundation Stage Curriculum, Te Whäriki and Reggio Emilia. *International Journal of Early Years Education*, 11(1): 57–67.

Southwood, I (2011) *Non-stop Inertia*. Airesford: Zero Books.

Stenhouse, L (1975) *An Introduction to Curriculum Research and Development*. London: Heinemann.

Sylva, K, Melhuish, E, Sammons, P, Siraj-Blatchford, I and Taggart, B (2010) *Early Childhood Matters: Evidence from the effective pre-school and primary education project*. London: Routledge.

Toren, Z, Maiselman, D and Inbar, S (2008) Curriculum integration: art, literature and technology in pre-service kindergarten teacher training. *Early Childhood Education Journal*, 35(4): 327–33.

Tyler, R (1949) *Basic Principles of Curriculum and Instruction*. Chicago: University of Chicago.

Whitty, G (2010) Revisiting school knowledge: some sociological perspectives on new school curricula. *European Journal of Education*, 45(1): 28–45.

Wood, E (2013) *Play, Learning and the Early Childhood Curriculum*, 3rd edn. London: Sage.

Yates, L (2009) From curriculum to pedagogy and back again: knowledge, the person and the changing world. *Pedagogy, Culture and Society*, 17(1): 17–28.

## Further reading

Kelly's *The Curriculum: Theory and practice* is still generally seen as an excellent introduction to this wider understanding of curriculum and the way in which it is shaped by political forces.

If you wish to think more widely around the English National Curriculum as an example of centralised curriculum planning and consider some of the tensions inherent in centralised structures then the special issue of *The Curriculum Journal*, volume 22, number 2, June 2011, includes articles relevant to considering sequencing and coherence of curriculum, the relationship of vocational to 'academic' education, the need for clarity of the principles of curriculum and the usefulness of subject disciplines.

If you are interested in investigating further ideas around democratic approaches to the curriculum then try the websites for the Free Democratic School Kapriole in Freiburg, Germany (**www.kapriole-freiburg.de/english/home/**) or the Sudbury Valley School in Framingham, Massachusetts (**www.sudburyvalley.org**). Alternatively see Fielding, M and Moss, P (2010) *Radical Education and the Common School*. London: Routledge.

# Chapter 6

# Assessment

## Nick Allsopp

**Introduction**

Assessment is important to everyone involved in or touched by education, whether you are a student, a teacher, a parent, a manager, someone involved in assuring the quality of provision or someone involved in employing those who have completed their studies. Assessment confirms or helps to form students' views of themselves as successes or not and also helps cement their views of their experience in school, college or university This can be seen clearly in the higher education sector's National Student Survey (NSS). According to the Higher Education Funding Council for England (HEFCE) website, the 'Assessment and feedback' section of the NSS received lower marks for overall student satisfaction (70 per cent) across all higher education institutions in 2012 than the sections on academic support (79 per cent), learning resources (82 per cent) and learning and teaching (86 per cent).

Assessment also helps employers make decisions about who they might like to interview as evidence from the Association of Graduate Recruiters' Graduate Recruitment Survey 2012 demonstrates: *the most common selection criteria by a significant margin is a minimum 2:1 degree classification (76.0%). The proportion of (employers) reporting use of this has increased…from 73.2% in 2010–11…(p.39).*

David Boud (1995, p.35) summarises this importance succinctly and starkly:

*students can, with difficulty, escape from the effects of poor teaching, they cannot (by definition, if they want to pass or graduate etc) escape the effects of poor assessment.*

*Pause for thought* | assessment

Assessment is often just taken for granted and seen as something everybody has to do. Consider the following questions:

- How are students/learners in the different sectors of education (primary, secondary, post-16, Higher Education) made aware of the way that assessment operates?

- Do you think that it matters if they are not made aware?

- What model of education might be underpinning the 'foregrounding' of the assessment process?

- What is your own experience? Were you made aware of the ways in which assessment criteria work and the importance of individual pieces of work to the final grade you receive for any specific qualification?

# What is assessment for?

If we accept that there is a great deal of assessment within all sectors of education, then surely that must mean that it is important, but what does it do exactly? Why do students spend so much time worrying and being motivated by assessment and why do teachers spend so much time engaged in it, often to the exclusion of other activities? What is assessment for?

This section will put forward two main views; you may think of many justifications for having assessment but the chances are that they will come back to two overarching reasons. Assessment is used to help students learn on the one hand or to safeguard standards on the other. Of course it is possible to argue that any individual act of assessment can cover both of these reasons but for the sake of clarity they will be treated separately here.

## Assessment to aid learning

Assessment is a key way that teachers help their students to learn, as Heron (1988) observes:

*external rewards and punishments tend to motivate learning rather than intrinsic factors such as authentic interest and involvement in the subject matter, the excitement of inquiry and discovery, the internal commitment to personally considered standards of excellence, self- and peer-determined debate, dialogue and discussion.*

(p.80)

Taking time out from delivering content to gauge how well students understand is vital if the next stage of learning is to be made appropriate to the students that are being taught. That was one of the key tenets of Black and Wiliam's original work on Assessment for Learning. In their seminal 1998 work *Inside the Black Box* they state:

*We start from the self-evident proposition that teaching and learning have to be interactive. Teachers need to know about their pupils' progress and difficulties with learning so that they can adapt their work to meet their needs – needs which are often unpredictable and which vary from one pupil to another.*

(p.2)

However, that aim does not help to explain the huge amount of energy expended on grading and marking students' work.

> **Pause for thought** | different ways of assessment
>
> Black and Wiliam argue that teachers have many different ways of finding out how well their students are progressing apart from formally assessing them. Make a list of these and consider their relative strengths and weaknesses.
>
> One of the key ingredients of *Assessment for Learning*, as originally conceived and tested by Black and Wiliam, was the idea of formative assessment. Here, evidence is gathered to help teachers adapt their work to meet the needs of their pupils. Formative assessment for Black and Wiliam did not include the giving of marks or grades, this latter act being seen as summative assessment. Over time, however, Assessment for Learning has become more

systematic and process driven and in many institutions the term is used for assessments that often do include the giving of marks. Ascribing marks to work done as the unit of work progresses is not truly formative assessment but instead might be seen as 'continuous summative' assessment since the tutor is making an assessment of the learning that has taken place and the marks go towards the final mark or grade for that unit of activity.

## Assessment to maintain standards

The second reason we assess students' work is to count and measure, make judgements and to safeguard standards. The prevailing direction over the last 30 years or so, it might be argued, has been to make the public sector more directly accountable for the funding it receives from the taxpayer. For this to occur, there has been an increasing drive to design ways of measuring that enable this to happen with relative ease and consistency. Thus children are tested at the various key stages in primary and secondary schools and judgements are made – primarily by Ofsted (The Office for Standards in Education, Children's Services and Skills) – about the quality of the school, its teachers and its leaders as a result of these tests.

In 2011 the Secretary of State for Education, Michael Gove, argued in a press release that external testing regimes drive up and safeguard standards of education. In accepting the recommended changes to primary assessment put forward by Lord Bew in July of that year he claimed that, *The system in future will be fairer for teachers and pupils. It will give parents the vital information they need and will hold schools accountable*. The changes made by successive governments have been justified by tying student achievement to economic competitiveness. So, the argument goes, the higher the level of attainment, the more educated and flexible will be the workforce, and the more flexible the workforce the more likely British industry is to win contracts and respond to change. It is perhaps paradoxical, therefore, that the British tabloid press should also become exercised about standards of education, but arguing that an increasing number of examination passes indicates not a rise in standards but quite the opposite: a dilution and reduction in quality.

### 'Dumbing down'

Melanie Phillips, writing in the *Daily Mail* in May 2012 following the publication of an Ofqual (The Office for Qualifications and Examinations Regulation) report into Science and Geography stated that:

*It's no surprise at all to learn that A-level and GCSE grades have indeed got progressively easier over the past decade. The only surprise is that, after more than two decades of denials, the education establishment has finally admitted it.*

*The exam watchdog Ofqual has found that science and geography papers are 'softer' and 'less demanding'. Teenagers now have more multiple choice questions and papers with less scientific content.*

*Ofqual warns that this deterioration is leaving pupils ill-prepared for university and there is less opportunity for good students to shine.*

Similarly, Graeme Paton, the Education Editor of the *Daily Telegraph*, discussed the rise in the number of 'good' honours degrees (1st and 2:1 classification) in UK higher education institutions in January 2012 thus:

*A record 53,215 undergraduates – one-in-six – finished courses last summer with top degrees, it was revealed. Figures published by the Higher Education Statistics Agency show numbers have increased by 14 per cent in just 12 months and 125 per cent in a decade.*

*The rise dramatically outstrips the overall increase in the student population over the same period, raising fears that some academics are coming under pressure to mark up students' work to boost universities' positions in league tables.*

The standards debate is thus complex and contradictory. There is a continual push on education providers to raise learner attainment as measured by external examination successes yet at the same time there is a negative reaction against any success in achieving this by some commentators at least, since they fear that this success has been completed by lowering the standards needed to achieve. These commentators seem concerned that the data showing success is in fact evidence of what is often called in the press 'dumbing down' – a phrase which itself encapsulates a positive vision of the past which the evidence does not seem to support.

## Research box

### PISA survey

The Programme for International Student Assessment (PISA) is a survey of the educational achievement of 15-year-olds in reading, mathematics and science conducted every three years for the Organisation for Economic Co-operation and Development (OECD). Sixty-five countries took part in the 2009 PISA survey and the report is used by government to make comparisons with other nations, highlight best practice and help form education policy. In England the Department for Education (DfE) produced a statistical analysis of the 2009 PISA; survey (DFE, 2010; OSR29/2010). This suggested *no significant change in performance compared with the results for 2006* but, because other nations had improved over the same time period, England's ranking in all three of the areas covered by PISA had fallen: in reading, from 17th out of 57 to 25th out of 65; in mathematics, from 24th out of 57 to 27th out of 65; and in science, from 14th out of 57 to 16th out of 65 countries.

The DfE highlighted 12 countries that *significantly* outperformed England in reading, 20 in mathematics and 10 in science. In all of these groups EU countries were in the minority with Finland being the only EU country to significantly outperform England in all three areas. The majority of those that outperformed England were from the Far East, especially in mathematics and science. Commentators have used this as evidence of the shift in global power now and in the future. Within England itself the DfE report claimed that the gap between those that score well and those that do not in both reading and science is greater than in many other countries. England was seen as *lacking in high achievers in mathematics*. In terms of gender, *girls scored significantly higher than boys in reading* while the opposite was true in mathematics and there was *no significant gender difference in science*. The report also highlighted a lack of qualified teachers in mathematics and a lack of adequate computer equipment in schools. With regard to socio-economic background, the report stated that *the performance gap between the most advantaged and disadvantaged pupils is relatively high in England compared with other OECD countries, (but) pupils in England are relatively well able to overcome the disadvantage of their background.*

An analysis of the same 2009 PISA data for an American audience by Miller and Warren (2011) at the National Center for Education Statistics put US performance on a par with that of England for reading, mathematics and science but behind Canada and Japan; illustrating where that country saw its key global rivals. As in England, boys outperformed girls in mathematics but quite the opposite in reading. The American analysis of the 2009 PISA survey also looked at the performance of students who were born in the USA, those with at least one parent born in America and those with no parents born there – their so-called *immigrant status*. The analysis showed that in reading American students with *an immigrant background scored lower, on average, than their native peers in all G-8 countries except Canada … and Japan*. Finally the American analysis confirmed that income is a key factor in educational achievement, stating that *in all reporting G-8 countries, adults with a higher level of education tended to earn more than those with a lower level of income* with 69 per cent of those who had completed American higher education earning more than the median income and 30 per cent earning twice this level. In comparison only 12 per cent of those who completed American higher education earned at or below half the median income, thus demonstrating the earning power associated with (higher) education in the USA.

To find out more about PISA, go to **www.oecd.org/pisa/faqoecdpisa.htm**

# Assessment and student achievement

It is now taken as a statement of fact that different student groups achieve differently. This is true within an individual institution or within the wider system of higher education. This section will consider those differences in achievement, whether positive or negative, and ask how this may be connected to the ways in which we assess students.

Inequalities in achievement in the UK have been analysed and discussed over many years, even decades. There is no doubt that these inequalities exist and that certain groups in society do less well in terms of educational achievement than others, as measured by examination success for example. The Triennial Review published by the Equality and Human Rights Commission (EHRC) in 2010, entitled 'How fair is Britain?' discussed educational achievement and concluded that overall things were improving:

*Educational attainment has been transformed in recent years. Around half of young people are now getting good qualifications at 16 (5+ A\*–C GCSEs or equivalent including English and Maths), and in 2008/09, 2.4 million students enrolled in higher education in the UK – a considerable change from a time when educational opportunities were only available to a minority of young people.*

(p.300)

While applauding this achievement the report also argued that class, race and gender continued to be significant contributory factors to pupil achievement:

*…in terms of both subjects studied, and in the obtaining of good degrees, differences persist. Women remain less likely than men to study Science, Technology, Engineering and Maths (STEM) subjects, (and) … The proportion of Black students getting first or upper second class degrees is still only at two-thirds of the level of White students.*

(p.300)

## Social class

The EHRC review argued that *educational attainment continues to be strongly associated with socio-economic background*. In claiming this they echoed the findings of another report in the same year by Perry and Francis (2010, p.2), which stated clearly that:

*Social class remains the strongest predictor of educational achievement in the UK, where the social gap for educational achievement is one of the most significant in the developed world.*

Both reports were in turn picking up on what Diane Reay (2006, p.289) termed *The zombie stalking English schools*. Reay argued that *social class (is) … the troublesome un-dead of the English education system*. Thus, despite any improvements in achievement, social class continues to be a significant contributing factor to pupil achievement.

## Ethnicity

In an Ofsted report entitled *Educational Inequality: Mapping race, class and gender*, Gillborn and Mirza (2000) had argued forcefully that the picture was complex and that as a result simple conclusions were less than useful. They presented data that showed, for example, that the achievements of individual ethnic groups differed across the country. White pupils were the highest achieving groups in 4 of the 81 local authorities that monitored for ethnicity and were the second highest in a further 26 authorities. Elsewhere, Bangladeshi children *did not attain highly in most surveys, but in one (authority) they emerged as the highest attaining group of all* (p.8) and African-Caribbean pupils *may be ranked poorly in national measures (such as the proportion attaining five higher grades (A\*-Cs) in their GCSE examinations), but the same group can be doing relatively well in some schools and in some LEAs* (p.7). The report provides evidence of the complexity of student achievement and argues that care must therefore be taken when forming conclusions that do not take account of this. In the final section of the report (p.78ff), however, the authors do produce a series of *broad conclusions concerning inequalities in relation to 'race', class and gender*:

- Ethnic inequalities of attainment vary from one area to another but, despite this variability, distinct patterns of inequality are consistently visible.
- Inequalities of attainment in GCSE examinations place African-Caribbean, Pakistani and Bangladeshi pupils in a disadvantaged position in the youth education, labour, and training markets, and increase the likelihood of social and economic exclusion in later life.
- Social class and gender differences are also associated with differences in attainment but neither can account for persistent underlying ethnic inequalities: comparing like with like, African-Caribbean, Pakistani and Bangladeshi pupils do not enjoy equal opportunities.
- Ethnic inequalities are not new but neither are they static. Evidence shows that in some cases the inequalities have increased in recent years. African-Caribbean and Pakistani pupils, for example, have not shared equally in the rising levels of GCSE attainment.

## Gender

When considering the achievement of pupils by gender the picture is equally complex. In 2006 Machin and McNally produced a report for the Centre for Economics of Education, an independent research centre funded by the then Department for Education and Skills, which argued forcefully that:

*In the UK, there is a marked gender gap in the educational attainment of boys and girls. At the end of compulsory education, 10 per cent fewer boys achieve 5 or more good GCSEs. This gap is by no means confined to GCSE. It is evident at all Key Stages.*

*Furthermore, some indicators suggest that the gap has widened over time. We find that it is in secondary school, rather than primary school, where the gender gap has widened most noticeably over time.*

This is perhaps the traditionally accepted view of student achievement by gender; however, Skelton et al. (2007) considered gender and achievement in a report entitled *Breaking Down the Stereotypes: Gender and achievement in schools*. In their findings they argued for a more complex understanding of student achievement, stating:

*The emphasis in recent years on boys' underachievement has resulted in an oversimplified view of the gender gap in achievement. Some groups of boys are achieving and some groups of girls are underachieving … Girls do not outperform boys in all subjects. On average, they do so in English and literacy... However, there is almost no gender gap in achievement in mathematics and science at KS2.*

(p.11)

---

*Pause for thought* | helping students achieve

We may now have reiterated what has been known for some time, that students' achievement is at least in part connected with factors outside of the classroom, but how can assessment be tied up in this? What, if anything, can the individual teacher actually do to help all of their pupils achieve? In considering your response you should bear in mind Biggs' (1999, p.23) argument that *if students aren't learning there is something wrong with our teaching/assessment method, not the student…*

---

One possible solution to this question is to conceive of pupils and students as part of the answer, as co-creators of the solution. Research by Rust et al. (2003) has shown very clearly that, for students in higher education, if they understood the assessment criteria being used, and wrote to the criteria, then they achieved more highly than those who were not helped to understand, and even co-construct, the assessment criteria. Rust et al. argue that a tutor should always explain clearly to the students why they are being assessed in a specific way and the pedagogic reasons behind the choice of assessment. Where possible, the tutor should also share any research or evaluation evidence of the effectiveness of the chosen assessment method. In this way the student understands the demands of assessment more clearly and can respond accordingly. By adopting this approach the student has a more active engagement in the assessment process rather than responding to it passively.

This in turn has echoes of a socio-constructivist approach to knowledge creation of the sort Vygotsky and Bruner described, where knowledge is shaped and evolves through increasing participation within different communities of practice.

Two practical examples of this approach would be:

- involving students in a marking exercise using the agreed marking criteria then discussing the results with other students and the tutor. Rust et al. suggest that this approach results in statistically significant improvement in students' subsequent work;
- tutors having an initial discussion with their peers regarding the meaning of the assessment criteria being used then a further discussion to refine their understanding after some marking has been undertaken using the criteria, followed by moderation discussions after all the marking has been completed. This, it is argued, increases the common understanding of what is wanted from an individual piece of assessment and thus results in better standardisation of marking.

In both examples, active engagement is a key.

## De Vita

Work by De Vita (2002) has examined the way in which groups of students from diverse backgrounds in one higher education institution worked when faced with a piece of group work. It had been noted previously that *home and international students do not spontaneously mix and would rather be involved in monocultural work groups* (p.153). Following a piece of research which involved examining the end result of students' group work – their achievement – and the way they tackled this – the make up of the group – De Vita made a number of perhaps surprising conclusions. Rather than the usual fear that working as a diverse group rather than a monocultural one might mean that results are pulled down by the weakest members of the group, this study found that the group work marks exceeded expectations when the group was culturally diverse. De Vita concluded that a group work mark is more likely to reflect the most able group member. The research also concluded that *assessed multicultural group work has a positive rather than negative effect on the individual average mark of all students* (p.153). The implications of this small-scale research are that working together as a group from diverse backgrounds and various nationalities can have a positive effect on attainment.

This study is important since it runs counter to many prevailing fears. It might also be a way of tackling a sense of unfairness in assessment arrangements identified by Black and Asian students in the NSS, as described in a report sponsored by the Higher Education Academy and the Equality Challenge Unit in 2008. 'Ethnicity, gender and degree attainment' looked at learning, teaching and assessment in a number of higher education institutions and noted that although, at a policy level, there was reference to inclusion and diversity, there was less reference to attainment by different groups of students and therefore little evidence that institutions were looking at student attainment through the lens of equality and diversity. Institutions were not ignoring differences in attainment, the report suggested, but were not looking for these differences deliberately and therefore could not know that they existed and could not take action to tackle them. The report acknowledged the sensitivities in *examining possible bias in marking* but suggested that teams, departments and whole institutions needed to explore *this sensitive terrain in order to ensure robust, fair and inclusive methods of assessment, marking and feedback.* You might like to consider what such an exploration might result in: changes in policy; curriculum content; assessment design; or practice? As the report suggested, this might result in less ethnocentric assumptions about student performance and perhaps a less Eurocentric and British-centric curriculum.

# Developing assessment literacy

The examples in the previous sections show the need for what Price et al. (2012) describe as *assessment literacy.* This is described as *a gateway or threshold to further learning* (p.7), which *enables one to engage deeply with assessment standards, to make a choice about which skill or which area of knowledge to apply, to appreciate which are/are not appropriate to a particular task and why* (p.10).

Another way of seeing the same idea is Miller and Parlett's (1974) notion of *cue seekers* – those students who make a proactive effort to find out what is wanted in an assessment and then act upon this information. While the student who achieves highly will probably be such a cue seeker, Miller and Parlett also acknowledge that there will be those students who are *cue deaf* or perhaps *cue conscious* but who are waiting for the tutor to inform them of what is required.

What joins all of these ways of thinking is an active engagement with assessment and this is open to all students, irrespective of previous educational experiences or attainment. This active approach is likely to help students to improve their attainment levels in any individual piece of assessment but, more importantly, will provide them with the skills needed to improve their attainment in all future assessments, irrespective of the subject discipline.

---

*Pause for thought* | role-play

Imagine yourself to be a teacher giving work back to a student. In pairs, role-play the situation. As the teacher, you should provide feedback that helps to explain the way in which the assessment criteria work. As the student, what would you want to hear that calmed initial nerves and provided ways of improving your work for the next time? How does this compare to your own experiences? You might want to record the role-play and use this as a means to feed back to the 'actors' and help to highlight both strengths and weaknesses.

---

# Developments in assessment

It is now a truism that the nature of the student cohort is changing, especially with the introduction of £9,000 tuition fees in 2012 for higher education study. Data from UCAS shows that the total number of applicants applying to higher education fell in 2012 by 46,524 (6.6 per cent) to 653,637 following four years of continual rises. In general terms the 2012 cohort was made up of similar proportions of students by age group as before (although slightly fewer 18 year olds applied), similar proportions by gender, by ethnicity (although slightly fewer Black students applied) and with similar numbers of students with a declared learning difficulty. It is not possible to comment on socio-economic groupings since the data UCAS released only went up to 2009. What higher education institutions feared would change was the attitude towards learning and achievement that these students, and those that follow them, come with and one of the questions for this chapter has been whether this perceived change in the student body has had any effect on the nature of assessment.

## The effect of the A level experience

The majority of applicants to higher education in 2012 were still 20 years old or younger (73 per cent) and as such they would, in general, have been assessed in their post-16 education using a different set of assessment tools to the ones they experience in the first year of their undergraduate experience. They would, for example, have worked with modular A levels offering multiple opportunities to resit the exam. The concern that this leaves students unprepared for higher education and results in the award of higher grades than a qualification that only tested at the end of two years of study is one of the reasons that the Secretary of State for Education, Michael Gove, has reformed the structure of A levels. Writing to the Chief Executive of Ofqual in January 2013 Gove argued that:

*The modular nature of the qualification and repeated assessment windows have contributed to many students not developing deep understanding or the necessary skills to make connections between topics.*

Applicants to higher education in 2012 would also have had more face-to-face contact time per subject than they would experience in HE and they would have been marked using a set of clearly differentiated marking criteria that made explicit what was required to achieve each grade. It is perhaps therefore not a surprise that these students, successful as they are by definition in order to be accepted into higher education, seem confused and even bewildered when they receive their first assignment back.

## The effect of £9,000 tuition fees

Many institutions have responded to the experience students have at A level and in other post-16 qualifications by spending time and energy in developing more robust assessment practices and grade descriptors that enable students to understand more clearly what they need to do in order to achieve and to improve. While this additional transparency is to be welcomed, it sits alongside an as yet unproven fear from tutors that the advent of £9,000 tuition fees will bring a more 'consumerist' attitude from students (see for example Molesworth et al., 2010). Students as consumers or customers goes hand-in-hand with changes to higher education to make it work much more like a market. In other words, universities act as suppliers of education and compete with one another for students, perhaps in terms of price or in terms of quality. Students then choose their university in a similar way to the way consumers or customers choose where to purchase other products. Frank Furedi (writing in Molesworth et al., 2010) argues that in some ways competition in education is nothing new. However, what is new is the way students are now seen as customers. Furedi and others see this as an ideological decision and one that is designed to specifically change the three-way relationship between the state, the student and the university. Critics of this development argue that student behaviour will inevitably change as they demand to know and experience where their money has been spent. This may be in the facilities that a university offers but it is also likely to be in the experience in the classroom. There are fears that students will expect better employment prospects from their degree now that they are paying directly for their education and that curriculum design and the teaching will reflect this. With specific reference to assessment this may result in a greater demand for quicker turnaround times for work to be returned, accompanied by more detailed advice on how the student might improve on the mark they were given. This might suggest a narrower view of education on the part of the student and, ironically, a risk of changes in the way students are assessed on the part of the tutor that lead to greater caution, less experimentation and thus to fewer advances in the ideas and practice surrounding assessment.

---

*Pause for thought* | students as consumers

In what ways does higher education already embrace competition like other parts of the economy? How does it demonstrate this consumerist behaviour? Think of the ways in which this analogy fails? What, if any, are the characteristics of education that make it different? What would all of those involved in education gain or lose from becoming more consumerist in their behaviour?

---

## Perceived rises in plagiarism

Alongside the developments – or the fear of little development – in pedagogy comes another change. There seems to be a change in student behaviour across all sectors of education that is characterised by an apparent rise in incidents of plagiarism (the deliberate attempt to pass another person's work off as your own as was discussed in the national press (Smithers, 2005). This may be due to factors such as the changes in the structure of assessments at GCSE and A level with fewer coursework opportunities and more writing in supervised settings or perhaps changes in expectation as students transfer to higher education. A now famous case in 2004 illustrates the point: it was alleged by a former teacher at Eton that she was told by a senior tutor to either help Prince Harry *answer questions enabling him to achieve a B grade* (BBC website) or had been ordered to write the text to accompany Prince Harry's Aboriginal-style paintings (Morris, 2005) in his A level Art coursework.

It is difficult to gain authoritative data from publically available sources to confirm whether incidents of plagiarism are indeed on the rise across higher education or whether now institutions are looking harder they are finding more cases. Academics are therefore left to form judgements based on their local circumstance and commentators, particularly in the media, are able to write hyperbolically without the fear of contradiction by hard data. Examples of the response of the media include the *Telegraph's* report of a research paper in 2010 with the headline *Half of university students willing to cheat, study finds* (Henry, 2010). The report centres on a small-scale research project, which suggested that students were favourably disposed to buying work wholesale and were 'sure' (or 'convinced' as the corresponding *Guardian* article claimed: Williams, 2010) that other students had cheated. However, the report and the article did admit that most students did not report their concerns and that there had been few proven cases of cheating, but put this down to a problem of detection rather than anything else. The following year, the *Telegraph* again ran a report on this subject with the headline the *cheating epidemic at Britain's universities* (Barrett, 5 March 2011). This stated that *more than 17,000 incidents of cheating were recorded by universities in the 2009-10 academic year – up at least 50 per cent in four years* but did admit that *only a handful of students were expelled for their misdemeanours* and that *lecturers deal with less serious cases* without them being escalated further within the university's systems.

These examples are illustrative of a reaction to changes in student behaviour and to the advent of both web-based services selling services such as essay writing to students and the almost ubiquitous use of similarity checking software such as Turnitin. A report by Badge and Scott in 2009 entitled 'Dealing with plagiarism in the digital age' acknowledged the increased interest in the media in suggested student plagiarism and focused specifically on what they described as *electronic detection software systems* which they defined as *automated systems which enable students' work to be compared one with another and with a variety of online sources*. This study concluded that there were still problems with the robustness and reliability of some of the software, giving rise to false positives and unfounded accusations against students. The report also concluded that the time taken in pursuing such cases might take teachers away from detecting genuine cases of plagiarism. Perhaps, the report suggests, time is better spent educating students in improving their writing and referencing skills. The biggest impact of the apparent rise in cases of plagiarism across all education institutions is likely to be on pedagogic practice in general and assessment practice in particular. As Badge and Scott state *no simple change in one element of practice will provide a long term solution to the problem of teaching our students how to be good scholars*. Equally, however, there is also a growing imperative on teachers to look again at the way that they design assessments for their students and to try to minimise the opportunities for plagiarism – often described as 'designing out' opportunities to cheat or appear so to do. There is much that is produced around this area and the work of Jude Carroll at Oxford Brookes University has helped to shape a great deal of thinking in this area (see **www.brookes.ac.uk/aske/index.html**) as has the work of the Plagiarism Advisory Service (now rebranded as **www.plagiarismadvice.org**). For some teachers it is as simple as rotating the questions asked in exams in consecutive years, for others it has been to increase the number of unseen examinations and for yet others it has involved the whole-scale redesign of modules or units of learning so that the emphasis is less on the regurgitation of facts and more on the demonstration of skills, competences and knowledge in a way that is suitable to the individual student yet still fulfils the learning aims of the module or course.

---

> ### *Pause for thought* | changes to discourage plagiarism
>
> Consider your own modules or units of learning: what do you think needs to change in the way that you are assessed to encourage you to become more aware of the issues surrounding plagiarism? What should your teachers alter to discourage students from plagiarising and what changes in the assessment design could be implemented to minimise the potential to cheat in this way?

---

## The rise in e-assessment

The increased volume of e-learning together with the rise in student expectations and the apparent rise in incidents of plagiarism or cheating of another kind have led many higher education institutions particularly to turn to software solutions. There is thus an increase in technology to enhance the learning, teaching and assessment experience in the university curriculum. According to a JISC report in 2010, e-assessment and e-feedback not only fit into the way young people (Prensky's [2001] 'digital natives') interact with the world but can also help students acquire important skills in *self monitoring and self-regulation* and can *prompt deeper and more effective learning,* all *without adding to the workload of practitioners* (p.6). The JISC report argues that using technology to enhance assessment and feedback will only succeed if the fundamentals of good assessment design and teaching practice are in place first of all. E-learning and e-assessment are thus not substitutes and not a panacea. With these basics in place, however, JISC argues (p.9), technology-enhanced assessment and feedback can provide greater variety in assessment design, improved engagement by the student and greater student choice in when assessments are started and completed. They also allow for more efficient submission and return processes and in some cases immediate automatic feedback to students. There will always be types of learning and assessment that are less able to be enhanced by the use of technology – group work and some types of practical work, for example. There is also a temptation to introduce new technology without firstly considering the need and as a consequence changing effective practice for the worse. However, the JISC report concludes that there will be an inevitable increase in the use of technology in all aspects of teaching, learning and assessment. As a result, everyone involved in these processes will need to change and adapt their ways of working and their expectations so that the principles of good assessment are not lost and that student learning remains at the heart of the educational process.

### Summary and conclusions

This chapter has highlighted the importance of assessment to many of the people involved directly and indirectly in education. We have considered what assessment is for and discovered that while educators might see the amount of time and energy they direct towards assessment as helping the individual to achieve success, there are other considerations, not least the economic standing of the nation in a global marketplace. The chapter has reiterated the unequal experience of various groups of students across all sectors of education and has suggested that one possible way forward is to increase students' understanding of the role assessment plays and then their active participation in the process. Finally, the chapter has considered some of the ways in which assessment seems to be developing, including the almost inevitable rise in electronic methods of assessment. The pressures on students to succeed in their assessments and for teachers to successfully prepare them for these means that the importance of assessment for all parties will only increase. This is already changing behaviours and that seems bound to continue apace.

# References

Association of Graduate Recruiters (2012) *Graduate Recruitment Survey 2012 Summer Review*. [Online] Available at: **www.cfe.org.uk**, accessed January 2012.

Badge, J and Scott, J (2009) Dealing with plagiarism in the digital age. Higher Education Academy Evidencenet. [Online] Available at: **http://evidencenet.pbworks.com/w/page/19383480/Dealing%20with%20plagiarism%20in%20the%20digital%20age**, accessed 23 March 2013.

Barrett, D (2011) The cheating epidemic at Britain's universities. *Telegraph* online. Available at: **www.telegraph.co.uk/education/educationnews/8363345/the-cheating-epidemic-at-britains-universities.html**

BBC News (2004) Royal Family denies Harry cheated. [Online] Available at: **http://news.bbc.co.uk/1/hi/uk/3730684.stm**, accessed 10 March 2013.

Biggs, J (1999) *Teaching for Quality Learning at University*. Maidenhead: SRHE/OUP.

Black, P and Wiliam, D (1998) *Inside the Black Box: Raising standards through classroom assessment*. London: Granada Learning.

Boud, D (1995) Assessment and Learning: Contradictory or complementary? in Knight, P (ed) *Assessment for Learning in Higher Education*. London: Kogan Page.

De Vita, G (2002) Does assessed multicultural group work really pull UK students' average down? *Assessment and Evaluation in Higher Education*, 27(2): 153–61.

Department for Education (2010) *Statistical Release: Programme for International Student Assessment (PISA) 2009: Results for England*. OSR29/2010: Department for Education.

Equality and Human Rights Commission (2010) *How fair is Britain? Equality, Human Rights and Good Relations in 2010*. London: Equality and Human Rights Commission. Available at: **http:// www.equalityhumanrights.com/key–projects/how-fair-is-britain**

Gillborn, D and Mirza, SH (2000), *Educational Inequality: Mapping race, class and gender*. London: Office for Standards in Education.

Gove, M (2011) *Key Stage 2 review of testing, assessment and accountability: Government response*. DFE press release. [Online] Available at: **www.education.gov.uk/inthenews/inthenews/a00192403/key-stage-2-review-of-testing-assessment-and-accountability-government-response**, accessed 20 February 2013.

Gove, M (2013) Letter to Chief Executive of Ofqual. [Online] Available at: **http://media.education.gov.uk/assets/files/pdf/l/ofqual%20letter%20alevels%20v2.pdf**, accessed 10 March 2013.

Henry, J (2010) Half of university students willing to cheat, study finds. *Telegraph* online. Available at: **www.telegraph.co.uk/education/educationnews/7840969/half-of-university- students-willing-to-cheat-study-finds.html**

Heron, J (1988) Assessment revisited, in Boud, D (ed) (1988) *Developing Student Autonomy in Learning*. London: Kogan Page.

Higher Education Academy (2008) *Ethnicity, Gender and Degree Attainment: Final Report*. York: HEA.

Higher Education Funding Council for England (2012) Highest ever student satisfaction rates in 2012 student survey. [Online] Available at: **www.hefce.ac.uk/news/newsarchive/2012/name,75522,en.html**, accessed 11 May 2013.

JISC (2010) *Effective Assessment in a Digital Age*. Bristol: JISC.

Machin, S and McNally, S (2006) *Gender and Student Achievement in English Schools*. London: CEE.

Miller, CMI and Parlett, M (1974) *Up to the Mark: A study of the examination game*. Guildford: SRHE.

Miller, DC and Warren, LK (2011) *Comparative Indicators of Education in the United States and other G-8 Countries: 2011*. Washington: National Center for Education Statistics.

Molesworth, M, Scullion, R and Nixon, E (eds) (2010) *The Marketisation of Higher Education and the Student as Consumer*. Abingdon: Routledge.

Morris, S (2005) Prince Harry, a weak student who was helped to cheat in exam, says ex-teacher. *Guardian* online Available at: **www.theguardian.com/uk/2005/may/10/schools. alevels2004** (accessed 10 March 2013).

Paton, G (2012) Warning over 'grade inflation' as first-class degrees double. The *Telegraph*, online version, 12 January 2012.

Perry, E and Francis, B (2010) *The Social Class Gap for Educational Achievement: A review of the literature*. London: RSA Projects.

Phillips, M (2012) Everyone knows exams have got easier over the last decade. The only surprise is that the educational establishment has admitted it. *Daily Mail*, online version, 2 May 2012.

Prensky, M (2001) Digital Natives, Digital Immigrants Part 1. *On the Horizon*, 9(5): 1–6.

Price, M, Rust, C, Donovan, B, Handley, K with Bryant, R (2012) *Assessment Literacy*. Oxford: ASKe.

Reay, D (2006) The zombie stalking English schools: social class and educational inequality. *British Journal of Educational Studies*, 54(3): 288–307.

Rust, C, Price, M and O'Donovan, B (2003) Improving students' learning by developing their understanding of assessment criteria and processes. *Assessment and Evaluation in Higher Education*, 28(2): 147–64.

Skelton, C, Francis, B and Valkanova, Y (2007) *Breaking Down the Stereotypes: Gender and achievement in schools*. Manchester: Equal Opportunities Commission.

Smithers, R (2005) Crackdown urged on web exam plagiarism. *Guardian* online. Available at: **www.guardian.co.uk/technology/2005/nov/22/news.schools**, accessed 10 March 2013.

UCAS data sets [Online]. Available at: **www.ucas.ac.uk/about_us/stat_services/stats_online/**.

Williams, R (2010) Internet plagiarism rising in schools. *Guardian* online. Available at: **www.guardian.co.uk/education/2010/jun/20/internet-plagiarism-rising-in-schools**.

# Chapter 7

# Community education: innovation and active intervention

## Viv Kerridge and Ruth Sayers

### Introduction

This chapter is concerned with education that occurs in the broader community rather than in a formal educational institution. It highlights the theoretical aspects of community education and considers its roots, function and importance. Set alongside the philosophical exposition will be a number of illustrations to place community education within a drama and theatre context as we perceive a constructive and vibrant connection between the two. There is a strong tradition of using drama and theatre in active community projects and a coherent theoretical basis which explains its usefulness and illustrates its effectiveness. The chapter introduces interventionist techniques designed to enable communities to recognise and negotiate external restrictions. Distinctions are drawn between theatre-in-education, community theatre and educational drama. The political perspective offered includes a consideration of the financial, social and political pressure placed upon the development of community education and the level of attention and funding given to mainstream theatre as opposed to 'people's theatre', including street arts. The professional perspective offers a practical guide to establishing community projects with regard to ethical, philosophical and logistical frameworks.

## Background

Formal education is a relatively new construct whereas some sense of community has always been fundamental to human development. Many of our life skills are absorbed *in situ* by informal means; that is by the family or the workplace. Humans learn many things effectively, if sometimes painfully, from observation and trial and error. Traditionally, crafts and trades worked on an apprenticeship basis through active learning, and formal theoretical assessment was not part of the process. There was, of course, nothing idyllic about this arrangement; it too was subject to economic restrictions and dictated to by the basic need to survive. Community co-operation and education are difficult to untangle. Even formal education generally takes place in the local community, and educational institutions form communities of their own in which personal relationships and individual identity play a significant part in the learning process. To this extent it is misleading to suggest that education, in its broadest sense, can be anything but a community issue. Indeed, a school community, or sub-set of it, might be considered a community of practice. Wenger (2004) suggests that engagement in a social practice is the fundamental process by which we lean and so become what we are. A community of practice for Wenger is a group which operates through joint enterprise, mutual engagement and shared repertoire. It must be able to negotiate its own enterprise, shape its own boundaries and evolve according to its own learning. Defining features of a community of practice are sustained relationships, shared practice, rapid flow of information, mutually defined identities, shared stories and jargon. So what is it that differentiates 'education in the community' from formal education?

Formal education is taken here to mean that which takes place in schools and other educational institutions. It undergoes constant development, or at least change, according to such criteria as pressures of finance, local and global pressures, government priorities and pedagogical fashion. Formal education can be flexible and fluid or very closely prescribed. Education in the community is also an umbrella term for a wide variety of activities, which vary in terms of formality from drop-in play sessions for mothers and toddlers to fully accredited lifelong learning courses. It is also closely connected with community development and the connection between social welfare, community and education.

A trawl of the internet uncovers a number of community education centres throughout the UK which still offer a vast array of services such as:

- education-business partnerships (which put schools in touch with potential business sponsors);
- links with local services (police, social services, health services);
- learning resource services (facilities such as desktop publishing, video editing, internet access);
- community cafes (or other relaxation areas where people can socialise and pick up information leaflets on local facilities);
- activities for the elderly;
- parents' groups (often with speakers and facilitators of parenting skills);
- basic skills sessions;
- youth organisations;
- professional advice (grant aid and advice on funding and training for community initiatives);
- citizens' advice sessions;
- free legal advice sessions;
- a range of classes at a variety of levels.

Some of these centres are based in community schools, libraries or other public buildings, while some have their own separate premises such as welfare halls and local institutes. These are open to all local residents. Some of the facilities are free and others are subsidised; many may be more 'community' orientated than 'educational'.

---

*Pause for thought* | community education

Look through the list of services provided by community education centres. How many of them seem to you to be educational? Which do you consider to be community based? Are any of them difficult to differentiate? Do you think that any of the functions on the list help to 'create' a sense of community, or do they 'service' a local area?

---

# The history of community education

This level of provision is not a new phenomenon. During the second part of the nineteenth and the whole of the twentieth centuries, there was a strong tradition of working people's clubs and institutes throughout the country. In his fascinating history of British working-class intellectual life, Rose (2002, p.237) referred to the miners' institutes of South Wales as *one of the greatest networks of cultural institutions created by working people anywhere in the world*. He mentions that, by the time of the Second World War, the Tredegar Institute Library, for example, circulated 100,000 books per year, and many similar institutes had cinemas and film societies and had staged numerous concerts and cultural performances. There is evidence that institute libraries stocked a vast range of books on a variety of subjects and that people's reading habits included the classics and social and political texts. While some of the people who benefited had aspirations beyond their cultural background, the majority used them as a form of personal enrichment and empowerment.

In addition to the wide range of cultural pursuits there was a strong tradition of political debate which often manifested itself through drama. Throughout the 1930s, radical theatre groups such as the Red Megaphones in Salford (MacColl, 1973) were producing agit-prop theatre performances for the working classes in order to raise awareness of political, social and ideological issues. They used street theatre as a way of delivering their message. Their work was inspired by similar experiments in the United States led by the 'Living Newspaper' units that had been established as part of the Federal Theatre Project during the 1930s (Witham, 2003).

Susan Mansfield (cited in Allen and Martin, 1992) traced both the lesser-known contribution that women made to the development of community education and the patriarchal values which manifested themselves as powerfully in community education as they did in the school system. The Suffrage Movement and the socialist Sunday Schools raised the political awareness and confidence of women; the Women's Cooperative Guild moved from an association concerned with women's traditional roles to a campaigning body which championed women's education. Later, movements such as the Townswomen's Guild and the Women's Institute included education programmes and campaigned for women's issues. The Suffragette Movement used drama in the form of propaganda sketches and full-length plays to further their political aims.

These movements and institutions and others like them across the country were largely self-generating and run by those they served. Rose (2002) noted that while the miners' libraries and other facilities were fed by the Miners' Welfare Fund set up by parliament to tax coal production and direct the revenue to the institutions, the miners themselves controlled the budget. They enjoyed a high level of cultural and intellectual freedom and were instrumental in the development of a culturally and politically aware populace beyond the jurisdiction of formal educational institutions. This is in contrast to many current community education centres, which offer similar facilities but are often run *for* the community rather than *by* them and rely on local authorities for subsidy. The system of applying to a variety of bodies for funding ensures certain standards but places a variety of obligations on the centres which may be counter-productive or restrictive. Such restrictions have been placed on theatre programmes that have been specifically designed to address community needs.

Theatre-in-education, often referred to as TIE, began in the UK in the 1960s. The history of TIE has been influenced by the political and economic context of each decade. Prior to the Education Reform Act of 1988, local education authorities were major funders. During the late 1970s and early 1980s there was little accountability and considerable freedom in designing programmes of work. A company was able to work for several days, or even weeks, with one class of students. With the implementation of Local Management of Schools as part of the 1988 Education Reform Act and its resulting restrictions, companies began to search for alternative sources of funding, often resorting to short-term projects designed to address a single issue quickly, and this continues to be the case.

# Emerging pressures

Michele Erma Doyle (cited in Richardson and Wolfe, 2001), referring to youth and community workers, remarked on the pressure of external expectations on the field of informal education. She noted that both adult education and youth work are under increasing pressure to focus on formal accreditation of learning. She recognised that community workers needed to be aware of the underlying educational theory to their work and lamented the 'how-to' nature of the current literature which detracted from their professionalism. This, she suggested, was a direct result of the impact of the National Curriculum and its concentration on what is learned and how it is learned:

*This 'product' approach to learning [is] in contrast to the traditional focus of informal education which ... has focused on relationships and thus on the process by which learning happens, rather than on what is learnt.*

(p.6)

These observations are reminiscent of the philosophy of Paulo Freire (1970) and his reference to formal education as *the banking concept of education*, a storing process where students build up deposits of knowledge supplied by the teacher. The 'banking concept' can be perceived as a restriction on the educator who is required to teach a highly prescribed curriculum. Freire called for educators to abandon the deposit system of education and to replace it with *the posing of the problems of human beings in their relations with the world*.

This approach is seen, at least in part, in a number of community initiatives. The national strategy plan for neighbourhood renewal launched in 2001 as a government initiative recognises that:

*neighbourhood renewal starts from a proper understanding of the needs of communities, and that the most effective interventions are often those where communities are actively involved in their design and development. This includes community of interest, such as people who are black or from minority groups, as well as geographically defined communities.*

(White, 2002, p.1)

Theoretically at least, the sense of grassroots participation in community planning and development is seen as a positive and necessary step. Lawton (2001) referred to the 'Third Way', a political philosophy adopted by the Labour government at the turn of this century which recognised the impossibility of sustaining the welfare state as chief provider, and sought to combine the complexities of capitalist globalisation and free markets with a social obligation on behalf of the state to support individuals and communities to help themselves:

*The basic idea entailed in the Third Way focus is on empowering individuals, families and communities to lift themselves out of poverty, unemployment and social exclusion by a combination of individual responsibility, education, social support and welfare to work initiatives.*

(p.95)

This recognises that, if people are to play an active part in local democracy, new skills and attitudes need to be developed. Government initiatives such as the citizenship curriculum in schools brought a new focus on community and active citizenship into the twenty-first century.

The 'Big Society' was the flagship policy idea of the 2010 Conservative Party general election manifesto, which was subsequently adopted as part of the Coalition agreement and it is now part of the domestic policy in England and devolved in Northern Ireland, Scotland and Wales. The government website states:

*The Big Society is about collective action and collective responsibility. We recognise that active local people can do better than state services at finding innovative and more efficient solutions to local problems .... we want communities to be part of the answer to the big social problems of our time.*

(Cabinet Office, 2013)

This advocates discussion, involvement and personal and group commitment. While obviously challenging, the approach to learning is empowering and life-enhancing on both an individual and community level. Freire (1970) referred to *problem-posing education* and contended that people, when challenged with problems that relate in a direct way to their own or their community's well-being, will feel obliged to respond to the challenge. By presenting challenges as personal and yet universal, the individual is encouraged to develop a sense of connection and personal involvement with the community. If this connection becomes proactive, it can in turn lead to the decentralisation of power and closer, interactive communities of responsible citizens who are involved and confident enough to make a difference. This approach has been developed in the work of Brazilian theatre practitioner Augusto Boal (1998, 1999). Boal's Marxist interventionist theories, influenced by Freire, were used frequently by TIE practitioners during the latter part of the twentieth century.

---

*Pause for thought* | proactivity

It is interesting to note that, for very different reasons, many western governments in pursuit of Lawton's 'Third Way' should mirror a number of the pedagogical recommendations of a revolutionary such as Freire. Consider for a moment what the advantages and disadvantages of proactive communities might be for:

- a community?
- a government?
- Cameron's Big Society?

---

# What is a community?

The concept of community is multifaceted and fluid. The term is often used to describe:

- physical proximity, as in neighbourhood;
- civic identity, as in a populace;
- collective identity, as in unity, co-operation and shared interest.

A sense of locality may well be fundamental to an individual's sense of identity, but this can be negative as easily as it can be positive. A sense of belonging, being recognised and accepted is psychologically healthy, but many people at some point in their lives feel marginalised or stifled by a community that is based purely on proximity. However, locality can provide a network of support. In addition to locality, there is a broader sense of community which operates on a less personal level. This includes such things as a wider regional or national identity or a shared language with loose classifications such as the 'black', 'gay', or 'asylum seeker' community. In normal, unstressed situations these broad classifications tend to remain on a level of recognition rather than meaningful engagement. Nicholson (2005) pointed out that these broader identities can obscure enormous differences and frequently ignore multiple identities. Each individual belongs to a number of communities, some of which satisfy a transitory need, others which are more lasting. Sometimes people from different locations and from different backgrounds find a common cause which initiates a sense of community, if only for a short time.

An increasing form of community identification, described by Nicholson (2005, p.84) as *the paradigm shift from communities of locality to communities of identity*, involves a sense of community dictated less by geography and more by interest and common experience, beliefs or values. This concept is made easier by effective communication services. To some extent this is an 'imagined' community of shared identity with no material existence.

---

**Pause for thought** | overlapping communities

The concept of community is not singular. Consider for a moment how many 'communities' you belong to and write them down. How far do they overlap? If you have left a community, how much of it have you absorbed and taken with you? Have you ever felt on the margins of a community? Have you ever felt restricted by a community you belonged to? Does community imply exclusiveness? Compare your ideas of community with someone else's.

---

# Community intervention

Asking communities to become more active and to take more responsibility socially, educationally and politically is a form of intervention. Its success depends on how far individuals are able to identify with community issues, which will depend to some extent on how clearly they understand them and on how much influence they believe they can have. People's apparent indifference to global, national and local issues often stems from a sense of powerlessness and a lack of confidence that they can have any influence whatsoever. Offering practical information or education about how society functions and how individuals and communities can access legal, financial and social services is helpful, but there are more empowering ways of educating people which enhance confidence, offer insight and actually build a sense of community identity. The notion of intervention, applying theatre and drama in the community for a particular purpose, has been one of the most significant areas of development as exemplified by Bayleiss and Dodwell's *Action Track Project* (2002) and Dwyer (2004).

Since 2000 there has been a shift away from educational drama towards applied theatre in books and journals. This appears to be endorsed by commentators such as Ackroyd (2000, 2007) and Bowell and Heap (2005, 2010) who believe that educational drama has been given less attention than applied practices. Issue-based theatre in education practice has received a great deal of attention in journals.

Neelands (2004) has developed the notion of social justice within the 'people's theatre', which he sees as participatory and active, belonging to all people within a community. Instead of defining form or genre, he refers to a living partnership between and within theatres, linking cultures together. He believes that stories are the building blocks of theatre and asserts that all communities share the common belief in the power of stories to help their youth make sense of the world. As well as being a stimulus for artistic action, Neelands has a vision of the 'people's theatre' within the social dimension, stating that this goes:

*beyond the recognition of cultural differences in our artistic work to include the opportunity for our social and economic differences to be publicly and socially negotiated in the interests of social justice.*

(p.33)

Any kind of interventionist strategy can potentially damage as well as liberate. Practitioners are accountable for the effect that their work has on the communities they service as these examples demonstrate.

## Research box

### monitoring the challenge

To what extent should participants be 'projected into' or 'protected from' controversial material and methodologies? The balance between challenge and support is the key to this issue. An exposition of the HIV/AIDS workshops developed through the perspective of the director Phil Morle (1993) provides a good example. In an 'anti-intellectual' approach to learning, the Kaos Theatre Company used theatre games, contact improvisation and sculpting and physical manipulation of participants. Morle encouraged participants to use their hands and eyes instinctively, without taking time to plan and think ahead. Although Boal's theories were evident in this process, the deliberate avoidance of intellectual engagement with the form does not appear to have adhered to his practice in all respects:

*If individuals think in their heads first and then attempt to translate this into physical imagery, the result is compromised by limitations of translation, causing a constraint of the potential image and ultimately the debate.*

(Morle, 1993, p.3)

Trusting in the language of imagery was central to the process in order to allow unconscious feelings to surface. The validity of such devices could be questioned since they do not offer protection to participants and encourage potentially embarrassing unguarded responses. Tensions could arise between the company delivering the workshop and the group leader entrusted with care of the group.

There are many examples of interventionist theatre programmes using Boal's Forum Theatre to address issues allied to the citizenship agenda (Dwyer, 2004). One such programme was the Brisbane Dracon project (O'Toole and Burton, 2005), which focused on the role of acting in helping young people towards a cognitive understanding of the nature, causes and dynamics of conflict and bullying. Students were given the skills to take control of their own conflicts and conflict agenda, with an assumption that educational drama techniques have *considerable potential to motivate and assist students to understand the causes of conflict.*

Community drama programmes claim to have had a positive impact in the area of social inclusion and social regeneration. Increasingly, such programmes have been expected to produce evidence of social outcomes as well as artistic realisation, taking theatre into new socio-cultural territory. Typically a company might be expected to produce statistical evidence about the participants and audiences serviced. London Bubble Theatre Company has placed these issues at the centre of its community programmes with the belief that the arts have the capacity to break down barriers of class, culture, age and gender. *The making of George* (Owen, 2004) was a collaborative project which sought to meet the objectives of the Southwark Community Cohesion Pathfinder Programme, a regeneration initiative. There was a meeting of social aims between funders and artists, but a tension emerged between a non-arts funding source and an arts programme. This community play could not rely simply on the benefits of bringing together people aged 15–75 from the area in a vibrant and innovative arts event. It also needed to produce evidence of social outcomes.

The community play is a medium for communities to take ownership of their own regeneration and is also an interventionist theatre form. The term defines a collection of voluntary, non-professional actors working together to create a performance, usually based on a local issue or story. It clearly falls under the mantle of educational theatre within the community and allows groups who inhabit the same cultural context to share their stories and learn to understand each other's problems, breaking down the barriers between groups and opening a dialogue with excluded groups in society. Van Erven (2001) wrote of a series of community plays throughout the world and suggested that the artistic processes involved in community theatre evolve under particular socio-cultural conditions. While scripts are often used in community theatre, there is an emphasis on oral stories and personal recollection. Spare Tyre Theatre Company, a community group formed to develop performance with people aged 65 to over 80 years old, offers an example of the function of the community play in social inclusion, empowering and valuing the experiences of a social group who might otherwise feel socially excluded (Irving, 2003).

The status of the community play and street arts when set against mainstream theatre belies its significance in the lives of individuals. Gardner (2003) commented that street arts events are virtually ignored. Yet the Streets of Brighton Festival draws in an audience of more than 100,000 people. In France, the Cinescenie at Puy de Fou is performed on the largest outdoor stage in the world, with 1,000 actors aged from 5 upwards, a team of 300 staff and 100 animals in each show. Almost 7 million spectators have seen the event since its inception in 1978. The pastoral setting is combined with cutting-edge technology to exciting effect, with surround-sound, lasers, pyrotechnics, water screens and projections. Despite its scale, reporting of such an event is minimal beyond the region in which it is performed. Kershaw (1999, 2003) advocated greater radicalism in street performance, wanting to move away from spectacle and towards dialogue which might result in greater critical attention.

## Setting up a community project

'Education in the community' offers an exciting opportunity to make a difference to the lives of others, especially when using vibrant interactive methodologies such as drama and theatre. It also places a number of practical and professional demands on those charged with establishing such projects. Effective protocols are required to ensure that etiquette, ethical concerns and equal opportunities are in place that will provide respect for participants. When education students work in the community, additional issues affect the project such as health and safety, assessment and support. The complexities involved in setting up an educational community project are outlined below.

If a facilitator undertakes a project with an established group, he or she suspends the relationship between the group and their usual leader. Initiating a positive relationship between the 'normal' group leader and the facilitator of the project is vitally important.

If a facilitator hopes to establish a freestanding community group, he or she must decide whether or not to approach an umbrella organisation in order to recruit volunteers. Gaining access to a target group within a church or prison, for example, could be achieved through access to regular meetings, enhanced through an advertising campaign. Both the emerging group and the facilitator in this situation have the security of working within clearly established rules and codes of practice. The facilitator will be required to observe the policies and procedures of the host organisation and will have the responsibility of ensuring that participants in the project do the same. A positive aspect of this situation is that individual rights and responsibilities are assured, with behaviour contracts in place and minority interests preserved. Individual needs are addressed through existing legislation and the whole group, including the facilitator, is protected by the organisation's public liability insurance, health and safety legislation and risk assessments.

It is possible, however, that the umbrella organisation may inhibit the behaviour of the participants and promote an atmosphere that the facilitator finds inappropriate. For example, there may be codes relating to appearance and use of language that meet the needs of the organisation in its day-to-day operation but prevent the facilitator from achieving the atmosphere required for learning outcomes to be realised. If interventionist drama theories are to be employed in the liberation of individuals from aspects of their lives that cause oppression, it is inappropriate to work within oppressive regimes. Yet if the organisation is sponsoring the work, its aims and values cannot be ignored even when they contradict those of the facilitator.

Given these negative possibilities, the facilitator may elect to establish a 'freestanding' community group, perhaps to celebrate a single event such as a community festival or national celebration. Arts events in this category could include a community play, torch-lit procession, street party, exhibition or entertainment for a village fete. Such events would be more likely to emerge from within a locational or geographical community group than an interest group. If the facilitator is an insider, then local loyalties, friendships and shared understanding will provide the pressure and motivation for the formation of the group. A disadvantage of the local leadership arrangement is that the group may fall victim to historical rivalries and disputes and may find it hard to attract funding.

Having identified a community group, the facilitator must produce a detailed project outline. This might include:

- targets;
- earning outcomes;
- identified target-group needs;
- timelines;
- budget;
- outcomes;
- legislative issues;
- research;
- risk management;

- workshop plans and content;
- resource needs;
- partners' interests;
- review processes.

A professional contract is needed in order to clarify roles, responsibilities and liability. It is essential that all partners are aware of the function, scope and expected outcome of the community project and that an appropriate balance is struck with participants between ownership and accountability.

## Summary and conclusions

There is a rich history of education within communities in non-formal settings. This goes beyond the accumulation of facts and information and deals with ideas, aspiration and personal and community identity. While it is vulnerable to outside manipulation, it is also responsive to positive intervention.

Intervention can be political, social or educational. Communities may be empowered to accept or reject intervention and can develop their own strategies for change from within. Theatre and drama structures are ideal for active intervention as they offer physical examples which can be viewed, deconstructed and re-negotiated. They also allow effective and cognitive responses to occur simultaneously, encouraging rounded engagement. Intervention is always value-laden and so any attempt to work within communities using active learning methods demands a level of self-awareness on the part of the facilitator in order to avoid imposing attitudes and assumptions.

It has been suggested that communities work most effectively when they form self-supporting units and also that theatre can be a powerful medium for initiating responses. Since theatre programmes can sometimes seem transitory and imposed, and also risk unearthing sensitive issues for vulnerable members of society, there is perhaps greater benefit in using sustained, active drama methodology to empower communities to solve problems. A well-prepared drama project in which a single facilitator moves into the community and works within it is an effective vehicle for building a confident, proactive community.

## *References*

Ackroyd, J (2000) Applied theatre: problems and possibilities. *Applied Drama Researcher* (1.2001 [PDF download]), **www.griffith.edu.au/arts-languages-criminology/centre-public-culture-ideas/publications/applied-theatre-researcheridea-journal/issues** (accessed 20 November 2009).

Ackroyd, J (2007) Applied theatre: an exclusionary discourse? *Applied Theatre Researcher*, (8 [PDF download]), **http://www.griffith.edu.au/arts-languages-criminology/centre-public-culture-ideas/publications/applied-theatre-researcheridea-journal/issues**

Allen, G and Martin, I (1992) Histories of community education: a feminist critique, in *Education and Community*. New York: Cassell.

Bayliss, P and Dodwell, C (2002) Building relationships through drama: the Action Track Project. *Research in Drama Education*, 7(1): 43–60.

Boal, A (1998) *Theatre of the Oppressed*. London: Routledge.

Boal, A (1999) *The Rainbow of Desire*. London: Routledge.

Bowell, P and Heap, B (2005) Drama on the run: a prelude to mapping the practice of process drama. *Journal of Aesthetic Education*, 39(4): 58–69.

Bowell, P and Heap, B (2010) Drama is not a dirty word: past achievements, present concerns, alternative futures. *Research in Drama Education*, 15(4): 579–92.

Cabinet Office (2013) *Big Society: Frequently asked questions*. London: Cabinet Office. [Online] available at: **http://old.cabinetoffice.gov.uk/content/big-society-frequently-asked-questions-faqs** (accessed 5 March 2013).

Dwyer, P (2004) Making bodies talk in Forum Theatre. *Research in Drama in Education*, 9: 9–23.

Freire, P (1970) *Pedagogy of the Oppressed*. London: Penguin.

Gardner, L (2003) Out of the ashes. *Street Arts: A User's Guide*, 1: 8–10.

Irving, E (2003) Old age ain't no place for sissies. *Mail Out: National Magazine for Developing Participation in the Arts*, 3: 9.

Kershaw, B (1999) *The Politics of Performance*. London: Routledge.

Kershaw, B (2003) Seeing through the spectacle. *Street Arts: A User's Guide*, 1: 10–13.

Lawton, D (2001) *Education for Citizenship*. London: Continuum.

MacColl, E (1973) Grass roots of theatre workshop. *Theatre Quarterly*, 9: 58–68.

Morle, P (1993) Art can save lives: drama and AIDS. *Journal of National Drama*, 12(1): 3.

Neelands, J (2004) The opening address to the 5th World Congress of IDEA. *Drama Journal*, 12(1): 31–8.

Nicholson, H (2005) *Applied Drama*. Hampshire: Palgrave Macmillan.

O'Toole, J and Burton, B (2005) Education acting against conflict and bullying: the Brisbane Dracon Project 1996–2004. *Research in Drama Education*, 10(3): 269–84.

Owen, L (2004) The making of George. *Drama Journal: One Forum, Many Voices*, 12(1): 5 7.

Richardson, LD and Wolfe, M (2001) *Principles and Practice of Informal Education*. London: RoutledgeFalmer.

Rose, J (2002) *The Intellectual Life of the British Working Classes*. New Haven, CT: Yale University Press.

Van Erven, E (2001) *Community Theatre: Global perspectives*. London: Routledge.

Wenger, E (2004) *Communities of Practice: Learning, Meaning and Identity*. Cambridge: Cambridge University Press.

White, L (2002) *Neighbourhood Renewal, Case Studies and Conversations*. London: NIACE.

Witham, B (2003) *The Federal Theatre Project: A case study*. Cambridge: Cambridge University Press.

# Chapter 8

# The Further Education and Skills sector

## Jim Crawley

### Introduction

The Further Education and Skills sector (FES) is one of the most complex and difficult parts of the education landscape to define and explain, but it is also a sector which offers a richness, diversity and range unlike any other part of education. Just the fact that the official title of the FES has changed around every five years for the past twenty years gives some indication of its complexity and changing nature. Successive governments have exerted an ever-growing influence in the FES to the point where it has been described as *the most highly-regulated and centrally-directed education system in Europe* (Orr and Simmons, 2010, p.78). The FES offers a breadth of learning opportunities and other services which is extensive and works with a great diversity of members of the community, industry, the public and private sectors. This range and scope is both one of its biggest assets and almost its biggest problem, as this chapter will indicate. The chapter will explain the key components of the FES and some of its achievements, and analyse its context, purpose and position within the UK education system.

## What is the FES?

The FES is complex, includes a broad range of subsectors, works with a diverse group of students, and operates in multiple locations. This makes it difficult to define, and indeed successive governments have changed the name of the sector with a regularity that suggests they also have difficulty defining it (Orr and Simmons, 2010). Crawley (2010) provides a helpful explanation when defining the FES as a community of subsectors, which make up the sector as a whole. The sector is defined by the education or training provision which takes place. When you are *in further education, community learning and development, workplace learning, 14–19 provision, sixth form colleges, public services training or offender learning which is not delivered by school teachers* (ibid, p.14) you are in the FES.

## What are the FES subsectors?

Within the subsectors, which make up this next part of the chapter, overlap and duplication exist, but the subsectors do have their own goals, target groups, professional groupings and associations, and employees working with students. The following descriptions provide the clearest explanation of what the subsectors are, what they do and who they work with which is currently available.

# Further Education (FE) colleges

There are 402 colleges in England in 2013 (Association of Colleges, 2013) and they offer academic, vocational and other programmes from entry level to higher education. They employ 117,000 teachers and lecturers. Every year colleges educate and train over 3 million people. 853,000 16 to 18 year olds choose to study in colleges (compared with 435,000 in maintained school and academy sixth forms). 45,000 16 to 18 year olds started an apprenticeship through their local college. Over 2 million adults study or train in colleges and 170,000 students study higher education in a college (Association of Colleges, 2012, pp.1–2). Many FE colleges operate from more than one campus, and it will not be unusual for teachers and learners to work across more than one in a normal day. Locations can include business parks, shopping centres, specialised vocational centres, community venues and industrial premises.

# Community Learning and Development (CLD)

CLD can include community-based adult learning; community development; community education, development education, family learning, working with parents and youth work. Much of the activity in the industry is voluntary. CLD employs over 1.2 million staff, and its funding comes from a variety of sources (Lifelong Learning UK, 2009). Participation rates in adult learning vary across the UK, and have been declining in recent years, but 3.1 million adults aged over 19 were enrolled on government-funded provision in 2010/11 (Data Service, 2012).

# Workplace learning

This subsector of the FES includes, as the title suggests, learning which is based in the workplace. This currently includes programmes such as apprenticeships, which have grown considerably from in the region of 270,000 participants in England in 2001/02 to 457,200 starts in 2010/11 (Data Service, 2012). This subsector could include anything from a major multinational company employing thousands of staff and providing its own learning centre on site, to a 'micro business' employing under 10 people, where all training is done on the job. The Association of Employment and Learning Providers (AELP) is a professional association for workplace learning, and *almost 300,000 employers across the country … helped 117,240 learners complete an apprenticeship* (AELP, 2012).

# 14–19 education

14–19 education is part of both the statutory school sector and the FES, and the FES part of this subsector takes place in Further Education Colleges, Workplace Learning Centres, and in centres jointly managed with schools. Over the past two decades, the FES has worked on an increasing basis with 14–19 year olds, which has been a significant shift from their work in the 1970s to 90s. 58,000 14 to 15 year olds enrol in further education courses each year, 3,000 full-time and 55,000 part-time. This is in addition to the 853,000 16 to 18 year olds (AoC, 2012, p.3). From September 2013, further education colleges will be able to recruit 14–19 year olds on full-time programmes without reference to a school.

# Sixth form colleges

Sixth form colleges are not part of the schools sector but independent, autonomous institutions. There are currently more than 150,000 students aged 16 to 18 studying at sixth form colleges. As the Sixth Form College Association (2013, p.1) indicates:

*Despite forming a relatively small part of the education landscape, with just 94 Sixth Form Colleges across England, the sector accounts for 14 per cent of acceptances to higher education – more than general FE colleges (11 per cent) and independent schools (10 per cent). Almost 90 per cent of the students at sixth form colleges are studying A-Levels.*

## Public and uniformed services training

One subsector often left out when defining the FES, but which works with hundreds of thousands of people each year, is that of public and uniformed services training. This includes the police, armed forces, fire and ambulance personnel; training often takes place within the premises of those services, and in the field or workplace. Students or trainees can be engaged in complex technical and vocational programmes, high-level professional learning, or basic skills to enhance their confidence and employability. Their training can even take place on the front line in a conflict zone. There is no nationally available data on the numbers of learners involved in this part of the FES, but it is significant.

## Offender learning

Another less-known subsector is that of offender learning, which can take place either in institutions where offenders are placed, or in the community after conviction. There were 90,100 offenders aged 18 or over in the prison system participating in learning in 2011/12, an increase of 1.4 per cent on 2010/11 (Data Service, 2013, p. 6).

As can be seen from these brief snapshots of the subsectors which make up the FES, they include many contexts and age groups, and they often overlap with each other. This diversity permeates the sector.

---

*Pause for thought* | are you new to the FES?

As you can see from the previous section, the FES encompasses a very broad range of educational activity and provision. But how new is this to you?

Read back through the descriptions of subsectors. How many of these had you already heard of? Have you or family members had any experience of learning with any part of the FES? Did you ever get to know what the sector was called?

---

# What does the FES teach?

There is no National Curriculum for the FES. As can be seen from the previous section, the range of subjects, contexts and types of educational or training programmes is extensive; for example, many FE colleges offer pure and applied sciences, languages, health and social care, arts and humanities, teacher training, media, computing and IT and access to higher education courses. The same organisation can often provide vocational qualifications, degrees, advanced level professional development and literacy and numeracy classes. Crawley (2010) suggests that there are at least 200 subjects on offer at any given time in just one medium-sized provider, which is quite different from schools. The age range of students in the FES is another factor which complicates the curriculum on offer. Children from 14 and adults over 65 can all be participating at the same time, and in the same location (and even in the same classroom under some circumstances). In the course of one day's teaching, an FES teacher could work with young people aged 14–16, professional adults aged between 25 and 55, offenders in a local prison, and senior citizens aged 65 plus.

***Pause for thought*** | subject search

There is one simple way to get a good idea of subjects available in the FES. Take a look at the website or prospectus of two different organisations in the FES, using the explanations in the earlier section. Search for, and count the subjects they have listed.

# A brief history of the FES

Blair (2009, p.96) suggests that *the function of FE has changed as the history of the society around it has unfolded.* The history of the sector is characterised by frequent and major change, recasting of government approaches, sector name changes and a tendency to be seen as less important than other branches of education. In 1563, the Statute of Artificers established apprenticeships as *the dominant form of work-related training up to the 1960s* (Armitage et al., 2007, p.245). In 1823, Mechanics Institutes were established, and they were working with 600,000 people by 1826. By the 1940s, Evening Institutes, and the Workers' Educational Association had been established, and the Education Act of 1944 legislated for there to be *adequate facilities* for full-time and part-time education *for persons over compulsory school age* and for *leisure-time occupation* (McNair Report, 1944). Industrial Training Boards (ITBs) were created in 1964 to improve the quality of training and remove skill shortages. By 1971, 27 ITBs covering 15 million workers were in place, and they were paid for by a levy on employers. The 1992 Further and Higher Education Act (Stationery Office, 1992) was implemented when Further Education Colleges came out of local authority control and became independent business corporations and polytechnics became full universities. In 2001, the Further Education National Training Organisation (FENTO, 1999) national standards were introduced and, for the first time, it became a requirement for teachers in the FES to gain a teaching qualification. In 2003, the first inspections of the FES were started by the Office for Standards in Education (Ofsted). In 2012 and 2013, change still takes place apace, with a key report on professionalism in the sector (Business Industry and Skills, 2012), and on adult and vocational teaching and learning (LSIS, 2013), one recommending the withdrawal of a requirement for teachers in the FES to gain a teacher qualification, only 12 years after it became a requirement. The other report proposes ways of enhancing vocational training. This is representative of the regularity and pace of change in the FES.

## Research box

### shifting sands: status and role of the FES

Various studies have tracked and commented on the nature and scope of the sector, and the pace of change it experiences. Blair (2009, p.96) exemplifies how the establishment of a consistent role over time for the lifelong learning sector (LLS) proves problematic when he states:

*(Continued)*

*(Continued)*

*The role of FE is changing, from supporting apprenticeships (1970s) to teaching arts and craft evening classes (1980s) to last chance/second chance (1990s) to the most recent developments in meeting the skill needs of society.*

Richardson (2007, p.409) presents a downbeat analysis of the place of FE in the LLS and in the overall education sector as follows:

*However these dynamics are understood, and despite the undoubted transformation of English FE in scale and breadth over the last 30 years, certain conspicuous cultural continuities remain. Above all, FE colleges in England have been weak institutions, unable to capitalise on their enormous growth in service to the community.*

He continues to suggest:

*…they remain just not important enough politically, when compared to secondary schools, to be given either equal funding for directly equivalent education provision per student or similar rates of pay for teachers.*

All of these factors generate a feeling of being second-class citizens in the UK education sector as a whole, and, unfortunately, statistics from research seem to confirm that viewpoint. Richardson (2007, p.409) explains some of this difference effectively:

*The shortfall compared to secondary schools in FE student funding per head is estimated at 13% … and in FE teachers' pay … at 9.5% … Beyond these direct, 'real-time' school/FE comparisons, FE also receives less funding for its 'second chance' work with students at Entry level, level 1 and level 2 when compared to schools.*

In the light of such analysis, Richardson (2007) concurs with Fletcher and Owen (2005, p.23) in describing the sector as *second class funding for second class people leading to second class institutions.*

There is evidence that change in the sector has accelerated towards the latter end of the twentieth century, and is continuing in the early twenty-first century. Since 2009 this has also coincided with a global recession and a new UK coalition government in 2010.

## Government involvement

The interest in, and involvement of, government in the work of the FES is a relatively recent development. Before the Second World War, the political Right *granted teachers autonomy on the basis that politics were kept out of education* (Avis et al., 2010, p.41). By the end of the Second World War, *curriculum and schooling were seen to be controlled by teachers* (ibid, p.42). This situation then began to attract criticism from the political Left who accused teachers of *complicity in reproducing inequality and failing to deliver social justice* (ibid, p.42). The Right became suspicious that teachers were becoming *progressive* and *anti-business* (ibid, p.42). In 1976 Prime Minister James Callaghan made a speech at Ruskin College (Callaghan, 1976) in which he commented that education was *funded by government, parents and industry* so those parties should not be excluded. The direct involvement of government in the FES grew after this speech, which set the tone for government involvement and could equally have been made by most governments since the late 1970s.

## Research box

### government involvement in the FES

Politics has become increasingly interested in teachers and teaching, and Avis et al. (2010, p.42) assert that:

*The result of these critiques, particularly those from the Right, was to refocus an interest in teacher professionalism, the ramifications of which are still being felt today.*

Avis et al. (2010) describe lecturers as:

*caught in a fast changing policy-practice dynamic in which their status has been 'casualised' and deprofessionalised by a process of market, funding-led and managerialist reform.*

(2010, p.438)

Avis et al. (2010, p.42) recognise that, *Various notions have been developed that seek to move professionalism in progressive directions* but that these:

*come up against the preferred model of the state which construes the FE teacher in particular as a service provider, at the behest of the market.*

(ibid, p.42)

In a sector which is used to turbulence, the current situation of continuing and unrelenting waves of government initiatives constantly impacts upon the working situation of those in it (Crawley, 2010; Coffield, 2008; Fisher and Simmons, 2010).

Orr and Simmons (2010) sum up the state of the FES effectively when they argue that it:

*...has also been subjected to unprecedented levels of state intervention and series of policy initiatives, relating to both strategic and operational matters. Virtually all aspects of FE are now highly mediated by the State.*

(ibid, p.78)

## Good news

There is, however, a range of positives about the sector and the teachers working in it which have regularly been acknowledged. Coffield et al. (2007), for example, emphasise the inclusive and 'second chance' nature of the sector. They use a brief example of a low-achieving school leaver who achieved well at college and then state:

*The above captures a very significant but unsung achievement of FE colleges. They take in students whom no one else wants to teach, namely, those who have failed to gain five good GCSEs at the age of 16, and, through sheer hard work and through forging more respectful and inclusive relationships, they restore them as human beings who begin to see themselves again as worthy of respect and who can and do succeed in gaining qualifications. Many of these students talk of being neglected and even insulted in schools.*

(Coffield et al., 2007, p.724)

There is an impressive range of achievements, which the FES can list despite its nature and complexity, government intervention, constant change and challenging working situation. A small proportion are listed below:

- Research shows students at sixth form colleges are more likely to get top grades at A-level than those in school sixth forms.
- Over three-quarters of people think that colleges make an important contribution to their local communities as an educator and employer.
- 130,000 FES students are aged over 60.
- 80 per cent of English for Speakers of Other Languages (ESOL) students study at a college.
- 220,000 unemployed people undertake education and training in the FES.
- Over 40 London 2012 Olympic competitors studied at a college and 14 of Team GB's London 2012 Olympic medals (6 of which were gold) were won by past and present College students.

(AoC, 2012, pp.1–6)

---

**Pause for thought** | find out more

Get a map of your local area and see how many FES organisations you can locate and list. You will need to use a variety of search techniques, but to start with a search term online of 'place name: e.g. Bristol' and 'college' followed by 'community learning' and 'workplace learning' should give you a good start.

---

## Summary and conclusions

The way in which the FES has developed to encompass such breadth and diversity is perhaps both its biggest strength, and one of its biggest challenges. The complexity represents a massive challenge to any attempts to unify, categorise or draw it together, and governments have tended to opt for control rather than allowing the diversity to flourish. Despite this context, the FES continues to rise to the challenge, making real contributions to the economy, welfare, employability, well-being and sense of community of millions of people each year who may otherwise not get that chance. Whatever it is called in the future, the chances are it will continue to undertake this crucial role in education.

## References

Armitage, A, Bryant, R, Dunnill, R, Flanagan, K, Hayes, D, Hudson, A, Kent, J, Lawes, S and Renwick, M (2007) *Teaching and Training in Post Compulsory Education* (3rd edn). Buckingham: Open University Press.

Association of Colleges (2012) *College Key Facts*. London: AoC.

Association of Colleges (2013) *College Key Facts*. Online Available at: **www.aoc.co.uk/en/research/college-key-facts.cfm** (accessed 19 May 2013).

Association of Employment and Learning Providers (2012) *AELP Fact Sheet*. Bristol: AELP.

Avis, J, Fisher, R, and Ollin, R (2010) Professionalism, in Avis, J, Fisher, R and Thompson, R (eds) (2010) *Teaching in Lifelong Learning – A Guide to Theory and Practice*. Maidenhead: Open University Press.

BIS (2012) *Professionalism in Further Education – Final Report (Lingfield Report)*. London: Department of Business, Innovation and Skills.

Blair, E (2009) A further education college as a heterotopia. *Research in Post-Compulsory Education,* 14(1), March, 93-101.

Callaghan, J (1976) *Towards a National Debate*, speech at a foundation stone-laying ceremony at Ruskin College, Oxford, 18 October 1976.

Coffield, F (2008) *Just Suppose Teaching and Learning Became the First Priority …* London: Learning and Skills Network.

Coffield, F, Edward, S, Finlay, I, Hodgson, A, Spours, K and Steer, R (2007) *Improving Learning, Skills and Inclusion*. London: Routledge.

Crawley, J (2010) *In at the Deep End – A Survival Guide for Teachers in Post Compulsory Education* (2nd edn). London: Routledge.

Data Service (2012) *Quarterly Statistical First Release*. Publication date: 29 March 2012. London: Data Service.

Data Service (2013) *Quarterly Statistical First Release*. Publication date: 29 March 2013. London: Data Service.

FENTO (1999) *Standards for Teaching and Supporting Learning in Further Education in England and Wales*. Coventry: Further Education National Training Organisation.

Fisher, R and Simmons, R (2010) What is the Lifelong Learning Sector? in Avis, J, Fisher, R and Thompson, R (eds) (2010) *Teaching in Lifelong Learning – A Guide to Theory and Practice*. Maidenhead: Open University Press.

Fletcher, M and Owen, G (2005) *The Funding Gap: Funding in schools and colleges for full-time students aged 16–18*. LSDA: London.

Lifelong Learning (2009) *Overview of Community Learning and Development*. Coventry: Lifelong Learning UK.

LSIS (2013) *Learning and Skills Improvement Service*. Coventry: LSIS. Available at: **http:// webarchive.nationalarchives.gov.uk/20130802100617/http://lsis.org.uk/about-lsis** (accessed 20 October 2013).

McNair Report (1944) *Teachers and Youth Leaders*. London: HMSO.

Orr, K and Simmons, R (2010) Dual identities: the in-service teacher trainee experience in the English further education sector. *Journal of Vocational Education and Training*, 62(1): 75–88.

Richardson, R (2007) In search of the further education of young people in post-war England. *Journal of Vocational Education and Training,* 59(3), September 2007, 385–418.

SFCA (2013) *Creating a Level Playing Field. White Paper.* London: Sixth Form Colleges Association.

Stationery Office (1992) *The Further and Higher Education Act 1992*. London: Stationery Office.

# Chapter 9

# University knowledge: the market and the state

## Stephen Ward

### Introduction

University education in the UK used to be for an intellectual elite, but policies for expansion and widening participation have led to a mass Higher Education system. The university is now said to be a business in the Higher Education market and higher tuition fees mean that students become 'customers' who pay for their education and can demand the same rights as shoppers who want value – a good degree for my money. Unlike schools, universities have traditionally enjoyed autonomy from government controls and academic freedom for their staff. This chapter examines Higher Education in universities and colleges and its role in UK society today. It looks at the ways in which universities traditionally defined knowledge and what counts as knowledge, and how this has changed with more government control. In particular it examines the ways in which market forces have affected what universities do and the ways in which they are run. Some of the issues discussed are:

- what knowledge should be studied;
- who should pay for it;
- whether universities should have academic freedom.

# What is Higher Education?

Higher Education (HE) is at the levels of study after Advanced Level and its equivalents at Level 3. It is taught in Higher Education Institutions (HEI) such as universities and colleges. A basic hierarchy of awards at different levels, with the usual length of full-time study includes:

- one-year Certificate in Higher Education (CertHE) (Level 4);
- two-year Diploma in Higher Education (DipHE) (Level 5);
- two-year Foundation Degree (FD) (Level 5);
- three-year Bachelor of Arts (BA) and Science (BSc) Degrees (Level 6);
- one-year Master of Arts (MA) and Science (MSc) (Level 7);
- three-year Doctorate (PhD) (Level 8).

There are also vocationally oriented degrees with specialist professional titles such as Bachelor of Education (BEd) or Masters in Business Administration (MBA).

HE is sometimes confused with 'Further Education' (FE), which is the term used to refer to education after the statutory leaving age of 16 but at a lower level than HE. What complicates things is that Further Education Colleges often teach Higher Education degree and diploma courses, validated and awarded by a university or other body. FE colleges which teach a lot of Higher Education students are now able to apply for degree-awarding powers themselves and may in the future become universities.

In this chapter the terms 'university' and 'university knowledge' will be used as shorthand for the various Higher Education institutions and courses.

*Pause for thought* | why do a degree?

Higher Education is an expensive business. Many people give up earning money in the short term and pay university fees. What are their reasons for doing this? Is it to have a better career and to earn more money later, or is it about education for its own sake? What made you decide to go into Higher Education? Was it because it was what your friends and family expected you to do? Was it part of your own vision for your career?

# Medieval origins of the university

The term 'university' derives from the Latin *universitas*, meaning 'a community', and the notion of a universal kinship of scholars underlies the original concept of Higher Education.

European universities began in Paris and Bologna in the thirteenth century and were internationally linked, borderless institutions sharing knowledge across Europe. This was made possible by two characteristics of the time: the relative weakness of national frontiers allowed academics to interact freely across geographical areas and the use of Latin as a *lingua franca* enabled their communication.

MacCulloch (2004, p.12) shows how the medieval university derived from *the burgeoning industry of intercession*: chantry foundations could employ a staff of priests, who needed an elaborate permanent organisation, and so formed an endowed association – in Latin, *collegium*. The formal university method of academic investigation, by a logical system of questioning and listing data from the authorities, was called scholasticism, and universities were *scholae*. The Higher Education system looks back fondly on the medieval university and its old symbols of knowledge and authority: masters, hoods, gowns and degrees with honours. It would be a mistake, though, to see the medieval university as a golden age of academic freedom in Higher Education. While the academic elite was free to engage as a scholarly community, the knowledge they were allowed to share was largely determined by the Roman Catholic Church. There was no original research, and privileges were guaranteed only so long as the tenets of the Church remained unquestioned.

In the sixteenth century, the Reformation began to free the universities from the Church to allow tutors to be recruited from civil society; less doctrinal teaching allowed new ideas and the development of knowledge. This was driven by the innovation of the printing press, the proliferation of texts, the development of humanism and the emergence of the notion of what now would be known as 'critique': to analyse texts and question their assumptions. It is significant in the later development of university knowledge and of the theory underpinning Education Studies (Ward, 2006). The source of these ideas was the re-discovered classical literature of Greece and Rome. However, as well as a change of curriculum in the universities, the Renaissance also brought the formation of nation states, border controls and the use of national languages in education. Universities lost their universal, borderless quality and became a function of national systems. The university became a national institution.

# The modern university

The modern university began with the Enlightenment and the industrial revolution. Whereas the Church was never seeking new knowledge but only the reinforcement of the traditional, the entrepreneurial society of the late eighteenth and early nineteenth centuries turned to the university for scientific knowledge and a trained professional elite. It was the politician Wilhelm von Humboldt who established the university of Berlin in 1810, which became the model for the modern European university. In this the state funds the university with academic freedom to carry out research, to create knowledge and teach: *The university became a privileged place where the future of society is forged through research* (Haddad, 2000, p.32). Berlin was the first university to provide the highly educated professionals required by industry and civil administration in exchange for freedom from the state and autonomy in the knowledge it produces.

The philosophical concept of the modern university derives from nineteenth-century German idealism, notably the work of Immanuel Kant. For Kant (1992) the basis of the university is reason, in contrast to superstition and tradition: ... *a perpetual conflict between established tradition and rational enquiry:*

*what distinguishes the modern university is a unifying principle that is immanent to the university. Kant ushers in the modernity of the university by naming this principle 'reason' .... And reason has its own discipline, that of philosophy, the lower faculty.*

(Readings, 1996, p.56)

In contrast, the higher faculties of theology, law and medicine draw from the *unquestionable authority* of the Bible, law on the civil code and the decrees of the medical profession. *The authority of the lower faculty is ... autonomous in that philosophy depends on nothing outside itself; it legitimates itself by reason alone, by its own practice* (p.56).

The 'conflict of the faculties' reflects the tension between superstition and reason. Kant does not see the university as divorced from culture and society, but he strikes a balance between the autonomy of reason and the power of the state. Kant argues that the role of the university is to produce technicians for the state – 'men of affairs'. However, .... *one of the functions of the University is to intervene at all times to remind these men of affairs that they must submit their use of knowledge in the service of the state and to the control of the faculties, ultimately to the faculty of philosophy* (p.58). Humboldt employed Kant's notion of creating and sustaining a national culture through reasoned critique in his model of the University of Berlin. Humboldt argued that *the state protects the actions of the university; the university safeguards the thoughts of the state. And each strives to realise the idea of a national culture* (Readings, 1996, p.69). The modern university, then, is a means of the realisation of state nationalism, culture and identity. Humboldt's genius was to create a system in which the state finances the university, but allows it autonomy and ensures academic freedom for its teachers. The Humboldt University of Berlin has been the pattern for European universities in the nineteenth and twentieth centuries.

Another way of characterising the idea of academic freedom is in the famous book by Cardinal Newman (1996) *The Idea of a University*. Newman, writing in the mid-nineteenth century, suggests that university knowledge should be 'useless knowledge' as against the 'useful knowledge' required by employment and industry. This is an extreme view of the university, sometimes known as 'the ivory tower'.

> *Pause for thought* | academic freedom
>
> The model of the Humboldt university is an attractive one for academics as they have complete freedom to determine what counts as knowledge and what should be learned. What are the advantages and disadvantages of university staff having academic freedom? Do you agree with the Humboldt university model, or should governments have more control and accountability for tax-payers' money? Should students have the right to decide on what is taught in the university?

# The postmodern university: knowledge, the state and the market

Critiques of the Humboldt model of the university come from Bourdieu (1988), Habermas (1971) and Parsons (1974). Parsons saw the university as a shared normative system and that there is a functional link between knowledge and citizenship. For Habermas, the university has an emancipatory function in society. Bourdieu, on the other hand, depicts the university as a self-preserving institution: an autonomous site in which different orders of power clash and struggle for self-reproduction. Using Foucault's (1972) notion of 'knowledge as power' in which the academic institution serves the interests of the dominant group, the university reproduces society and legitimates inequalities. Education is the means that modern society has devised for the transmission of cultural capital, which are the cognitive structures of the dominant cultural models in society. This differs from Parsons's notion of a shared normative system since culture, in being pervaded by power, is forced to be a site of contestation. Kant's conflict of the faculties is between knowledge and rationality; for Bourdieu the conflicts are between different sorts of capital: cognitive or cultural.

Delanty (2001) argues a new role for the university in the context of cultural and epistemological changes in society with the democratisation of knowledge:

*By democratisation I mean the participation of more and more actors in the social construction of reality. Given that the university is no longer the crucial institution in society for the reproduction of instrumental/technical knowledge and is also no longer the codifier of a now fragmented national culture, it can ally itself to civil society.*

(p.6)

Cowen (1996) sees the university in terms of global economics and market forces and proposes: …. *a rebalancing of the relationships between the state, the productive economy and universities* (p.3). The university loses its autonomy from government. The effect is a shift from knowledge as truth to knowledge as 'performativity': that which is useful in the economic terms of student employment. It is a part of the epistemological change described by Lyotard (1986) as the post-industrial, postmodern collapse of meta-knowledge and the contestation of the nature of knowledge itself. Cowen explains the change in terms of government claims of economic crisis. Universities have become part of the training for business in order to cope with the move from material production to the techno-sciences of the global economy. Cowen's conclusion is that, through the pursuit of performativity, the university is reduced, or *attenuated,* in a variety of ways: spatially, financially and pedagogically.

Barnett (2000) rejects Cowen's notion of the completely attenuated university. He acknowledges attenuation through performativity in the types of research and teaching which are packaged for consumption. However, Barnett does not see the university as reduced: it is the 'multiversity' with multiple roles. For Barnett there are no limits to the postmodern university:

*The contemporary university is dissolving into the wider world ... The postmodern university is a distributed university ... It is a multinational concern, stretching out to and accommodating its manifold audiences. It is ... no longer a site of knowledge, but, rather a site of knowledge possibilities .... The university is no longer to be understood in terms of the category of knowledge but rather in terms of shifting and proliferating processes of knowing.*

(pp.20–1)

# University knowledge as preparation for employment

Barnett criticises the conversion of university knowledge into performative skills: there are no longer historians, only graduates who possess a range of transferable skills for society and industry. In Lukasiewicz's (1994) notion of 'the Ignorance Explosion' the proliferation of knowledge is text-based and there is more of it than can possibly be comprehended. Knowledge production is out of step with knowledge comprehension and the relationship between academics and their audience has broken down. So there is a new illiteracy: students are reduced to having data-handling skills, and the human mind is reduced to data-processing skills.

> ### *Pause for thought* | university knowledge
>
> Stefan Collini's recent book is entitled *What are Universities for?* (2012) Can you answer this question? Is university knowledge about providing graduates with employability skills, or does the university still have a role in educating intellectuals with knowledge for its own sake? How does research fit in?

There is, though, optimism in Barnett's possibilities for the future of the university. It may be able to retain some of its modernist role. Although industry demands skills, and the university responds to the demands, the wider society longs for knowledge, breadth, critical reason and freedom:

*society is hesitantly intimating that it needs the universities to live up to their rhetoric of guardians of reason. The university seems intent on constructing itself in narrower frames of self-understanding. A trick is being missed.*

(Barnett, 2000, p.34)

For Readings (1996) 'culture' is no longer the watchword of the university:

*The university is no longer Humboldt's, and that means it is no longer* The *university.*
*The Germans not only founded a University and gave it a mission; they also made the*
*University into the decisive instance of intellectual activity. All of this is in the process*
*of changing: intellectual activity and the culture it revived are being replaced by the*
*pursuit of excellence and performance indicators.*

(p.55)

This 'discourse of decline' is countered by those who see universities as the partners of socio-economic and cultural development. The last decades have seen attempts to link university research and teaching to the world of work with new teaching methods and widening access. Haddad (2000) argues that universities have moved from elitist groups in ivory towers and become closer to society and suggests that they need to go further in developing openness and producing research for peace, human rights and a sustainable future. He points to the mixture of respect and distrust there has always been about universities and suggests that society now has a better idea of university roles and responsibilities.

The expansion of Higher Education changes the original role of the university, which was to educate an intellectual elite. It must now engage with a broader range of the population (50 per cent of the 18–30 cohort).

## Research box

### the infantilisation of Higher Education and the decline of the intellectual

Furedi (2004) argues that government control of universities has become stronger through academic auditing by the Quality Assurance Agency (QAA). Academics from different universities are employed by the QAA in policing subject quality. This makes it appear that the universities retain autonomy, but Furedi suggests that this process has converted academics into 'professionals' who serve as inquisitors on behalf of the QAA and others who act on behalf of the university. This leads to the denigration of intellectual life, a diminished level of individual freedom and a decline in the search for 'objective truth'. Intellectuals should influence the politics of the real world; instead they are trapped as professionals in the institutional bureaucracy of the university.

*Professionalism promotes values and forms of behaviour that may well be inconsistent with*
*those of the intellectual. Activities such as offering a critique of the status quo, acting as the*
*conscience of society, or pursuing the truth regardless of the consequences are not what*
*the job of a professional is all about.*

(p.39)

The shifting balance between state control and control by the institution results in the diminishing of academic freedom and the independence of university knowledge.

Do you agree with Furedi?

# British universities and the market

Until the 1960s Higher Education comprised the five per cent elite who attended the small number of chartered universities. In 1963 the Robbins Commission (Committee on High Education, 1963) recommended the expansion of Higher Education in Britain with the creation of more chartered universities and Higher Education in the colleges. The policy which was developed was the so-called 'binary divide' between universities with a royal charter and polytechnics and colleges controlled by the local education authorities (LEAs). Anthony Crosland, Labour Secretary of State for Education in 1965, set up the system with the ambition of creating separate but equal branches of Higher Education to serve different purposes. There would be the twin virtues of academic independence for the existing universities and, for the new polytechnics, local accountability and an emphasis on applied knowledge for industry.

Although the binary system permitted some financial independence for the polytechnics and colleges, it saw distinctly different forms of academic control between the two types of institution. The established universities with their royal charters were largely self-governing in their curriculum, while knowledge in the polytechnics and colleges was rigorously controlled by the Council for National Academic Awards (CNAA). This was a government-funded organisation which operated to ensure the implementation of strict guidelines for curriculum structure, content and methods. Degree courses to be taught in the polytechnics were to be approved by the Council and were required to meet all its criteria. Although it employed Higher Education 'peers' to implement its directives, it exercised a high level of control over Higher Education knowledge with rigorous scrutiny (Silver, 1990). The existence of this body signified the relationship of the institutions to the state. While the chartered universities enjoyed the Humboldt model with the trust of the state to define and codify knowledge, the polytechnics and colleges were under its watchful eye, with every item of knowledge rigorously audited and approved or rejected.

Freedom from LEA control was granted by the Education Secretary of State, Kenneth Baker, in 1989 with incorporation of polytechnics as independent financial institutions, but the request for university title as 'Polytechnic Universities' was refused. However, things were to change rapidly in 1991 with the new Secretary of State, Kenneth Clarke, who was reported to have said, 'Let's take the great plunge and make them all universities, let's get rid of all the arguments' (Kogan and Hannay, 2000, p.139). With that, the binary system was abolished at a stroke.

While this might appear to foreshadow an increase in independence for the Higher Education institutions, the outcomes were not so simple. The end of the twentieth century brought the New Right in British politics with a different view of the management of public organisations and the professions. These are characterised by New Public Management (NPM) in 'the evaluative state' (Henkel, 1991). NPM is intended on the one hand to devolve power to institutions, but on the other hand to retain central control in order to reduce the power of professional bodies which is depicted as 'professional hegemony'. Margaret Thatcher's 1980s reforms were supposedly intended to roll back the state in a *shift from academic control towards both the market and to the incorporation of universities in the generality of state control* (Henkel, 1991, p.55). Cawson (1982) argues that freedoms were offered to universities only in exchange for working within the state and Kogan and Hanney explain that *the boundary between what should be funded publicly and what earned privately shifted, so that the acceptable sources of higher education funding became multiple and virtually unbounded* (2000, p.55).

Kogan and Hannay present the abolition of the binary system as a whimsical, cavalier action by Kenneth Clarke in the horse-trading with the polytechnic principles. Readings (1996), however, sees the move as part of a larger process of converting the whole British university system into the 'excellence' model to imitate the United States' model of Higher Education. The conversion of polytechnics into universities, he argues, was not an ideological commitment to expanding Higher Education as such, but a mechanism to bring all institutions into the same competitive market in which the successful – as measured by the performance indicators – are rewarded by higher grant allocations.

This marks the move towards government control through market forces, or more particularly, the use of government controls to enable a free market: not a magnanimous egalitarian gesture towards the polytechnics, but an example of pure Thatcherism. Gray (1998) helps to explain this apparent contradiction in Conservative government policy where 'rolling back the state' appears to mean the removal of government controls, but actually involves controls on institutions through nationally prescribed curriculum and criteria. Gray maintains that strong government intervention is always required to permit a completely free market, pointing out that,

*encumbered markets are the norm in every society, whereas free markets are a product of artifice, design and political coercion. Laissez-faire must be centrally planned: regulated markets just happen. The free market is not, as New Right thinkers have imagined or claimed, a gift of social evolution. It is an end-product of social engineering and unyielding political will.*

(p.17)

The removal of the binary system, then, should be seen as a move to the American free market in Higher Education and the mixture of freedoms and controls which that has brought. Readings (1996) argues that the very foundations of the traditional western university are crumbling in post-modern chaos. The hollowing out of the nation state through global capitalism and trans-national corporations led to the ruin of the modernist university, for the primacy of the nation state is in the role of the university:

*The modern university was conceived by Humboldt as one of the primary apparatuses through which this production of national subjects was to take place in modernity, and the decline of the nation-state raises serious questions about the nature of the contemporary function of the university.*

(p.46)

> ### Pause for thought | academic and vocational higher education
>
> The binary higher education system was designed to create universities providing 'academic' degrees and polytechnics providing vocational studies. Do you agree with the principle of there being two types of university: those which teach purely 'academic' subjects such as philosophy, the arts and humanities, and those which teach 'vocational' subjects such as engineering and teaching?

# English tuition fees and university knowledge

The Blair government's introduction in 2005 of 'variable' tuition fees with a maximum of £3,000 was another step towards the American model of market-led Higher Education. Because the demand for Higher Education was so high, all apart from two charged the maximum fee and so the attempt to introduce market competition failed. At the time there was bitter opposition among Labour MPs to the fees. Blair's attempt to introduce the necessary legislation almost led to his government losing the vote in the house. The limit of £3,000 was a symptom of the government's weakness in not being able to introduce a proper competitive market; again, as Gray (1998), notes, strong government is needed to establish a market.

Universities complained that the £3,000 fee did not provide sufficient income to provide high quality education. The Browne Report (Browne, 2010) introduced the proposal of unlimited tuition fees. The 2010 Coalition Government tried to take this up, although a limit of £9,000 was imposed as a result of the Liberal Democrat influence within the coalition, the party having opposed tuition fees in the 2010 General Election. A strong Conservative government would have made no limit on fees in order to engender a fully-fledged competitive market. In the event, most universities charged the maximum £9,000 fee. There were two reasons for this: first, they needed the income to sustain teaching quality, and second, because most universities did not want to be seen as 'cut-price' or 'down-market' institutions which would deter student applications. So again, the notion of a market based on differential pricing collapsed. The Coalition Government made some desperate efforts to encourage universities to charge lower fees by offering additional numbers in 2012 which could only be used at a £6,000 fee, but few institutions responded to this, most being Further Education colleges teaching HE courses.

The Coalition Government, of course, presented the increase in fees as a fiscal measure to reduce the national financial deficit. However, as Steve Smith points out, (Morgan, 2011) the government saves little from the arrangement: it will have to find all the funding for student loans, much of which will never be repaid. Tuition fees should, then, be seen as continuing marketisation, putting the control of higher education into the hands of the student.

*Pause for thought* | who pays for university degrees?

Some people argue that Higher Education should be free. Others argue that graduates benefit from their degrees and should contribute to their education. What are the economic arguments for and against these positions?

The National Student Survey (2013) allows students to report on the quality of their education, and universities must respond to this, or they will lose their 'customers'. What is the case for students having power over their university in this way? Can you see any problems with it?

The discourse about tuition fees has been exclusively in terms of finance and the controversy about access to higher education for the financially disadvantaged. There is little discussion of how marketisation bears upon university knowledge. The increased power of the student voice through the market has forced a change in the nature of the university curriculum and in who makes decisions about it. This occurs at two levels: first is the selection of subjects included in the university with the decline of traditional subjects such as philosophy, Kant's basis of knowledge in the modern university, and the rise of 'popular' subjects: sports science, dance, commercial music. The second is the student's choice of modules within a subject where popular and 'easy' knowledge is selected. Within an Education Studies programme it is difficult to include philosophy modules or modules with a strong sociological content to underpin analysis. Students prefer 'softer' topics such as early-years and child development.

Students exercising their choice is, of course, Delanty's (2001) 'democratisation of knowledge' described on page 97. But it raises the larger question of whether we should be willing to let Humboldt's vision of the relationship between the state, knowledge, culture and the university slip into the hands of a blind market. The commitment of successive British governments to neo-liberal free market economics as a means of managing all public services should be challenged, and universities should be leading on confronting this. While the university operates as a business in a free market with the first priority of attracting fee-paying customers, it is difficult to see an optimistic future for the university's definition of knowledge. While Kant worried that university knowledge should not be 'for the service of the state', we should now, surely, be arguing that knowledge should not simply be at the service of the market.

*Pause for thought* | the university in ruins

Readings (1996), in his book entitled *The University in Ruins*, suggests that, while universities are assembling impressive new buildings, their epistemological – or knowledge – foundations are crumbling. He argues that what counts as knowledge is now being determined by the mass market: what students prefer to study. So we have degrees in media studies and sports science which are sometimes criticised for not being 'proper' university knowledge. As students pay higher fees they will demand to be treated as customers. Do you agree that market forces are a good thing for universities, or does it lead to the 'dumbing down' of degrees?

### Research box

## what are universities for?

In his book, *What are Universities for?* Collini (2012) gives a stinging critique of the government's vision of Higher Education as a mechanism for economic growth. The postmodern university is designed to provide Higher Education purchased *by* the individual and *for* the individual student's benefit. And that is the basis of the case for tuition fees. However, Collini points out that university education is more than for the individual: it is a *public good*. The whole of society benefits from having an educated population, and so the state should continue to contribute to pay for Higher Education. Do you agree with Collini?

### Summary and conclusions

The chapter has outlined the changes which have taken place in Higher Education with the move from the 'modern' to the 'post-modern' university in the market place. Higher Education continues to be in a state of rapid and perhaps irreversible change and more is to come as the student population increases and successive governments enable the influence of the market on education. The key issues are:

- changes to university knowledge as a result of market forces;
- how Higher Education relates to the economy and whether it becomes more vocational;

*(Continued)*

*(Continued)*

- the expansion of Higher Education and whether this leads to 'dumbing down';
- the relationship of Higher Education to the national economy and the global economy;
- increasing state control and the potential denigration of university knowledge;
- the loss of academic freedom and the decline of the intellectual.

It has been shown that Higher Education is becoming increasingly allied to the economy. Debates are related to whether universities are serving the economy by providing sufficiently skilled workers. However, the debates about the economy tend to mask one of the virtues of higher education: the development and self-realisation of the individual through academic study. That this is now open to more people must itself be a matter for celebration.

# References

Barnett, R (2000) *Realizing the University in an Age of Supercomplexity*. Buckingham: Society for Research into Higher Education and Open University Press.

Bourdieu, P (1988) *Homo Academicus*. Cambridge: Polity Press.

Browne, J (2010) *Securing a Sustainable Future for Higher Education: An Independent Review of Higher Education Funding and Student Finance*. London: DfE.

Cawson, A (1982) *Corporatism and Welfare*. London: Heinemann Educational Books.

Collini, S (2012) *What are Universities for?* London: Penguin.

Committee on Higher Education (Robbins) (1963) *Report*. London: HMSO.

Cowen, R (1996) *World Year Book of Education: The evaluation of higher education systems*. London: Kogan Page.

Delanty, G (2001) *Challenging Knowledge: The university in the knowledge society*. Buckingham: HE/Open University.

Foucault, M (1972) *The Archaeology of Knowledge*. London: Routledge.

Furedi, F (2004) *Where Have all the Intellectuals Gone? Confronting 21st century philistinism*. London: Continuum.

Gray, J (1998) *False Dawn: The delusions of global capitalism*. London: Granta.

Habermas, J (1971) The university in a democracy: democratisation of the university, in *Towards a Rational Society*. London: Heinemann.

Haddad, G (2000) University and society: responsibilities, contracts, partnerships, in Neave, G (ed) *The Universities' Responsibilities to Society: International perspectives series*. Oxford: Pergamon.

Henkel, M (1991) *Government, Evaluation and Change*. London: Jessica Kingsley.

Kant, E (1992) *The Conflict of the Faculties*, Trans. Mary J. McGregor. London: University of Nebraska.

Kogan, M and Hanney, S (2000) *Reforming Higher Education*. London: Jessica Kingsley.

Lukasiewicz, J (1994) The Ignorance Explosion: Understanding Industrial Civilization. Ottowa: Carleton University Press.

Lyotard, JF (1986) *The Postmodern Condition: A report on knowledge*. Manchester: Manchester University Press.

MacCulloch, D (2004) *Reformation: Europe's house divided*. London: Penguin.

Morgan, J (2011) UUK head: cuts reality 'rather different to the headlines', *Times Higher Education,* 17–23 March 2011.

National Student Survey (2013) [Online] Available at: www.thestudentsurvey.com/ (accessed 28 February 2013).

Newman, JH (1996) *The Idea of a University,* ed. Frank M. Turner. New Haven, CT: Yale University Press.

Parsons, T (1974) The university 'bundle': A study of the balance between differentiation and integration, in Smelser, N and Almond , G (eds) *Public Higher Education in California: Growth, structural change and conflict.* Berkeley, CA: University of California Press.

Readings, B (1996) *The University in Ruins.* Cambridge, MA: Harvard University Press.

Silver, H (1990) *A Higher Education: The Council for National Academic Awards and British Higher Education 1964–8.* Lewes: Falmer Press.

Ward, S (2006) *Undergraduate Education Studies as an Emerging Subject in Higher Education: The construction and definition of university knowledge,* Unpublished PhD Thesis. Bristol: University of the West of England.

# Chapter 10

# Alternatives to mainstream schooling

## Will Curtis

### Introduction

It is easy to take for granted the principles that underpin our education system and the models and approaches to schooling that we adopt. Yet it is worth reminding ourselves that our state-run schooling system has been in place for less than 150 years. Compulsory education for all 16 year olds was only introduced, along with comprehensive schooling and A-level grades, in the mid-1960s. Many of the universities you study at were opened during the same period. Many other institutions gained university status in the 1990s or later. Among the assumptions we now make are that:

- education is for children and young people between the approximate ages of 5 to 18;
- learning takes place in specific institutions at specific times;
- there are clear dichotomies between – the teacher and the learner; the assessor and the assessed; the 'expert' and the 'novice', the formal and informal learning environments; the pre-school, school, college and university;
- schools are good for children and for society.

This chapter sets out to interrogate these assumptions and others. It begins by proposing a number of critiques of mainstream schooling – that schools are, to a greater or lesser extent, harmful to both individuals and societies. Second, it considers alternative approaches to schooling – reflecting on different models that currently exist alongside mainstream schools. Third, it considers a growing number of possibilities to learn outside of a formal school environment. Increasingly, families are electing to home educate and changes in society and technology provide new and inventive learning opportunities. Finally, the chapter reimagines mainstream education – drawing on current innovations to explore approaches that circumvent the earlier critiques.

## Toxic schooling?

There was a period between the late 1960s and early 1980s when radical critiques of formal schooling were relatively commonplace. The work of educational theorists such as John Holt, Ivan Illich, Everett Reimar, RF MacKenzie, Paul Goodman and Paulo Freire was well known and influential. Clive Harber's recent book, *Toxic Schooling* (2009), outlines much of this work. As Semel and Sadovnik (2005) remind us, many of these 'progressive' and 'child-centred' critiques continue to have resonance today. Moreover, recent political and cultural changes have given rise to further criticism (see Abbott and MacTaggart, 2010). What follows is a brief outline of some of the more significant critiques.

# Schools are outdated

Current educational structures and practices were designed in, and for, late nineteenth- and early twentieth-century requirements. As a consequence, many argue that established models have become incongruent with, and inappropriate for, our twenty-first century ways of living. By the late 1960s, Postman and Weingartner were arguing that the pace of change meant that the transmission of established knowledge was no longer useful or meaningful – because these 'facts' were continuously being superseded by new ideas and new information (1971). Since then, the rapidity of change has only intensified. From this perspective, transformations in society, culture, economy, politics, employment and knowledge require us to rethink fundamentally how we perceive and organise our educational systems. Chief among these changes is the development and ubiquity of the internet – transforming, as it does, the ways we access and experience information. In this context, arguably, we need teachers to help us navigate and evaluate the mass of information available to us, rather than to transmit a series of prescribed 'facts'.

# Teaching fear, confusion, boredom and dependency

Educationalists including John Holt and John Taylor Gatto have long argued that formal schooling develops qualities in pupils that inhibit learning. Holt's accounts in particular have shaped the current 'unschooling' movement, by arguing that formal schools controvert children's natural love of learning (1982). According to Holt, children are confused by fragmented classes and curriculum and taught to fear failure – perhaps the single most powerful impediment to effective and independent learning. Gatto (1992) outlined how classroom and assessment practices teach children to become emotionally and intellectually dependent on their teachers – unable to evaluate their own work without their teacher's comments and reliant on external approval for their self-esteem.

# 'Cookie-cutter' curriculum

We have developed a 'one size fits all' approach to schooling that neatly bundles knowledge into a series of distinct subject areas. This bears little resemblance to the 'real world' and forces children and young people to study in prescribed times, topics and techniques. While this might suit some children, it cannot suit them all. Critics argue that the 'cookie-cutter curriculum' is subject-centred rather than person-centred. But each child is unique, developing at different paces, with different skills, abilities and interests. A standardised and universalised curriculum cannot cater for this multiplicity of curiosities and capabilities.

# 'Teaching to the test'

Since the highpoint of external testing, with SATs at each of the four key stages before A levels, the number of assessments have reduced somewhat. Nevertheless, English children are still assessed more than children in many other countries. High levels of assessment might impact negatively on learning in a number of ways:

- Continual preparation for assessment reduces timetable space for learning new material.
- Classroom activities are limited and distorted by impending external examination – teachers 'teach to the test'.

- Stress and anxiety are increased – for students and teachers alike.
- Children learn to be motivated by external rewards – that learning is valuable only in as far as it helps pass tests (perhaps this causes the ritual whereby school-leavers destroy their workbooks after they finish their final exam).

## Deskilled and deprofessionalised teachers

Until recently, teachers had considerable autonomy – to develop classes in independent and original ways. The national curriculum brought with it standardisation and, since then, teachers' practices have become increasingly prescribed and monitored. 'High stakes testing', whereby school and teacher performance are measured and published, have reduced flexibility and increased surveillance. This has led many commentators to argue that teaching has ceased to be a profession and become technicised, deskilled or deprofessionalised – with increasingly casualised staff reduced to enacting narrowly prescribed procedures. Moreover, press and politicians make open association between wider social disorder and a breakdown of discipline in schools. Not long after the 2011 riots, newspaper editorials were blaming teachers' inability to control their classes. Such simplistic pronouncements unfairly discredit and further undermine the profession. More recently, the coalition government has reduced pay and worsened working conditions. A discourse that 'anyone can teach' has been heightened by policies that fast-track military personnel into the classroom, remove PGCE and teacher education from universities and relax the requirement for teachers to possess a teaching qualification. The latter is no longer a requirement for teachers in academies or free schools – and, consequently, there are more than 5,000 state schoolteachers who do not possess a teaching qualification today.

# Turning children off learning

The impact of much of the above is a concern that schools turn children off learning. Evidence suggests that this is not limited to the children who perform poorly in school. As Table 10.1 illustrates, international comparative data reveals an interesting paradox – seemingly the better children perform, the less interested they become. Analysis of science scores indicates an inverse correlation between test score and interest in the subject (see Table 10.1).

**Table 10.1**   The test score/interest paradox (Avvisati, 2011)

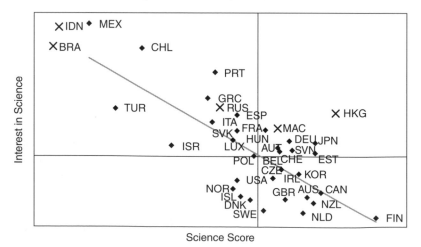

**Pause for thought** | your own education

Think about your own experiences of school, college and university.

- Are critiques like those outlined above an accurate reflection of your experiences?
- What were the benefits of your own education in formal settings?
- What could have been done differently – to make you get more from your formal education?

# Alternative approaches to schooling

There are a variety of approaches to schooling – based on quite different philosophies and principles to mainstream education. Alternative schools have traditionally received no state funding – so the majority are independent, fee-paying schools. Among the more influential approaches are:

## Steiner schools

Steiner or Waldorf schools are based on the philosophy of Rudolf Steiner, an Austrian-born educationalist who developed his ideas in the early twentieth century. Steiner schools have become the largest type of alternative education with more than 1,200 independent schools and 2,000 early years institutions in 60 countries worldwide. There are 38 schools in the UK (SWSF, 2013). Recently, Steiner state schools were established in England – in Hereford, Somerset and a third opening in September 2013 in Devon. Schools and teachers have high levels of autonomy and they focus on children's physical, moral, social, emotional, creative and spiritual development. Typically, one teacher will take a class from the age of 7 to 14, enabling deep personal relationships to develop. Artistic expression and imagination are emphasised in a curriculum that integrates the practical, creative and academic thematically. Subject specialism is not introduced until children turn 14.

## Montessori

Another highly influential early twentieth-century educationalist was Maria Montessori – an Italian doctor who worked in special education, where she developed her innovative classroom approaches. Montessori schools are child-centred and holistic, emphasising children's natural curiosity and personal development. Schools encourage children to exercise freedom within structured and planned settings, believing that self-motivated children are happy and self-confident. Among their more notable characteristics, a typical Montessori classroom will consist of children from different age groups – with the older ones encouraged to support the younger. Children experience blocks of uninterrupted play and can choose their activities from a number of options as set out by their teacher. Resources and furniture are child-sized (see **www.monstessori.org.uk** for further details). Montessori approaches have proved influential in early years and primary school mainstream education.

## Free schools

The notion of 'free school' has come to mean something quite different with the coalition government's funding and support for 'independent state schools'. The term 'free school' used to indicate schools that followed AS Neill's philosophy of 'free range childhood'. From this perspective, children should not be coerced or disciplined. Adults should not impose their own rules and regulations on children. Rather, children should be free to make their own choices about what, and even whether, they learn. Summerhill, the independent school in Suffolk that Neill himself established in the 1920s, is perhaps the most famous and long-standing school of this type. But 'free range childhood' was not the preserve of the privately educated, with celebrated post-war schools like Risinghill and St George-in-the-East rooted firmly in the state sector (Michael Fielding has done much to bring the latter to our attention today). Dulwich Natural Childhood Group's 'Children's Charter' affords a simple and compelling contemporary example of the tradition:

> *Flourish*
>
> *Thrive*
>
> *Be truly alive*
>
> *Not hurried or stressed*
>
> *Or rushed to get dressed*
>
> *Give them space not schedules*
>
> *Sunlight not screens*
>
> *Throw out the targets, timetables and tests*
>
> *Let curiosity do the rest*
>
> Natural Childhood
>
> (www.naturalchildhood.co.uk/about-us/childrens-charter/)

## Democratic schools

The notion of 'democratic education' is closely connected with the original 'free school' ideals – with many 'radical' or 'progressive' schools portraying themselves as both free and democratic. The key principle of democratic schools is that all members are equal and, as such, distinctions between teachers and students are blurred. Prescribed schedules and curriculum are replaced with dialogue, negotiation and consensus. Originating in the USA, Sudbury Schools are run by direct democracy, with teachers and students possessing equal status in decision making. In the UK, Leicestershire's Countesthorpe College was a prominent democratic state school until the 1980s, in which students and teachers at the 'moot' (school meeting) agreed school policy. Some of the school's 'democratic' traditions – like calling teachers by their first names and no compulsory uniform – remain today.

## Forest schools

Recent years have witnessed growing interest in opportunities to learn outside, as opposed to within the confines of the classroom. A natural woodland environment provides the basis for cross-disciplinary study and the development of technical, personal and social skills. Forest schools originated in the 1920s in the US, but were not introduced in the UK until the 1990s. Since then, they have rapidly grown in popularity. The Forest Schools (2013) directory has more than 200 listings from across the country. In general, forest schools run alongside mainstream schooling, providing children with the opportunity for woodland study for part of their school week.

***Pause for thought*** | more alternatives

There are many other alternative approaches to education. You might want to look in more detail at some of the following examples:

***Sands school*** – an independent democratic school in Ashburton, Devon;

***Brockwood Park school*** – an independent school in Bramdean, Hampshire, based on the teachings of the Indian thinker Jiddu Krishnamurti;

***The Dharma primary school*** – an independent school in Brighton and the only one in the UK based on Buddhist teachings;

***The Alternative School (TAS)*** – a school in Barnoldswick, Lancashire for children who have not engaged with mainstream education;

***The Social Science Centre*** – a higher education organisation based in Lincoln, offering democratic and cooperative learning opportunities.

Think about the alternative approaches identified above.

- How do these alternatives differ from mainstream schooling?
- Are there similarities between them – both in terms of their underpinning philosophies and their practices?
- How are they funded and organised?
- Can you think of any instances from your own schooling that correspond with any of these alternatives?
- Can you imagine any/many of these ideas becoming part of mainstream educational thinking and practice? Why?

# Alternatives to schooling

While schooling remains the most prominent institution in which (formal) learning takes place, increasingly, alternative spaces for learning are developing. In this section we consider the increasing popularity of home schooling and we look at how changes in society and advances in technology are giving rise to new learning opportunities.

## Home schooling

It is difficult to know the number of children who are home educated in the UK. This is because, unless a child has been removed from mainstream schooling, there has been no requirement on families to register their home-educated child. A major report into elective home education in 2009 discovered 20,000 registered children, but estimated that there are up to 80,000 in reality (Badman, 2009). This lack of compulsory registration led the report's author to conclude that the UK was the *most liberal in its approach to elective home education* (2009, p.37). Drawing on evidence from the USA, where home education is more commonplace (approximately 1.1 million children), it is possible to identify patterns. While you might consider a home-educated child to be permanently removed from school, it is quite common for home education to be a temporary and even part-time arrangement.

Isenberg (2007) noted high attrition rates in home-educated families – with more than a third home educating for less than a year. Moreover, according to this research, a fifth of children combined home education with schooling. While evidence is patchy, it is difficult to argue with the fact that the number of families electing to home educate has increased rapidly in recent years.

Families choose to home educate for a variety of reasons. One of the more influential classifications was proposed by Van Galen, who distinguished between ideologues and pedagogues (1991). Ideologues reject the formal school curriculum. Most commonly, ideologues have strong religious or spiritual beliefs and dislike the secular nature of much mainstream education. On the other hand, pedagogues dislike conventional teaching methods and *actively question the professionalization and bureaucratization of modern society* (Van Galen, 1991, p.72). Particularly in the USA, pedagogues are likely to favour the ideas of 'unschoolers' like John Holt – desiring that their children's learning is led by natural curiosity, rather than inhibited by the constraints that formal institutions impose.

Alongside these values-based motivations to home educate are a number of pragmatic or practical reasons – and these may account for a large proportion of home-educated children in the UK. These include:

- concerns about the quality of local schooling;
- removal of a child from school because they are exhibiting behavioural problems in the setting;
- the avoidance of bullying or negative peer exposure;
- a perception that mainstream schooling is poorly equipped to support children with special educational needs;
- concerns that 'gifted and talented' children are not adequately stimulated in the classroom (see Winstanley, 2009).

Pragmatic decisions like these are more likely to result in temporary withdrawal from schooling.

The 2009 review of elective home education recommended a number of significant changes to policy. Among Badman's 28 recommendations were:

- the development of a compulsory registration scheme, requiring a parental statement of educational approach, intent and outcomes and with local authority guidance, support and monitoring;
- local authority officers being given the right to visit the home and meet with the home-educated child on her own;
- mainstream schools being encouraged and supported to offer opportunities for flexi-schooling;
- local authorities being given authority to refuse registration on the grounds of safeguarding (Badman, 2009).

Badman's recommendations proved highly controversial. Home-educators felt it further stigmatised a choice that was already difficult. The Labour government had intended to implement the recommendations, but it lost the 2010 election. The coalition government has not legislated, though it has argued in favour of flexi-schooling. While the Welsh government has been consulting on a policy of compulsory registration, there is currently no plan to do so in England.

*Pause for thought* | home schooling

Visit these websites providing information and support for home-schooling families.

- Homeschooler
- Oxford Homeschooling
- The Home Education Network UK
- Education Otherwise (UK)
- Freedom-in-Education

Consider the following:

- What do these sites tell you about home education in the UK?
- Do you think it might be easier to home educate today? Why?
- Why are many home-schooling families resistant to recommendations like those proposed in the Badman Review?
- What are the advantages and disadvantages of flexi-schooling – where children might study in school for part of the week and at home for the rest of the week? Consider from the perspective of:
  - o flexi-schooled children;
  - o their peers in the school;
  - o their home-educating parents;
  - o their schools;
  - o their teachers.

## Community education

As Leadbeater importantly reminds us, learning can take place in many settings other than formal institutions. And these alternative settings might prove more beneficial for learners.

*More learning needs to be done at home, in offices and kitchens, in the contexts where knowledge is deployed to solve problems and add value to people's lives.*

(Leadbeater, 2000, pp.226–7)

Community education begins from this perspective – and the idea is not new. Henry Morris proposed one of the most influential visions for community education in the 1920s. Morris, in his role as Secretary for Education in Cambridge, developed the notion of the 'village college':

*The village college could lie athwart the daily lives of the community it served; and in it the conditions would be realised under which education would not be an escape from reality, but an enrichment and transformation of it.*

(Henry Morris (1925) *The Village College. Being a Memorandum on the Provision of Educations and Social Facilities for the Countryside, with Special Reference to Cambridgeshire;* cited in Smith and Jeffs, 1998)

Today, community education takes multiple forms – from extra-mural or 'lifelong learning' accredited provision in universities to virtual 'peer-to-peer' communities like 'Mumsnet' (2013); from traditional church organisation classes to radical learning opportunities in the *Free University, Tent City University* or the *Really Open University;* using spaces from the traditional classroom to the garden shed (Men's Sheds Assoc., 2013) or the local street (Playing Out, 2013). The previous government developed SureStart centres – with the aim of providing communities with the resources and support to develop educational provision in, by and for the local community. Austerity policies have meant much of this provision has declined or disappeared and the coalition government's notion of a 'big society' – to empower local communities and people – has yet to take off.

Central to much community education is the belief in the capacity of education to transform and empower. Based on the seminal writing of Brazilian adult educator, Paulo Freire (1995; 2005), teachers seek to build communication and co-operation on a local level, and to use educational activities to emancipate disempowered communities. Education is not perceived as a process of memorising prescribed facts; it is focused on developing the skills and confidence to enable people to act and to make a difference. Explicit in the work of Freire and current writers like Jean Anyon (2005) and bell hooks (1994) is a belief that education enables us to transform an unequal and oppressive world. From this perspective, community education both *humanises* (helps us to learn about ourselves and one another) and *conscientises* (helps us develop critical consciousness).

## Digital alternatives

Unquestionably, technological developments offer opportunities for learning outside of mainstream education. The last few years have witnessed remarkable advances that have the potential to transform our relationship with knowledge fundamentally and to disrupt our reliance on formal institutions as providers of learning experiences. Three such developments are considered below.

### • Online networks

If you want to learn how to play a new guitar chord, replace a light fitting, or make the most delicious macaroni cheese you are likely to make use of an online search engine. In each case, high up on your search return will be a video with somebody showing you what to do. The internet provides the tool to facilitate what Illich (1971) referred to as 'learning webs' – networks of learners and teachers identifying one another to develop widespread, voluntary and informal educational experiences. Social networks allow users to become authors, to share and collaborate – to publish their skills and knowledge to a massive audience. Local and global 'skill exchanges' are becoming increasingly popular, through which members can offer their teaching skills in return for learning opportunities (see **www.swapaskill.com** for example).

### • OERs (Open Educational Resources)

Put any topic into an internet search engine and you will find multiple links, numerous irrelevant or worthless ones, but many very useful. Increasingly, these links will take you to peer-reviewed papers or work by established and published authors. Previously, the majority of published work was protected behind a password wall – requiring registration (and payment) to gain access. Today, many of those barriers have been removed. OERs have become freely accessible – available to read and, frequently, to comment on and contribute to. The publishing world is changing and new licenses enable *the sharing and use of creativity and knowledge through free legal tools* (Creative Commons, 2013).

## • MOOCs (Massive Open Online Courses)

As their name suggests, MOOCs offer freely accessible internet-based programmes of study. Typically, MOOCs include video lectures, structured activities and peer-to-peer forums. Among the most prominent and popular are *Coursera, EdX* and the *Khan Academy.* MOOCs emerged in 2008 and have expanded at a tremendous rate since then. For instance, there are more than 3 million registered students on *Coursera.* In the UK, a group of 20 research-intensive universities are developing *FutureLearn* – an online platform that will offer free courses in a range of subject areas – with the first courses beginning in September 2013.

At present, these digital learning opportunities exist alongside mainstream formal education. They are complementary rather than alternative. As MOOCs do not currently possess formal accreditation, they are commonly undertaken as a taster to further 'accredited' study. For instance, the University of Edinburgh is investing in MOOCs – largely as a tool for advertising their provision on a global stage. Formal institutions utilise OERs, MOOCs and social networking to enhance their students' learning experiences – to extend opportunities to learn together and to access rich, wide-ranging and contemporary information. These technologies are employed to facilitate 'seamless learning', whereby educational experiences are continuously available, as and when required.

---

*Pause for thought*  |  MOOCs

Explore one or two of the MOOC sites listed above. Sign up for a course that interests you. As you go through the course, consider:

- How do your experiences as a MOOC learner differ from your normal learning experiences? What, if anything, is lacking?
- What makes you trust/distrust the material you cover?
- What do you see as the main advantages and disadvantages of MOOC study?

At present, around three-quarters of people who sign up to study on MOOCs already possess a first degree.

- Why do you think this might be?
- From your experiences of MOOC study, how could the courses be modified/developed to attract a wider range of learners?

---

Such changes make the prospect that we can learn what we want, when we want and how we want entirely feasible. 'Seamless learning' breaks down some of the borders between formal and informal learning – providing opportunities to learn before, alongside and after formal educational experiences. It is, however, entirely possible to conceive of a time, perhaps not too far away, where the formal element shrinks, or even disappears. New tools like *Mozilla Open Badges* (www.openbadges.org) have begun to offer users the opportunity to gain recognition for courses they complete online. Already people are asking: Why pay £9,000 to study face-to-face when I can study for free online? Why learn what I am compelled to study in school, when I can learn what I want to on my computer? These technologies are very new, but they are already causing many to rethink our dependency on formal structures and institutions.

# Reimagining mainstream schooling

The chapter began by outlining a number of the more influential critiques of mainstream schooling – most damningly perhaps, the claim that schools turn children off learning. While you might find some of these critiques enthralling, it is important to acknowledge that the term 'mainstream' covers a wide variety of schools – with distinct principles, priorities and practices. Recent policy changes are likely to have expanded this diversity – many new school models coming into existence, and initiatives like the academy programme giving head teachers far more autonomy than they previously had to shape school policy. Most significantly, neither academies nor free schools are required to follow the national curriculum today.

Nevertheless, many modern schools share much in common with their precursors of 60 to 100 years ago. While the current Secretary of State for Education, Michael Gove, is probably the most radical reformer to hold the post for 25 years, he appears intent on emphasising knowledge, key facts and discipline. Gove is an admirer of the American writer Eric Hirsch. Hirsch rejects child-centred education and is a passionate advocate for content-based delivery and the teaching of 'key facts' (2010). The new primary curriculum for 2014 is underpinned by this philosophy. Among the free schools that Gove has supported are Toby Young's West London Free School and Annaliese Brigg's Pimlico Free School (opening in September 2013) – and both are inspired by Hirsch's traditional approach. For instance, West London free school emphasises strong discipline and its 'classical' curriculum includes compulsory Latin until the age of 14.

While the majority of approved free schools follow a traditional knowledge-based curriculum, recent policies do offer the potential for 'alternative' state provision. The Royal Society for the encouragement of Arts, Manufactures and Commerce (RSA) developed 'Opening Minds'– an alternative competence-based curriculum that is now taught at Key Stage 3 in more than 200 schools across the country (RSA, 2013). 'Urban village schools' or 'schools within schools' are developing at a rapid pace – emphasising positive relationships, children's voices within 'human scale' communities, personal well-being and enquiry-based learning (Wallace, 2009).

Many educators are calling for more wholesale transformations – to make educational structures and practices fit for purpose in the twenty-first century. Sumatra Mistra challenges us to reimagine examinations – to move away from outmoded conventions that sit individuals in isolation, attempting to recall memorised facts:

*Teaching in an environment where the internet and discussion are allowed in exams would be different. The ability to find things out quickly and accurately would become the predominant skill. The ability to discriminate between alternatives, then put facts together to solve problems would be critical.*

(Mistra, 2013, p.30)

Other educationalists want to go further still. Critical pedagogists argue that the twenty-first century is characterised by corporate greed, war, poverty and ever-increasing inequality. In a climate like this, a new pedagogy is called for that raises awareness and critical consciousness and heightens engagement and participation (see Fischman et al., 2004). In the UK, Fielding and Moss (2011) make a compelling case for the 'common school' – based in the community and serving all local children, a human scale and person-centred public space for all citizens.

Research box

## the school I'd like – what educational experiences would children wish for?

In 1969, Edward Blishen published *The School That I'd Like*, a collection of children's thoughts about their ideal school. In 2001, Burke and Grosvenor replicated the research for the *Guardian* newspaper. More than 15,000 young people submitted their ideas. The collection of essays, pictures, poems and plans make for particularly interesting reading – both as a critique of current provision and as evidence for future policy and practice.

The *Guardian* continued with the project and, in 2011, it published an updated *Children's Manifesto* (Birkett, 2011). The manifesto outlined a case for schools that are: active, calm, comfortable, creative and colourful, expert, flexible, friendly, listening, inclusive, international, outside, technological. Other characteristics included a choice of uniforms to express personality, a flexible curriculum and fewer tests.

Look at the ideas that have been generated from *The School I'd Like* research.

- How have children's perspectives changed between the 1960s, 2000s and 2010s?
- How similar or different are the ideas from mainstream schooling?
- Can you find evidence of a disconnect between what children value/wish for and what schools provide?
- What qualities would the school you favour possess?
- What should school be for?

Summary and conclusions

Mainstream schooling plays a vital role in the development and flourishing of both society and the individuals who constitute it. Outside the family, it is the predominant institution through which young people become socialised and inculcated into wider culture. Children learn fundamental capacities, skills and dispositions. We expect a tremendous amount from our schools and teachers – to foster academic, personal, spiritual, social, moral, cultural and physical development.

Nevertheless, mainstream education is not without its critics. Schooling has been shown to turn large numbers of children off learning – teaching pupils dependency, fear of failure and that learning has value only in as far as it translates into cultural or material reward. Narrowly prescribed and fragmented curriculum, as well as frequent tests and exams, are seen to alienate teachers and students and impoverish learning. Increasing numbers of families are electing to educate their children outside of mainstream schooling, either in alternative provision or in a non-school environment. Advances in technology provide more and more opportunities for learning outside formal institutions. In a contemporary society, where vast amounts of information are accessible at the push of a button, mainstream schooling must move away from its concentration on the transmission of established facts. Twenty-first century schools ought to teach young people to love learning, to be comfortable and confident in uncertainty, to evaluate competing knowledge claims, to work together, and to solve problems and enquire. Disappointingly, current policies propose a move in the opposite direction.

## References

Abbott, J and MacTaggart, H (2010) *Over Schooled but Under Educated: How the crisis in education is jeopardizing our adolescents*. London: Continuum.

Anyon, J (2005) *Radical Possibilities: Public policy, urban education and a new social movement*. Abingdon: Routledge.

Avvisati, F (2011) 'Effective Teaching for Improving Students' Motivation, Curiosity, and Self-Confidence in Science: Evidence from PISA 2006.' *Education for Innovation: the Role of Arts and STEM Education OECD/France Workshop – Paris, 23-24 May 2011*. OECD Centre for Educational Research and Innovation (CERI).

Badman, G (2009) *Review of Elective Home Education in England*. London: The Stationery Office.

Birkett, D (2011) The children's manifesto. The *Guardian*, 3 May 2011.

Blishen, E (1969) *The School That I'd Like*. Harmondsworth: Penguin.

Burke, C and Grosvenor, I (2003) *The School I'd Like: Children and Young People's Reflections on an Education for the 21st Century*. London: Routledge.

Creative Commons (2013) 'What is Creative Commons?' Available at: **http://creativecommons.org/about** (accessed 5 May 2013).

Fielding, M and Moss, P (2011) *Radical Schooling and the Common School: A democratic alternative*. Abingdon: Routledge.

Fischman, G, McLaren, P, Sunker, H and Lanksheer, C (2004) *Critical Theories, Radical Pedagogies and Global Conflicts*. Lanham, MD: Rowman and Littlefield.

Forest Schools (2013) Welcome to Forest Schools. Available at: **www.forestschools.com/** (accessed 10 May 2013).

Freire, P (1995) *Pedagogy and Hope*. London: Continuum.

Freire, P (2005) *Education for Critical Consciousness*. London: Continuum.

Gatto, J (1992) *Dumbing us Down: The hidden curriculum of compulsory schooling*. Gabriola Island: New Society Publishers.

Harber, C (2009) *Toxic Schooling: How schools became worse*. Nottingham: Educational Heretics Press.

Hirsch, E (2010) *The Making of Americans: Democracy and our schools*. New Haven, CT: Yale University Press.

Holt, J (1982) *How Children Fail*. New York: Delta/Seymour Lawrence.

hooks, b (1994) *Teaching to Transgress: Education as the practice of freedom*. London: Routledge.

Illich, I (1971) *Deschooling Society*. Harmondsworth: Penguin.

Isenberg, E (2007) What have we learned about homeschooling? *Peabody Journal of Education*, 82, 2007: 387–409.

Leadbeater, C (2000) *The Weightless Society*. New York: Texere.

Men's Sheds Association (2013) Welcome to the Men's Sheds network. Available at: **http://menssheds.org.uk** (accessed 10 April 2013).

Mistra, S (2013) It's time to totally rethink our approach to education. *The Observer*, 16 June 2013.

Mumsnet (2013) Mumsnet: by parents for parents. Available at: **www.mumsnet.org** (accessed 12 April 2013).

Playing Out (2013) Playing out: active street play in your local area. Available at: **http://playingout.net** (accessed 10 April 2013).

Postman, N and Weingartner, C (1971) *Teaching as a Subversive Activity*. Harmondsworth: Penguin.

RSA (2013) RSA: Opening Minds. Available at: **www.rsaopeningminds.org.uk/** (accessed 2 May 2013).

Semel, SF and Sadovnik, AR (eds) (2005) *Schools of Tomorrow, Schools of Today: What happened to progressive education* (2nd edn). New York: P Lang.

Smith, M and Jeffs, T (1998) Informal Education. Available at: **http://infed.org/mobi/henry-morris-village-colleges-and-community-schools/**

SWSF (2013) Steiner Waldorf Schools Federation. Available at: **www.steinerwaldorf.org.uk/** (accessed 5 May 2013).

Van Galen, J (1991) Ideologues and pedagogues: parents who teach their children at home, in Van Galen, J and Pitman, M (eds) *Homeschooling: Political, historical and pedagogic perspectives*. Norwood, New Jersey: Ablex Publishing.

Wallace, W (2009) *Schools Within Schools: Human scale education in practice*. London: Calouste Gulbenkian Foundation.

Winstanley, C (2009) Too cool for school? Gifted children and homeschooling. *Theory and Research in Education,* 7(3) November 2009: 347–62.

## *Further reading*

Facer, K (2011) *Learning Futures: Education, technology and social change*. Abingdon: Routledge – explores educational potential of technological advances and considers the changing role of formal institutions.

Lees, H (2013) *Education without Schools: Discovering alternatives*. Bristol: Policy Press – a new book about elective home education, including a critique of formal institutions and suggesting a reconfiguration of formal structures.

Wrigley, T, Thomson, P and Lingard, B (2012) *Changing Schools: Alternative ways to make a world of difference*. Abingdon: Routledge – a reimagining of mainstream schooling, drawing on the practices and philosophies of inspirational schools around the world.

**Infed.org** 'The encyclopedia of informal education' – a fantastic resource on theories, concepts and practices of informal education.

# Chapter 11

# Devolved education? Policy in Scotland, Wales and Northern Ireland

## Mark Murphy and Anna Beck

### Introduction

Since devolution in the late 1990s, education policy has diverged across the four home nations. This is not surprising for a number of reasons, one of the more significant ones being that the political system has diverged. As Gareth Rees points out (2011, p.58), the Conservative party is *essentially an English party in their capacity to win seats*. The Conservative party is essentially a spent force in Scotland, and the politics of Wales and Northern Ireland have their own historical debates that set them apart from England. As in most policy arenas, localism has a strong part to play in the education system, with a stronger emphasis in Wales for example in collaboration between different stakeholders. However, it should be emphasised that the education system – its numbers, governance and complexity – dwarfes its neighbours. So localism is always bound to play a much stronger role in the non-England countries.

This chapter explores some of the key differences and similarities between the home nations, with particular regard to: education governance, education provision and the education profession. Space does not allow for a comprehensive sweep of the whole education sector, so this chapter will focus on the compulsory education sector (see Hodgson et al., 2011 for an overview of home nation differences in the post-compulsory education sector).

## Devolution and education governance

Both before and after the 2006 Act, a distinctive agenda was established for education and training in Wales, with the Welsh Assembly Government (WAG) pursuing its own agenda (Rees, 2011, p.59). For example, Wales is similar to Scotland in that it has a united Ministry for school and post-school education, with a stronger focus on cradle to grave learning (Hodgson and Spours, 2011, p.10). Wales has a number of key organisations that influence education governance – alongside the Department of Education and Skills, a department of the Welsh Assembly, there is also ESTYN, the Office of Her Majesty's Inspectorate of Education and Training in Wales, and also the Teacher Training Recruitment Forum for Wales.

Northern Ireland, like England, has a split governance arrangement for education: as part of the Northern Ireland Executive, the Department of Education (DENI) is responsible for compulsory schooling (covering pre-school, special education, primary and post-primary), while the Department for Employment and Learning is responsible for further and higher education. Governance at the local level is also significant – across Northern Ireland there are five education and library boards, which administer education at the regional level. There is also an association called Classroom 2000 (E2K), which looks after ICT issues for all schools.

In terms of governance, *religion* still plays a major role in education in Northern Ireland, with schools being split between what are called 'controlled' schools and Catholic schools (there are also a small number of integrated schools in Northern Ireland, overseen by the Northern Ireland Council for Integrated Education – running since 1992). However, given the fact that 95 per cent of pupils still attend either controlled or Catholic schools (mostly Protestant or Catholic respectively), this educational division is ingrained. Under the management of the Schools Board of Governors, controlled schools are in principle open to all faiths, but it is still the case that Catholics tend to go to Catholic schools. Historically, controlled schools had strong links to the three large Protestant churches (Presbyterian, Church of Ireland and Methodist – known as transferors), and still maintain strong links through representations on the boards of governors. Currently, four out of nine governors are linked to the churches. This right to representation is currently being re-examined under the review of public administration (RPA).

About half the pupils in Northern Ireland are educated in Catholic schools, which have their own governing body, the Council for Catholic Maintained Schools (CCMS – a result of the 1989 education reform order). The Council is an important player in education matters, being a large employer of teachers and also contributing to policy on issues like curriculum, selection and leadership. The Council includes representatives from the Department of Education, trustees, parents and teachers.

Education in Scotland is often considered to be distinct from that elsewhere in the UK. Under the terms of the Act of Union (1707), which united Scotland with England at the level of Parliament, the distinctive nature of Scottish law, the church and education was recognised and protected. For over 300 years, therefore, long before political devolution in 1999, Scotland has developed and maintained its own education system, which is both separate and, at times, quite different, to the education systems of Wales, Northern Ireland and England. In this sense, education has played a key role in the shaping and maintaining of Scottish national identity (Paterson, 1997; Scotland, 1969).

Nevertheless, prior to devolution, Scottish education was required to operate within the context of the UK government. The Scotland Act (1998), however, allowed the Scottish Parliament to gain legislative control over all education matters. Since formation of the minority SNP government in 2007, a strong emphasis on presenting an independent approach to policy development can be identified. Indeed, this position was strengthened by the formation of an SNP majority government as a result of the national election in 2011. This can be considered as playing a key role in the SNP's ambition of achieving complete political independence from the rest of the UK.

In 2007, a Concordat was signed between the Scottish Government and Scotland's 32 constituent Councils that not only guaranteed the allocation of grant-aided expenditure but also allowed a degree of autonomy to prioritise budget spend. This was viewed as a landmark agreement because it heralded the beginning of a new relationship between national and local government, *based on mutual respect and partnership* (Scottish Government, 2007, p.1), placing emphasis on the 'partnership' approach, which is often associated with Scottish policy making. However, the co-construction of education policy has not been without its complications (see Seith, 2009).

With a relatively small population of 5.295 million, one key characteristic of Scotland's education policy community is that it is tightly networked, with many of the key policy actors being personally known to each other (Humes, 1997). This model of policy making is quite different from the model adopted elsewhere in the UK, and has often been described as 'democratic' and 'consultative'. However, the extent to which these values are put into practice has been the subject of some discussion (Humes and Bryce, 2008; Paterson, 1997; Humes and Paterson, 1983).

# Devolution and education provision

The formal school system in terms of age span is roughly similar across all home nations, compulsory up to the age of 16 and the GCSE, and non-compulsory up to 18 and A level stage. There are some minor variations; in Scotland, for example, the compulsory phase of school education is sub-divided into primary, which usually comprises seven years, and secondary, which usually lasts four years with an option for two additional years. Children normally begin primary school between the ages of 4.5 and 5.5 years, depending on birth date. The earliest age at which a young person can normally leave education is 16, although there are various routes offered to secondary pupils that are not necessarily delivered in a school setting.

In terms of school provision, a significant policy intervention was the National Curriculum, introduced with the Education Reform Act of 1988 and governing all parts of the United Kingdom, with the notable exception of Scotland. One of the major aims of the National Curriculum was to ensure that all state schools (apart from academies and public schools) would have a common curriculum. This however does not preclude room for manoeuvre, as deviations from the curriculum certainly exist in the cases of Wales and Northern Ireland. When it comes to school accountability and assessment, for example, one distinctive aspect of provision in Wales is the abolition of key stage testing and associated league tables (at national level anyway).

Alongside these divergences are others such as in the Welsh case a commitment to *non-selective, community-based comprehensive schools*, and new curriculum provision for 14–19 year olds through the Learning Pathway and the Welsh Baccalaureate. In September 2008 Wales implemented a school curriculum for 3–19 year olds, the idea being to establish a curriculum for the twenty-first century. This incorporates what are called 'learning pathways', designed to transform the way in which Welsh pupils are educated 14–19. Three key elements are:

- an *individual learning pathway* meeting individual needs;
- wider choice and flexibility of courses (leading to qualifications for a local curriculum);
- wider learning from the *learning core* regardless of pathway.

Wales has also made changes at the other end of the curriculum, with the introduction of the Foundation Phase, covering the ages 3–7. The phase is seen to be a progressive approach to education as its curriculum design is based on experiential learning in small groups – learning by doing being the mantra for early years education. At the other end of the scale, the Welsh Baccalaureate (introduced in 2007) is also available as a qualification option although ungraded.

---

***Pause for thought*** | what kind of school structure is best?

Academy schools are growing in numbers in England, while other parts of the UK are clinging onto the comprehensive ideal. Academies, it must be said, have proven in some quarters to be controversial, and question marks remain about the ideological underpinning of such a policy move – but some, however, have welcomed the opportunity for greater flexibility in the system, allowing more local input and curriculum development to meet local needs. This stands in contrast to the rest of the UK, and it will thus be interesting to see how these two diverging systems work side-by-side in the UK policy arena.

## exploring the impact of devolution on education, equality and human rights

An important function traditionally for state education is its role in the promotion of equality and human rights – a role that takes on greater significance in the context of devolution. Chaney's work (2011) explores the way these matters have been addressed in the policy and law making programmes of the UK's devolved administrations. Chaney uses a form of policy discourse analysis to analyse each administration's education policies in relation to initiatives to promote equality and human rights, a method that *allows an appreciation of how policy-makers formulate and construct problems; enables focus on their claims and rhetoric; and acknowledges that policy documents are complex exercises in agenda-setting power* (p.433).

Overall, his analysis suggests that devolution in the UK has seen the political reprioritisation of the promotion of equality and human rights in schooling following the governments' commitment to mainstreaming. This shift in priorities resulted in a range of new policy initiatives, devolved enactments, and the development of governance structures to enable this policy priority. Nevertheless, Chaney argues that there is a continuing distance between the devolved administrations' espousal of mainstreaming and policy outcomes, with significant challenges remaining *before the mainstreaming rhetoric is fully realized in the devolved education systems of the UK* (p.447).

Language remains a more significant issue in the Welsh education system than elsewhere: a significant minority of students (nearly a quarter) there are taught mainly or solely via the medium of the Welsh language. Also the study of Welsh is compulsory for ALL pupils until the age of 16. Northern Ireland also makes specific provision for linguistic differences: there are a number of institutions which teach via the medium of the Irish Gaelic language, with the 1998 Education (Northern Ireland) order placing a duty on DENI *to encourage and facilitate the development of Irish-medium education*.

Unlike England, and paralleling Scotland to some extent, Wales maintains a faith in the community-based comprehensive schooling system. There are some private schools in the country but no academies. Proportionally, Northern Ireland has quite a large number of grammar schools still (69 as opposed to 164 in England) and it was only recently that the 11 plus (in the guise of the 'transfer test') was phased out (2008). At the same time, many of these grammar schools now set their own entrance examinations, a fact that is somewhat controversial given that this is in contravention of recent government regulations. Some have gone as far as to say that NI policy is more similar to England than elsewhere, with for example, Horgan and Gray (2012, p.475) arguing that *since the 2011 election, government in Northern Ireland continues to follow an agenda set in London*.

In terms of special educational needs (SEN), the provision is largely similar in Wales to that in England. But Wales does have its own SEN code of practice (with a separate SEN tribunal also) – approved by the National Assembly in 2001 and LEAs have been required to uphold it since. However, proposals for reform of the legislative framework are currently being debated (the consultation ended late 2012, see Welsh gov.uk site). Scotland has seven state-funded national schools that offer specialist educational provision to children and young people with certain additional support needs. These schools are mainly located in the Scottish central belt and equality of access has been a criticism often raised by the more remote Scottish Authorities. Over time, following the Melville Report (Scottish Education Department,

1973), which led to the Education (Scotland) (Mentally Handicapped Children) Act 1974, and more recently, the enactment of the Education (Additional Support for Learning) (Scotland) Act 2004, there has been an increasing drive towards the inclusion of children and young people with additional support needs in mainstream schools. Although this has not been without its challenges (Allan, 2010), inclusive education has become a key policy objective for the Scottish Government.

> ### Research box
>
> ## the effect of tuition fees on student mobility: comparing the home nations
>
> Given the recent hike in university tuition fees in England in particular (as opposed to the other home nations), it is a shame that little research has been carried out not just on student mobility but also the effect of tuition fees on mobility. One notable example is that of Wakeling and Jefferies (2013), who explored the relationship via an analysis of data on student enrolment destinations across the home nations (and Ireland) for the period 2000–2010. A key finding of their research is that little evidential support exists for the idea that students move to secure more favourable tuition fee rates:
>
> *As with studies in the USA, Canada and Germany, it seems that any disincentive effects are small and that for some institutions and/or subjects, demand is price-inelastic. Potentially, this means that fresh fears about 'fee refugees' from the further substantial increases in tuition fees introduced for England by the Conservative-Liberal Democrat coalition may not be realised.*
>
> (Wakeling and Jefferies, 2013, p.19)
>
> However, they also note that, in terms of the massive fee increase in England in 2012, *very early indications suggest some shift in behaviour, albeit partly extending already evident trends* (Wakeling and Jefferies, 2013, p.20).

One distinguishing feature of Scottish educational provision is the high number of state-funded faith schools (McKinney, 2007), almost all of which are of a Catholic denomination (there are three Episcopalian schools and one Jewish school). The independent school sector in Scotland provides pre-school, primary, secondary and special school education for children and young people, however, it is particularly small and somewhat limited; the majority of independent fee-paying schools are located in Edinburgh (see Sischy, 2008, for further information).

The national curricula framework in Scotland has recently undergone a significant period of transition with a 'Curriculum for Excellence' (CfE) replacing the previous longstanding 5–14 curriculum (Scottish Executive, 2004). The CfE is considered by its creators to be *one of the most ambitious programmes of educational change ever undertaken in Scotland* (Scottish Government, 2008, p.8). CfE aims to ensure that all children and young people in Scotland develop the attributes, knowledge and skills that are essential in life, learning and work, and it is envisaged that these attributes will allow for the demonstration of four key capacities: to be successful learners, confident individuals, responsible citizens and effective contributors.

At the point of writing, CfE has been at the heart of educational change in Scotland for over ten years, and it is interesting to note that it is has not yet been implemented fully in all schools, neither has it been fully embraced by all members of the teaching profession. Tensions arise from an increased emphasis on the professional input of teachers as developers of the curriculum with a corresponding absence of curriculum prescription. As a result, CfE has been criticised for its vagueness in terms of content, processes and pedagogy (see Priestley, 2010).

---

### Research box

## the impact of devolution on educational outcomes

Research carried out by Andrews and Martin (2010) explored the impact of policy divergence in England, Scotland and Wales on public service outcomes. This is a significant area of research, given that devolved government is supposed to deliver more effective and better quality public services at a regional level. Their analysis of statutory performance indicators does reveal statistically significant differences between public service outcomes in the regions – interestingly the most significant variations were in hospital waiting times and school examination results – lower and higher respectively in the case of England relative to Scotland and Wales. Based on these findings, Andrews and Martin argue that:

*Since health and education are the two largest services for which devolved administrations in Scotland and Wales now have direct responsibility, it is likely that these differences are attributable, at least in part, to policy divergence in the three countries since devolution in 1999. These variations, therefore, have implications for assessments of the impacts of devolution and public service reform strategies.*

(Andrews and Martin, 2010, p.919)

This leads them to conclude that *the 'top-down' model of public services reform adopted by the UK government in England appears (in general) to have been more effective in driving up performance than the more consensual approaches adopted by the devolved administrations in Wales and to some extent in Scotland* (p.929).

This finding could well be viewed as controversial in some quarters, especially given the resistance to the 'top-down' model among education professionals. However, Andrews and Martin do state that such findings *do not imply that devolution is necessarily a bad thing*, and that it may be the case that *the creation of the devolved administrations has had other benefits – for example, in terms of improvements in accountability, public engagement, and economic development policies* (Andrews and Martin, 2010, p.929).

---

# Devolution and the teaching profession

Teacher education is broadly similar to that of England in the other home nations in that students either complete an initial teacher training (ITT) – known as initial teacher education (ITE) in Scotland – course (which gives them QTS) or go down the graduate PGCE route. Like Scotland, Wales is not signed up to the SCITT scheme – i.e. the groups of schools that have formed school-centred ITT consortia. In fact, all PGCE courses in Wales and Scotland are based in universities or colleges of higher education (with a different system for Northern Ireland). Interestingly, the Welsh government has recently given the go-ahead for Teach First to operate in Wales from September 2013. They will be called Teach First Cymru and will be recruiting 40 graduates to teach according to their website 'in some of Wales' most disadvantaged communities'. They have been awarded a contract from the Welsh government initially for three years to recruit 150 trainee teachers.

There is a General Teaching Council for Wales, which is the statutory self-regulating professional body for Wales, and like Scotland has the power to investigate incompetence and to introduce disciplinary procedures against individual teachers. It has been involved in helping put together a professional development framework for Wales. The General Teaching Council for Scotland (GTCS) was established in 1965, some 35 years earlier than its counterparts elsewhere in the UK. The GTCS was the world's first independent self-regulatory body for teaching and plays a central role in the promotion and regulation of the teaching profession nationally. Its independent status was recognised by the Scottish Government in 2012, coincidentally at the same time as the GTC for England was abolished.

---

*Pause for thought* | who should deliver teacher education?

The current UK government's Minister for Education, Michael Gove, would like to see teacher training taking place in schools or in school consortia rather than in universities or colleges of HE. As indicated above, such consortia only exist in England and it looks unlikely they will take hold in other parts of the UK. But it raises the question: what is the best way to deliver teacher education? And how significant is the theoretical input provided by universities to the education of future teacher professionals?

---

The Welsh government delivered its revised 'professional standards for educational practitioners in Wales' (Circular 2020/2011) – which makes some adjustments to standards for higher level teaching assistants, practising teachers and head teachers.

Since devolution, teacher education policy in Scotland has been considered by some to be following an increasingly divergent path from that elsewhere in the UK, particularly England (Hulme and Menter, 2011). There is a developing consensus that the profession of teaching is viewed differently, north and south of the border. In Scotland, there is a move to view teaching as a profession based on academic learning, within which university education plays a significant role. In England, pedagogy is sometimes considered as a collation of acquired technical skills where teaching is viewed more as a trade or craft rather than an occupation based on academic achievement such as in law or medicine.

The provision of ITE in Scotland is delivered by seven schools of education, which are based within universities. These universities are therefore responsible for the design, facilitation and delivery of ITE, with assistance from local authorities in the form of school placement practice. In 2010, the Scottish Government established a Review of Teacher Education in Scotland, led by Professor Graham Donaldson, former Senior Chief Inspector for Her Majesty's Inspectorate of Education (HMIE) which resulted in 'Teaching Scotland's Future' (perhaps more commonly referred to as the Donaldson Report) (Donaldson, 2011). The report contains 50 recommendations for the improvement of teacher education in its entirety. All 50 of the recommendations were accepted by the Scottish Government and are currently being implemented. Donaldson has a vision of teachers as expert practitioners, who are themselves the engines of professional progress. He believes that they should be empowered as professionals, and distinguished by their capacity for self-determination and judgement. What is interesting to note about this particular teacher education reform, is the importance placed on the role of the university, not just in ITE, but also in models of career-long professional learning and leadership education.

Elsewhere in the UK, issues in teacher supply and quality have led to the development of market-driven routes into teacher education, which do not require university sector input, such as 'Teach First'.

## Research box

### teacher education north and south of the border

Hulme and Menter (2011) conducted a comparative textual analysis of education policy in England and Scotland. They analysed two key texts: 'Teaching Scotland's Future' (TSF; Donaldson, 2011) and 'The Importance of Teaching' (IoT; Department for Education, 2010) in order to understand how policy on teacher education is being developed post-devolution.

They discovered that although there were many commonalities between the two texts on the surface, they differed with regard to their philosophical stance and conceptualisation of teaching. Some of the main differences were:

- *Teacher professionalism*: IoT describes teaching as a 'craft' and focuses on the teacher as a 'discipliner', whereas TSF sees teaching as a complex and intellectual profession.
- *Teacher education*: The role of universities and the importance of a 'knowledge base' are referred to throughout TSF. IoT depicts teaching as a profession, which requires very little professional preparation and disregards the role of the university, favouring schemes such as 'Teach First' instead.
- *Evidence/research*: TSF highlights the need for teaching to be an evidence-informed profession and emphasises the crucial role of educational research. IoT completely omits this concept.
- *Partnership*: TSF stresses the importance of collaborative partnerships between key stakeholders in education, whereas IoT appears to be centred on a more individualistic approach and self-governance.
- *Social justice*: Both texts reveal different visions of a socially just education system, with TSF stressing the importance of collective responsibility.

## Summary and conclusions

The chapter explored some of the ways in which education policy has converged and diverged across the home nations. Using governance, provision and profession as the three guiding themes, it becomes clear when studying UK policy that the local context matters: language in Wales plays an important part in provision, religion in governance in Northern Ireland, and political ideology in Scotland when it comes to all aspects of education policy. While still a United Kingdom (the outcome of the referendum on Scottish Independence may drastically alter the political landscape), there is strong evidence of a *disunited* kingdom when it comes to some key features of an educational ethos – not least the role of league tables, inspections, funding, and what it means to be an educational profession.

*(Continued)*

*(Continued)*

At the same time it is important not to overstate the case for divergence. It could be argued that, looking at the bigger picture, there is as much convergence as divergence taking place, if not more so – all home nations have a strong focus on increasing professionalisation of the sector (standards, frameworks, professionalising roles such as teaching assistant and head teacher), and also codes of practice (accountability, regulatory and risk frameworks). Such convergence in the system alongside the examples of difference detailed above suggests that students of education policy should take seriously both regional and national systems as key players in the complex process of policy making.

# References

Allan, J (2010) Questions of inclusion in Scotland and Europe. *European Journal of Special Educational Needs*, 25, 199–208.

Andrews, R and Martin, S (2010) Regional variations in public service outcomes: The impact of policy divergence in England, Scotland and Wales. *Regional Studies*, 44(8): 919–34.

Chaney, P (2011) Education, equality and human rights: Exploring the impact of devolution in the UK. *Critical Social Policy*, 31: 431–53.

Department for Education (2010) *The Importance of Teaching. The Schools White Paper 2010*. London: The Stationery Office.

Donaldson, G (2011) *Teaching Scotland's Future*. Edinburgh: Scottish Government.

Hodgson, A and Spours, K (2011) National education systems: the wider context, in Hodgson, A, Spours, K and Waring, M (eds) (2011) *Post-compulsory Education and Lifelong Learning across the United Kingdom: Policy, organisation and governance*. London: Institute of Education.

Hodgson, A, Spours, K and Waring, M (eds) (2011) *Post-compulsory Education and Lifelong Learning across the United Kingdom: Policy, organisation and governance*. London: Institute of Education.

Horgan, G and Gray, A (2012) Devolution in Northern Ireland: A lost opportunity? *Critical Social Policy*, 2012, 32: 467.

Hulme, M and Menter, I (2011) South and North – Teacher education policy in England and Scotland: a comparative textual analysis. *Scottish Educational Review*, 43, 70–90.

Humes, WM (1997) Analysing the policy process. *Scottish Educational Review*, 29, 20–9.

Humes, WM and Bryce, T (2008) The distinctiveness of Scottish education, in Bryce, TGK and Humes, WM (eds) *Scottish Education: Beyond devolution* (3rd edn). Edinburgh: Edinburgh University Press.

Humes, W and Paterson, L (1983) *Scottish Culture and Scottish Education 1800–1980*. Edinburgh: John Donald.

McKinney, S (2007) The faith school debate: Catholic schooling in Scotland. *Pastoral Review*, 3(4).

Paterson, L (1997) Policy-making in Scottish education: A case of pragmatic nationalism, in Clark, M and Munn, P (eds) *Education in Scotland: Policy and practice from pre-school to secondary*. London: Routledge, pp. 138–55.

Priestley, M (2010) Curriculum for Excellence: Transformational change or business as usual? *Scottish Educational Review*, 42, 23–36.

Rees, G (2011) Devolution, policy-making and lifelong learning: the case of Wales, in Hodgson, A, Spours, K and Waring, M (eds) *Post-compulsory Education and Lifelong Learning across the United Kingdom*. London: IOE.

Scotland, J (1969) *The History of Scottish Education* (2nd edn). London: University of London Press.

Scottish Education Department (1973) *Training of Staff for Centres for the Mentally Handicapped: The Melville Report.* Edinburgh: Scottish Education Department.

Scottish Executive (2004) *Curriculum for Excellence.* Edinburgh: Scottish Executive.

Scottish Government (2007) *Concordat between the Scottish Government and Local Government.* Edinburgh: Scottish Government.

Scottish Government (2008) *Building the Curriculum 3: A framework for learning and teaching.* Edinburgh: Scottish Government.

Seith, E.(2009) Political battle continues. *TES*, 4 December. Available at: **www.tes.co.uk/ article.aspx?storycode=6029188.**

Sischy, J (2008) The independent sector, in Bryce, TGK and Humes, WM (eds) *Scottish Education: Beyond devolution* (3rd edn). Edinburgh: Edinburgh University Press.

Wakeling, P and Jefferies, K (2013, iFirst) The effect of tuition fees on student mobility: the UK and Ireland as a natural experiment. *British Educational Research Journal.* Available at: **http://onlinelibrary.wiley.com/doi/10.1080/01411926.2012.658022/pdf** [accessed 24 May 2013].

# Chapter 12

# Education and the economy

## Jane McDonnell

### Introduction

The economy seems to be at the forefront of everybody's minds at the moment. Turn on the TV or pick up a newspaper and it won't be long before you come across a story about the economic downturn and its effect on people's lives. Politicians disagree over the root causes of the problem and the best route to recovery. What doesn't seem to be in dispute is that the economy presents a real problem at the moment that needs to be tackled. But what is the economy and how does it relate to education? More importantly, what are the key issues for education and the economy in the UK today? One of the most obvious ways in which education and the economy are related is in the way schools prepare young people for the world of work. But there are other important questions too – such as the amount of public money available to spend on education in times of austerity, how education can contribute to economic growth and the extent to which educational sectors and individual establishments should operate according to business principles. In this chapter, we will explore these questions by looking at a number of key issues affecting education and the economy today. By the end of this chapter, you should have a deeper understanding of the nature of the economy and its relationship with education, and be able to critically reflect on some of the key issues in the field today.

## The economy

If you were asked to think about the economy, you might start by considering some of the issues that affect your everyday life – the price you pay for your weekly shopping for example, the interest rate you pay on your car loan or mortgage, or your career prospects in the graduate job market. This makes perfect sense because the economy is made up of all the financial decisions that people make as they go about their everyday lives. Economists are concerned with the collective impact that these decisions have on markets and economic policy, as well as with how wealth is produced and distributed. Economic thinking tends to operate on the principle that people make rational decisions as they seek to maximise their own benefit in a world of scarce resources (Mankiw and Taylor, 2011). One important concern for economists in modern western societies therefore has been the balance between efficiency and equity in the production and distribution of resources. Economists are concerned with how well the economy makes use of resources to produce new wealth and contribute to economic growth, but also with how equitably these are distributed among the population (Mankiw and Taylor, 2011). Economists also study broader questions about how an economy should be run, e.g. on free market principles or on a more of a centrally planned basis (Sloman, 2003).

*Pause for thought* | economic planning

In the UK, a pattern can be traced from a 'classical' or 'liberal' approach to the economy (emphasising market forces) in the early part of the twentieth century, to a post-war consensus that the economy should be more centrally planned. Following the oil crisis of the 1970s there was a return to classical liberal (or neo-liberal) economic thinking, which has arguably held sway with successive governments ever since. Recently, however, in the wake of the financial crisis, there has been a resurgence of interest in economic theories which advocate greater government involvement – in particular the work of John Maynard Keynes. Writing in 1936, Keynes challenged the dominant view at the time that a market economy is self-correcting. Instead, he argued that governments could 'spend their way' out of a recession, even if that meant running at a deficit for a time, i.e. spending more money than comes in through taxes and exports (Sloman, 2003).

Imagine you were tasked with coming up with an economic plan for the UK. What would it look like? In a small group, try to come up with a five-point plan for the economy to present in poster form to your classmates. You might want to consider the following in your plan:

- What role should government play in the economy?
- How much support should be given to businesses by the government?
- Which sectors of industry and the economy should be prioritised?
- Where should the balance lie between big and small businesses?
- To what extent should public services be run according to business principles?

## Important issues for economists of education

Many of the above principles are reflected in the issues that are of interest to economists of education. Allen (2011) has outlined what have been some of the most important concerns for educational economists since this was established as a distinct field of study in the early 1960s. She traces the origins of the economics of education to an interest in human capital theory, involving the study of how investment in people through education and skills can lead to individual and societal benefits. Alongside this interest in the relationship between human capital and economic growth, Allen (2011) cites efficiency in the production of educational resources, equity in the distribution of these, labour markets for teachers and market reforms in education as some of the main areas of interest that concern economists of education today. She notes that there has recently been a growth of interest in educational policy among economists of education, which can be attributed to the growing impact of market-based reforms of education. As financial planning has been devolved to schools and choice has been introduced to the public sector, economists of education have offered analysis of specific educational policies for governments (Allen, 2011, p.86). Important questions tackled by economists of education include the relationship between average years of schooling and economic growth, the impact of class sizes on educational outcomes, ways of ensuring fairness within the education system, teachers' pay and productivity (including performance-related pay), and the impact of reforms such as voucher systems designed to introduce choice and market values into education. In the following sections, we will explore some of these questions further as they relate to key issues for education and the economy today, including the economic independence of schools and other educational establishments, public spending on education in the context of economic crisis, the relationship between education and work and the role of education in contributing to industry and economic growth.

# Schools as economically independent entities

An important development in education over the past 30 years has been the devolution of financial responsibility to schools. The impetus for this can be traced back to the 1988 Education Reform Act, which restructured the educational landscape in favour of choice and market forces. Following this legislation, the Local Schools Management system (LSM) was introduced, allocating funds to schools based partly on pupil numbers, and new kinds of schools were created – such as Grant Maintained Schools – funded directly by government. Although not a full voucher system as operated in many other countries such as Chile and Sweden (see below), this led to increased competition between schools and effectively meant the operation of a quasi-market in state education (Chitty, 2011). The introduction of market forces into the system under the then Conservative government has since been strengthened – first under New Labour, with the establishment of academies, and more recently under the Coalition government, with the expansion of these and the introduction of free schools. The educational environment in the UK now consists of a range of schools, with varying degrees of economic independence from local authorities, from among which parents are encouraged to choose.

Research conducted in the wake of these reforms has charted their impact on educational practice and cultures within schools and colleges. Sinclair et al. (1996), for example, conducted research in schools in England, which pointed to an increased 'casualisation' of labour within the teaching profession, and the intensification of teachers' workloads through measures such as the increased use of substitute teachers and the diversification of roles and responsibilities. They argue that a combination of market reforms and shrinking budgets led to the emergence of a new managerial culture as school managers began to act as though they were running private businesses (1996, p.645). The introduction of performance-related pay for teachers in 1999 can be read as a continuation of this cultural shift, as policy makers began to look at the potential rewards of offering financial incentives to teachers (Chamberlain et al., 2002). Today, this managerial culture can be seen in proposals to abolish the mandatory pay scale for teachers (DfE, 2013) and in the greater freedom given to academies and free schools over teacher recruitment. Academies do not have to adhere to the School Teachers Pay and Conditions Document that governs pay in other schools and, like free schools, are allowed to recruit staff without Qualified Teacher Status (DfE, 2012). Some academies pay more to teachers who can demonstrate they spend a significant amount of time on extra-curricular activities. The impact of the market reforms outlined above was not only to introduce a competitive economy *between* schools but also to change the cultures and economic structures *within* them.

This shift towards schools as economically independent entities within a quasi-market of state education has perhaps found its fullest fruition in the free schools policy introduced in 2010. Funded directly by government rather than local authorities, free schools can be set up by anyone and have a higher degree of autonomy than other schools (for example in terms of curriculum and teacher pay and recruitment – see also above). Swedish free schools have often been cited as a key influence on the free schools policy in England. Free schools in Sweden were introduced in 1992 under legislation that allowed new schools to be established and receive funding directly from the government, based on the average cost per pupil in the local area. Schools were also allowed to make a profit by charging top up fees. While the first free schools in Sweden were mostly not-for-profit, by the late 1990s, the fastest growing types of free school were those run for profit by private companies. The largest of these made over 120 million Swedish Kronor in 2005/2006 (roughly £12 million), a third of which went to the owner of the company (Wilborg, 2010). Free schools in England are run as not-for-profit organisations but there has recently been some debate about whether this should change. It has been suggested that the Conservative party would include this in their manifesto to be implemented if they won the next general election in 2015 (Grice, 2013).

## learning from the Swedish free schools model

Research into free schools in Sweden has offered a mixed picture of their educational, economic and societal impact. Wilborg (2010) notes that the free schools have resulted in greater costs for municipalities and have led to 'market-orientated' behaviour among teachers as well as widening existing social inequalities. She cautions against a straightforward adoption of the model in England, noting some important differences between the two contexts. While the introduction of free schools in Sweden was genuinely innovative, providing choice in what was an overwhelmingly state-dominated system, private education and choice within the state sector have long been features of education in England. She argues that establishing similar kinds of schools in this context could risk an even greater increase in inequality than has been the case in Sweden (2010, p.21). Sahlgren (2010), however, points to evidence of an increase in some aspects of school performance following the introduction of free schools in Sweden. He claims that a similar policy in England could offer important benefits but crucially claims that the profit motive was integral to the success of Swedish free schools. He argues that this, and a commitment to allow failing schools to close, must be integrated into the model applied in England for it to be effective (2010, p.31).

The introduction of for-profit schools in England would perhaps represent the logical end point of the market reforms introduced in 1988. As Sahlgren (2010) has pointed out in relation to the Swedish context, this could have important benefits for educational attainment. However, it would also raise difficult questions about the political desirability of private companies making a profit from state education. For example, is it right that the tax payer should subsidise private gains from education? Would such schools be more interested in profit than in the quality of education provided? And what kind of values would they promote?

## *Pause for thought* | profit-making free schools

Imagine a motion to introduce profit-making free schools was put forward in parliament. Write a letter to your MP expressing your views on the issue. Try to do some research into the impact of similar schools in other countries to help inform your response (you could look at charter schools in the USA for example). You might want to consider the following in your letter:

- Raising standards.
- Private profits and public money.
- Impact on other schools.
- Impact on teacher pay and labour markets.
- School autonomy.
- Parental voice.

# Public spending on education

The amount of public money available to spend on education is often a contentious issue, and perhaps never more so than in the context of the current economic climate. The impact of the global financial crisis of 2008 – including recession, slow growth and rising unemployment have been of major concern in the UK over the past five years. The economy has gone into recession twice since 2008 and the government has employed a policy of austerity, implementing massive cuts in public spending. This of course has significant implications for public spending on schools, colleges and universities. The Institute for Fiscal Studies has estimated that public spending on education will fall to 4.6 per cent share of national income by 2014–2015, down from a high of 6.4 per cent in 2009–2010. The areas forecast to be hit the most are further and higher education, early years education, youth services and capital spending (e.g. on buildings and infrastructure). Day-to-day spending in primary and secondary schools will be relatively protected from the cuts although they are unlikely to see any increase in spending, experiencing instead a 'freeze' in the level of expenditure (Chowdry and Sibieta, 2011).

Since the introduction of mass schooling nearly a century and a half ago, successive governments have taken different approaches to public spending on education, often reflecting broader trends in the economy as a whole. The 1940s and 1950s saw the emergence of a 'post-war consensus' around the need for more central planning and government investment and a steady increase in public spending on education as the school leaving age was raised to 15. However, this consensus was overturned from the late 1970s onwards, following a return to classical, liberal (or neo-liberal) economic thinking under the Conservative government of 1979–1997. We have already seen that the 1980s saw the devolution of economic autonomy to schools and the introduction of market forces in education. Tomlinson (2005) has written of this period as the move towards a 'post welfare society', in which education came to be seen as a commodity rather than a public good. Public spending on education during this period continued to increase in real terms (after accounting for inflation), but at a slower rate, and it actually decreased as a share of national income (Chowdry and Sibieta, 2011). Under New Labour, a 'third way' approach to public spending was championed, and collaborative partnerships between the public and private sector were encouraged. The Public Funded Initiative (PFI) scheme (launched by the Conservative government in 1992 and allowing private companies to build new schools in partnership with local authorities) was embraced by the New Labour government. Overall, government expenditure on education increased during this period. By 2010, it was back to a high of 6.4 per cent of national income – a figure not seen since 1976 (Chowdry and Sibieta, 2011).

Despite overall cuts in the level of spending on education under the Coaltion government, there are similarities between its priorities in this area and that of the previous New Labour government (Chowdry and Sibieta, 2011). Higher education has suffered successive budget cuts as both governments have shifted the balance in university funding from the state to individual students and graduates. Measures such as the introduction of variable tuition fees under New Labour have been consolidated by the lifting of the cap on tuition fees under the Coalition government and the almost total withdrawal of the teaching grant formerly paid to universities. Total public spending on higher education is only 0.9 per cent of national income in the UK – the lowest rate of any country within the Organisation for Economic Co-operation and Development (OECD) (Locke, 2011). One major difference between the approaches of the two governments is in capital spending. This was the fastest growing area of public spending under New Labour but now faces the steepest cuts.

> ## *Pause for thought* | building schools for the future
>
> One of the casualties of the current austerity measures has been the 'Building Schools for the Future' programme. The scheme was set up in 2004 and allowed schools to work with architects and developers to redesign their buildings. The scheme was beset by bureaucratic difficulties and involved a lot of investment both in time and money – the total government spend for the programme was estimated at £55 billion. The Coalition scrapped the scheme in 2010, announcing that only a handful of projects already under way would continue to receive funding. They cited wastefulness and inefficiency as reasons for cutting the programme in straitened economic times.
>
> This case illustrates a number of the issues relating to public spending on education outlined above. With a classmate, discuss the following:
>
> * Where should the balance lie between public and private investment in education?
> * Is it more important to spend money on buildings or day-to-day services?
> * Where should education sit on the list of the government's spending priorities?

# Education and work

The role of schools in providing skilled workers for the economy has been an important issue since the introduction of mass education in the 1870s (Sanderson, 1999). As work shifted from the fields to the factory in the wake of the industrial revolution, a new breed of workers with basic skills in numeracy and literacy was required to fill new jobs (Dufour, 2011). In the years that have followed, education and schools have often been blamed if there appears to be a 'skills gap' between the attributes of school leavers and the requirements of employers. The relationship between education and work often comes under closest scrutiny in debates about vocationalism. There has long been a divide between academic and vocational education in the UK, with academic qualifications historically favoured over the vocational by schools, parents, universities and employers (Hyland, 2002; McCulloch, 2002). Public debate over the purposes of state education, the extent to which it should meet the demands of employers and its accountability to the tax payer can be traced in part to the 'great debate' launched following a speech made by the then Labour Prime Minister James Callaghan at Ruskin College, Oxford in 1976. In it he voiced concern over the extent to which the curriculum met the needs of a modern economy and prepared young people for careers in industry (Bartlett and Burton, 2007). In the years since, the issue of how well schools prepare young people for work in the current economy has been an important aspect of public discourse about education.

An ambitious attempt to overcome the academic/vocational divide was formulated in the findings of the Tomlinson review. This was set up alongside a raft of educational reforms for 14–19 year olds set up under the New Labour government in 2002. These offered greater access to vocational qualifications in schools and introduced new, more applied courses worth the equivalent of two established GCSEs (Haynes, 2008). The review advocated doing away with GCSEs, GNVQs, A levels and NVQs altogether, and offering instead a diploma system, which would provide both vocational and academic routes of equal status. However, these recommendations were not implemented in full, and diplomas were introduced only alongside existing qualifications. Many have seen this as a missed opportunity and educationalists have highlighted the ongoing difficulty of achieving parity of esteem between academic and vocational qualifications in the UK (Tomlinson, 2005; Pring et al., 2012). It is worth noting that, in many ways, this is a specifically British problem. In Germany, for example, where manufacturing has retained a significant stake in the economy, vocational education is highly prized (Lauder et al., 2012, p.20).

---

### *Pause for thought* | vocational courses

In 2011, the government announced plans to cut a number of vocational courses from inclusion within school league tables and to remove their status as equivalent to GCSEs. The number of courses included in the tables was finally cut from over 3,100 to just 125 in January 2012, following questions about their credibility highlighted in the Wolf report (2011), which was commissioned by the current government. Some quite strong opinions were provoked by this decision and questions were asked about why courses such as horse care and nail technology were ever on the curriculum in the first place (it could equally be asked why people were so angry about it!). One newspaper headline from the time referred to the *axing* of *thousands of mickey mouse courses* (Clark, 2012).

Why do you think the decision to scrap these qualifications provoked such strong reactions? If you had to draw up an ideal curriculum for 14–19 year olds, what would it include and why? Present your ideas to your class for feedback.

---

# Education and economic growth

At the beginning of the chapter we noted how an interest in human capital and economic growth had been an important issue in the study of the economics of education. Tomlinson (2005) has noted a resurgence of interest in human capital theory towards the end of the twentieth century, linked to globalisation. With rapid economic growth in 'developing' countries such as China, Brazil and India and more migration of workers across national borders, western countries have felt increasingly impelled to compete on the global economic stage. This was compounded by the emergence of a 'knowledge economy' in the late twentieth century, involving both the shift from an industrial economy to one based on knowledge, services and information, and the growing acceptance that knowledge itself is an important commodity. Leadbetter (2000) in his book *Living on Thin Air* famously captured this movement, highlighting the growing importance to the economy of areas such as finance, services and the creative industries. In this context, education has increasingly been charged with contributing to overall economic growth.

As a consequence, UK governments have adhered to a belief in 'credentialism', i.e. the view that gaining more qualifications is beneficial both for individuals and for the economy as a whole. Lauder et al. (2012, p.2) have expressed this in the simple equation *learning = earning*. Under New Labour, this resulted in what Casey (2012, p.2) has described as the emergence of the *learner-worker of the learning economy/society*. Under the Coalition, an emphasis on facts and traditional academic subjects has equally been linked to economic competitiveness. However, the perceived link between education and economic success has been challenged (Wolf, 2002) and many have questioned its continued relevance in a post-financial crisis world (Lauder et al., 2012).

> ### Research box
>
> ## Tomlinson 'Ignorant yobs: low attainers and the global knowledge economy'
>
> Tomlinson (2013) has raised an important question in relation to the trends described above, i.e. what becomes of 'low attainers' and children with special educational needs in the new knowledge economy? Based on a review of the literature, discussion with academics, comparative data from visits to other countries and observation of students on vocational courses, Tomlinson argues that the dominant 'knowledge economy' and credentialism narrative ignores the real experiences of many young people today. She points out that while there has been an insistence on the need for ever more knowledge and qualifications, the reality is that many students will acquire only a few qualifications and go on to work in low skilled jobs. For Tomlinson, these *'low attainers' are particularly affected by beliefs that there is a global knowledge economy in which they are unlikely to participate* (2013, p.20) and are often demonised as *yobs, louts* and *workshy scroungers* (p.2).

The concerns voiced by Tomlinson (2013) are particularly pertinent in the context of the growing number of young people aged between 16 and 24 who are 'not in education, employment or training' (NEETS). According to figures from the Institute for Public Policy Research (IPPR), the number of young people in this situation in 2011 was 21.9 per cent – over a fifth of the youth population (Tomlinson, 2013, p.22). The term NEETs was introduced in the early 1990s following policy changes that disqualified 16 and 17 year olds from claiming unemployment benefit, and therefore both described a new social reality and allowed for the targeting of specific policy interventions (Furlong, 2006, as cited in Inui, 2009). It is also symptomatic of broader changes in the nature of employment. Beck (2000) has argued that young people have been most affected by such changes which have involved a casualisation of labour through, for example, the increase in temporary and part-time contracts (Beck, 2000, as cited in Inui, 2009). In sociological terms, the categorisation and subsequent demonisation of young people in this way could be seen as part of an exclusionary process. The sociologist Zygmunt Bauman has used the term 'waste' to describe how people who are deemed incapable of choice are excluded from society because they present a danger to consumerist priorities of modernity (Poder, 2008). This could be seen as a helpful way of thinking about the situation of young unemployed people today, as the lack of ability to 'choose' employment trajectories within the knowledge economy based on poor qualifications leads to their marginalisation. In any case, support can certainly be found for Tomlinson's view that these young people are demonised as workshy and lazy (Inui, 2009). The issue of youth unemployment is likely to become increasingly contested in light of developments such as the removal of the Educational Maintenance Allowance (EMA) in England and plans to make schooling compulsory up until the age of 18.

# Higher education and the economy

Universities are an interesting case within this 'education for economic growth' narrative. They have been seen both as a means of providing higher levels of knowledge and skills within the population, and as generators of economic wealth in and of themselves. Under New Labour, the widening participation agenda saw a drive to include more students from non-traditional backgrounds within higher education and a target was set of 50 per cent of the population attending university by 2010. While seen as an issue of equality of opportunity and access to the university experience, this agenda was also framed within a narrative about improving the economic competitiveness of the country as a whole (Kettley, 2007). More broadly, universities have been seen as a key driver in the knowledge economy and in the promotion of entrepreneurial skills (Olssen and Peters, 2005). Having been moved across a variety of government departments since the 1960s, higher education now tellingly comes under the remit of the Department for Business, Innovation and Skills.

Higher education has also been framed as an important contributor to economic growth and recovery as an industry in and of itself. Earlier in the chapter, we noted the impact of the 1988 Education Reform Act on schools and colleges. But it is not only in schools that the increasing impact of market forces in education has been felt. Legislative changes to higher education from the 1980s onwards also saw a shift towards the financial independence of institutions and the increasing impact of market forces in the sector (Barr and Crawford, 2005). With the introduction of tuition fees in 1998 and subsequent increases in the levels universities are able to charge, student fees have become a huge source of revenue and the recruitment of students from outside the EU has become a major source of funding. Higher education has become somewhat of an export industry, with foreign students attracted from around the world to study at UK universities.

Opinions on the relative opportunities and threats associated with this development are mixed. Locke (2011) has cautioned against the over recruitment of foreign students where there is inadequate support once they arrive in the UK. Others, however, have been very vocal in defending the position of higher education as a booming export industry that can help the country recover from the current economic slump. The university sector currently contributes £27 billion to the economy annually, with £3 billion of that coming from fees from international students, and a further £8 billion estimated from their spending in the surrounding economy (Morgan, 2012). Some of these issues came to a head in September 2012 in the decision by the UK Border Agency (UKBA) to withdraw sponsor status from London Metropolitan University, revoking its licence to support visas for foreign students from outside the European Union (EU). Universities UK (the body that represents the sector as a whole) has lobbied in parliament for international students to be excluded from the government's new migration targets, based on the argument that higher education is an important contributor to economic growth.

> *Pause for thought* | higher education as an industry
>
> With a classmate or in a small group, list all the benefits of higher education you can think of. Now try to rank them in terms of importance. How many of your reasons have to do with the economy and where do these lie in terms of importance? Looking at your ranking, discuss in your group the extent to which you think higher education should be seen as an industry.

## Summary and conclusions

In this chapter we have explored a number of topical issues relating to education and the economy. Interesting aspects of our discussion have included the possibility of private companies making a profit from education, the ideological battle over the extent to which universities should be run as businesses, and the thorny question of where 'low attainers' fit within a narrative of education for economic success. These issues expose new fault lines in educational debate in the UK today. As the country struggles to recover from the worst economic downturn in a century, these are likely to become even more prominent. Important decisions will have to be made about where education fits within the economy and society as a whole, how much it ought to contribute to economic growth and recovery, and what kind of investment we are prepared to make in schools both for individuals and society as a whole. An awareness of these issues should help to make sense of current educational debate as the UK faces the challenge of both a globalised, knowledge economy and a global economic crisis, the like of which hasn't been seen since the 1930s.

## References

Allen, R (2011) The economics of education, in Dufour, B and Curtis, W (eds) *Studying Education*. Maidenhead: Open University Press.

Barr, N and Crawford, I (2005) *Financing Higher Education*. London: Routledge.

Bartlett, S and Burton, D (2007) *Introduction to Education Studies* (2nd edn). London: Sage.

Casey, C (2012) *Economy, Work and Education. Critical Connections*. Oxford: Routledge.

Chamberlain, R, Wragg, T, Haynes, G and Wragg, C (2002) Performance related pay and the teaching profession: A review of the literature. *Research Papers in Education,* 17(1): 31–49.

Chitty, C (2011) The politics of education, in Dufour, B and Curtis, W (eds) *Studying Education*. Maidenhead: Open University Press.

Chowdry, H and Sibieta, L (2011) Trends in education and spending. Institute for Fiscal Studies [Online] Briefing note 121. Available at: **www.ifs.org.uk/publications** [accessed 19 April 2013].

Clark, L (2012) Thousands of "Mickey Mouse" courses will no longer count towards GCSE league tables. *Daily Mail*, 1 February [Online] Available at: **www.dailymail.co.uk** [accessed 29 March 2013].

Department for Education (2012) *Academies to have same freedom as free schools over teachers*. [Online] Available at: **www.education.gov.uk** [accessed 19 April 2013].

Department for Education (2013) *New advice to help schools set performance related pay*. [Online] Available at: **www.education.gov.uk** [accessed 19 April 2013].

Dufour, B (2011) The history of education, in Dufour, B and Curtis, W (eds) *Studying Education*. Maidenhead: Open University Press.

Grice, A (2013) Exclusive: Revealed – Tory plans for firms to run schools for profit. *The Independent*. 10 January [Online] Available at: **www.independent.co.uk** [accessed 18 April 2013].

Haynes, G (2008) Secondary headteachers' experiences and perceptions of vocational courses in the key stage 4 curriculum: some implications for the 14-19 Diplomas. *Journal of Education and Work,* 21(4): 333–47.

Hyland, T (2002) On the upgrading of vocational studies: analysing prejudice and subordination in English education. *Educational Review*, 54(3): 287–96.

Inui, A (2009) NEETs, Freeters and Flexibility. Reflecting precarious situations in the New Labour market, in Furlong, A (ed) *Handbook of Youth and Young Adulthood: New perspectives and agendas*. Oxford: Routledge.

Kettley, N (2007) The past, present and future of widening participation research. *British Journal of Sociology of Education*, 28(3): 333–47.

Lauder, H, Young, M, Daniels, H, Balarin, M and Lowe, J (2012) *Educating for the Knowledge Economy? Critical Perspectives*. Abingdon: Routledge.

Leadbetter, C (2000) *Living on Thin Air: The new economy*. London: Penguin.

Locke, W (2011) False economy? Multiple markets, reputational hierarchy and incremental policymaking in UK higher education, in Brown, R (ed) *Higher Education and the Market*. Oxford: Routledge.

Mankiw, NG and Taylor, MP (2011) *Economics* (2nd edn). London: Thomson learning.

McCulloch, G (2002) Secondary education, in Aldrich, R (ed) *A Century of Education*. London: RoutledgeFalmer.

Morgan, J (2012) Fire sale feared as London Met faces flood of red ink. *The Times Higher Education Supplement*, 6 September. [Online] Available at: **www.timeshighereducation. co.uk** [accessed 26 March 2013].

Olssen, M and Peters, MA (2005) Neoliberalism, higher education and the knowledge economy: from the free market to knowledge capitalism. *Journal of Education Policy*, 20 (3): 313–45.

Poder, P (2008) Bauman on Freedom – Consumer freedom as the integration mechanism of liquid society, in Hviid Jacobsen, M and Poder, P (eds) *"The" Sociology of Zygmunt Bauman: Challenges and Critique*. Aldershot: Ashgate.

Pring, R, Hayward, G, Hodgson, A, Johnson, J, Keep, E, Oancea, A, Dees, G, Spours, K and Wilde, S (2012) *Education for all: The future of education and training for 14–19 year olds*. Abingdon: Routledge.

Sahlgren, GH (2010) Schooling for money: Swedish education reform and the role of the for profit motive. *Institute of Economic Affairs*. [Online] IEA discussion paper no. 33. Available at: **www.iea.org.uk**. [accessed 22 February 2013].

Sanderson, M (1999) *Education and Economic Decline in Britain, 1870 to the 1990s*. Cambridge: Cambridge University Press.

Sinclair, J, Ironside, M and Seifert, R (1996) Classroom struggle? Market orientated education reforms and their impact on the teacher labour process. *Work, Employment & Society*, 10(4): 641–61.

Sloman, J (2003) *Economics* (5th edn). Edinburgh: Pearson Education.

Tomlinson, S (2005) *Education in a Post Welfare Society*. Maidenhead: Open University Press.

Tomlinson, S (2013) *Ignorant Yobs? Low attainers in a global knowledge economy*. Abingdon: Routledge.

Wilborg, S (2010) Swedish free schools: do they work? *Centre for learning and life chances in knowledge economies and societies*. [Online] Available at: **www.lakes.org**. [accessed 22 February 2013].

Wolf, A (2002) *Does Education Matter? Myths about education and economic growth*. London: Taylor & Francis.

## *Further reading*

Casey, C (2012) *Economy, Work and Education. Critical Connections*. Abingdon: Routledge.

Lauder, H et al. (2012) *Educating for the Knowledge Economy? Critical Perspectives*. Abingdon: Routledge.

Tomlinson, S (2005) *Education in a Post Welfare Society*. Maidenhead: Open University Press.

Tomlinson, S (2013) *Ignorant Yobs? Low attainers in a global knowledge economy*. Abingdon: Routledge.

Wolf, A (2002) *Does Education Matter? Myths about education and economic growth*. London: Taylor & Francis.

# Chapter 13

## Gender and education

### Alice Pettigrew

## Introduction

Reading through the newspaper headlines which regularly accompany the annual publication of English secondary school exam results, you would be forgiven for thinking that a never-ending battle of the sexes characterises our classrooms: 'The boys are left standing'; 'Boys fighting back'; 'Girls trouncing their male classmates', reported the *Daily Mail* newspaper, for example, during the summers of 2002, 2009 and 2012 respectively. Here girls and boys are presented as pitted against each other, as though one group's academic success depends upon the other's decline. Perhaps not everyone would agree with the battlefield comparison. However, headlines such as these – and the newspaper stories that accompany them – draw on and feed into widely shared assumptions that there are inevitable differences between males and females and the effectiveness of various teaching styles, classroom resources or forms of assessment critically depend upon whether a student is a girl or a boy.

In this chapter, we shall investigate these assumptions and some of the deeply held thinking that underpins them. The chapter argues that 'gender' is a socially constructed category and therefore always open to competing interpretation and possible change. We will consider that what it means to be a man or woman, girl or boy, has varied throughout history and by socio-cultural context and will look at the roles that formal systems of education can play in reinforcing – or challenging – established gender norms. We shall return to explore recent trends in girls' and boys' end of year examination performance and interrogate some of the explanations regularly offered for these. Finally, we will reconsider the common forms of binary – or either/or – thinking that continue to inform much contemporary discussion of gender within education and explore potential alternatives to these.

## 'Gender' and 'sex': socio-cultural or biological distinctions?

When trying to investigate and account for differences in girls' and boys' – or men's and women's – experiences, many commentators begin by separating the concepts of 'sex' and 'gender'. Most commonly, 'sex' is used as a biological classification distinguishing 'males' from 'females' on the basis of the absence or presence of ova or testes, or the XY and XX chromosome. Today there are in fact an estimated 100,000 individuals in the UK who would be more accurately described as 'intersex', having both male and female physiology and so, even at the level of biology, the either/or distinction is not always entirely accurate or clear. 'Gender' on the other hand, commonly refers to social and cultural expectations typically associated with those biological distinctions. While this division of sex from gender can be very useful analytically, it is important to note that *often biological and social influences are very tangled* (Gove and Watt, 2004, p.44) and the total separation of biology from culture is not always possible – or entirely helpful – to sustain.

Throughout this chapter, we will primarily refer to *gendered* identities and *gender* relations and prioritise socio-cultural analysis over arguments made on the basis of biology. Some physical characteristics distinguishing male and female bodies might appear entirely clear-cut and uncontroversial: it is true, for example, that the average male is likely to be taller and heavier than the average female. Others, however, such as variation in hormone levels or brain structure (as discussed further in the Research Box below) are notoriously difficult to measure accurately or conclusively interpret (Fausto-Sterling, 2000). Even among less contentious physical characteristics that do appear to bear a clear male/female correlation, there is commonly considerable variation *within* each group: *all* men or boys are by no means taller or heavier than *all* women or girls. There are therefore strong grounds to question the extent to which biological sex is ever a particularly instructive basis on which to predict an individual's potential aptitude or capability.

## Research box

### all in the mind? Neuroscience or neurosexism?

Since the European Enlightenment, various scientific disciplines have been drawn on to advance the arguments that: 1) there are inherent differences in male and female temperaments and capabilities; and 2) there is a biological – and thus unalterable – basis to these. During the nineteenth century, physiology and medicine were used to argue that women were biologically designed to stay at home and raise children. Some commentators expressed serious concern that encouraging females out of their natural, domestic, environment and into schools or universities could seriously damage their health risking future fertility and a woman's ability to breastfeed (Paechter, 1998).

In the early twenty-first century, the mantle of such biological essentialism appears to have been taken over by interpretations and claims made on the basis of neuroscience, the study of the human brain. Bestselling popular science titles such as *Why Mars and Venus Collide* (Gray, 2008), *The Essential Difference: Men, Women and the Extreme Male Brain* (Baron Cohen, 2003) and *Why Men Don't Listen and Women Can't Read Maps* (Pease and Pease, 2001) promulgate the argument that scientific understanding now 'proves' there are fundamental differences in the ways that males and females think and behave. *The female brain is predominantly hard-wired for empathy,* while *the male brain is predominantly hard-wired for understanding and building systems* the Cambridge psychologist Simon Baron Cohen informs his readers (2003, p.1) before suggesting that those with the 'male brain' make the best scientists, engineers and lawyers, while those with a 'female brain' are better suited to the caring professions such as nursing, primary teaching or counselling (ibid, p.185). Exactly these sorts of argument have also made their way into educational discourse and debate. The specialist educational consultant Geoff Hannan, for example – regularly cited in the British media as an 'expert', or 'guru' in the field of improving boys' school achievement – advises teachers that boys' and girls' mental competencies develop along different pathways and they therefore require different learning styles and modes of communication in classrooms in order to succeed (Raphael Reed, 1999).

However, much of the 'evidence' which these arguments are built upon has recently been very thoroughly critiqued (Fine, 2010; Jordan-Young, 2010; Eliot, 2009). The weight of existing scientific inquiry and interpretation does in fact support *some* of the observations that Baron Cohen, Hannan and others make. For example, there *are* sex differences in the relative size of individual brain structures, likely to be caused by male and female foetuses' exposure to different levels of testosterone while still in the womb. This scientific discovery might well prove to be profoundly significant and could have important implications for medicine and other related fields. However, using neuroscience to argue that there is a biological, 'hardwired' explanation for the disproportionately low numbers of women with successful careers in high level science, for example – as was controversially claimed by a former president of Harvard University – is deeply problematic. As a number of neuroscientists would themselves be at pains to point out, no single study has yet been able to demonstrate convincingly a clear and unequivocal causal relationship between brain structure and behaviour, that is, that difference in brain structure *causes* difference in behaviour over and above multiple alternative potential socio-cultural influences or constraints (Eliot, 2009). On the contrary, just as many scientists argue that causality could as easily work in the opposite direction, social and cultural influences could themselves potentially impact hormone levels and ultimately lead to changes in the function and structure of the brain (Fine, 2010).

If biological arguments tend to present differences between the sexes as impossible fundamentally to alter, contributions from the fields of sociology, philosophy and feminist psychology focus instead on attempting to explain how and why such notions of difference have been socially constructed. They therefore open up the possibility of potential transformation and change. In fact, it is one of the central tenets of gender theory that differences between males and females have been purposefully, misleadingly, presented as 'natural' in order to make people accept them as inevitable, even if they sometimes recognise and resent the restrictive limitations that gendered expectations are likely to place upon their lives (Bem, 1993).

It was, therefore, politically very powerful when the feminist theorists of the 1970s and 80s began to draw on anthropological evidence to illustrate that, far from being 'biologically determined' or essential, what it means to 'act like a man' or 'behave like a woman' can vary considerably in different socio-cultural contexts. In Ann Oakley's seminal 1972 text, *Sex, Gender and Society,* for example, she argued that gender roles and relations varied to such a great extent across the globe that they could not possibly be considered 'natural' or 'inevitable'.

Nor do our understandings of characteristic behaviour for men or women remain constant over time. Consider some of the transformations in the roles typically performed by women and girls within British society over the last 150 years. At the beginning of the twentieth century, respectable 'femininity' was considered incompatible with paid employment, at least among the upper and middle classes. Only 15 per cent of all married women worked outside of the home. By 2008, that figure had risen to nearly 75 per cent and even within just the last 30 years, everyday attitudes to women's employment have significantly changed. Statistics collected and analysed by the British Social Attitudes (BSA) programme and European Social Survey (ESS) indicate clearly that *the traditionalist view of men as 'breadwinners' and women as 'homemakers' has declined* (Park et al., 2012, p.110): in 1989, 32 per cent of men asked within the BSA survey agreed with the statement, 'a man's job is to earn money; a woman's job is to look after the home and family'. By 2002, only 20 per cent agreed (Crompton, 2006, p.43). Responding to a slightly different question within the European Social Survey in 2004, only 16 per cent of men in paid work believed that men have more right to a job than women and by 2010, this had fallen further still to only 10 per cent (Park et al., ibid).

Using examples such as these, gender theorists have argued powerfully that 'typical' masculinity and femininity are conceptions that society itself constructs: they are built upon learned actions and behaviours which, on closer inspection, often support and reflect particular political or economic interests or needs. They are therefore neither inevitable nor innate. However, to argue that gender roles are socially constructed rather than naturally occurring is not to deny their profound, continued importance in both men and women's lives. Gender, like all social identities, describes a relationship between an individual and wider society: it refers both to how an individual sees themselves – and chooses to present that self to the world – and to how their choices and actions are received. On this basis, gender theorists have also argued that our shared ideas about gender perform a strong regulatory function: there are very clear, often unspoken but quickly internalised, rule-like expectations regarding how males and females should and should not behave.

---

*Pause for thought* | subverting gendered norms?

In December 2012, a picture was posted on the Facebook website, reportedly showing a five-year-old American boy in his parents' car on the way to his first day of school. The photograph and connected post became the subject of much heated discussion and debate because the boy in question was wearing a pair of 'girly' pink shoes. Some commentators suggested that the boy's parents were irresponsible in allowing him to do so, arguing that whatever the family themselves might believe about individual freedom of expression or the need to challenge gender stereotypes, their young son would predictably become an obvious target for ridicule and bullying as soon as he arrived at school. Based on your own experience, what do you think the likely consequence of a boy wearing 'girls'' shoes to school would be? Why? Do you agree that the boy's parents were irresponsible? What if their son had wanted to wear a dress? Do you think the age of the boy is important? What do you think the response from the school should be?

---

# Gender theory and potential for change

Three further related insights from gender theory are significant to highlight as each may further aid our analysis of male and female school experience and educational outcome: gender as binary, gender as hierarchy and gender as an enduring system of inequality.

In most Western societies, gender is commonly conceived of on a binary basis: 'masculinity' and 'femininity' are not just considered to be different but are presented as though antithetical or mutually exclusive. They are defined in opposition to each other: behaving 'like a boy' means, necessarily, not behaving 'like a girl'. Reality of course is far more complicated than such either/or categorisations allow. The inadequacy of such either/or thinking is perhaps most clearly exemplified by the increasing number of individuals who identify themselves as 'transgendered' rather than exclusively male *or* female. Most individuals combine a variety of supposedly 'masculine' and 'feminine' characteristics or traits but binary thinking tries to hide and deny this sort of complexity. It exaggerates difference and creates distance in place of recognising variation *within* groups or emphasising common ground. When girls and boys are directed to choose between two, colour-coded, sections of a clothes shop, for example, pointed towards 'boys' interest' or 'girls' interest' toys and bookshelves or routinely told to form a separate girls' line and boys' line before coming back into a classroom after playing outside, the message they are receiving is that there is an inevitable and omnipresent significance to a binary gender divide.

Dominant forms of gendered thinking are also hierarchical. Throughout history 'masculinity' and 'femininity' have been differentially valued with 'masculine' attributes and male experience typically awarded greater priority. Psychologist Sandra Lipsitz Bem (1993) argues that this has led to a prevailing 'androcentrism' or male-centredness in how we commonly experience and interpret our social worlds: even if many people now reject or challenge the crude notion that males are inherently superior to females, male experience is still commonly assumed to be the default position, as though gender neutral. 'Feminine' behaviours or female experiences are encountered as a deviation from the norm. Thus male perspectives, male characters and male voices continue to dominate most recent film releases, television programmes and works of literature, including those aimed at children and used in schools (see, for example, the Geena Davis Institute of Gender and Media's analysis of gender representation in recent family films).

The feminist theorists of the late twentieth century drew attention to the social construction of gender primarily in order to highlight and challenge what they saw as the endemic patriarchy of Western societies, that is, the systematic oppression and disadvantaging of women by men. While many would argue that full equality for girls and women remains elusive, today gender theory is increasingly deployed to show how the processes of binary thinking, differential valuing and the presentation of gendered difference as natural, inevitable and unalterable combine to produce restrictive limitations on *both male and female* lives (see Frosh et al., 2003 and Foster et al., 2001 below).

## Reproducing or challenging gendered inequality? The role of education

As will have been made evident in earlier chapters and elsewhere in your studies, formal systems of education have a critically important – albeit complex and potentially contradictory – relationship with wider society. It is largely through schools, colleges and universities that individuals are equipped with the skills, formal qualifications and/or personal confidence required for different occupations and their associated social, political and economic roles. Schools are also considered to be a pivotal site for socialisation: as the French sociologist Emile Durkheim most famously elaborated, it is through formal education that children begin to internalise the shared beliefs, expectations and values required to confidently function with others outside of their immediate family home (Durkheim, 1956). In both respects, the implications for the maintenance of gender norms and production of gendered inequality are clear: the over-representation of men or women in certain sectors of the workforce, for example, is at least in part a consequence of schools differentially equipping students on the basis of their gender, either in terms of formal qualifications or internalised expectations of what males or females are able to do and be.

For these reasons, feminist movements throughout history have identified classrooms and college campuses as crucially important territory. Mary Wollstonecraft's 1792 *A Vindication on the Rights of Women* was in large part a treatise for girls' equal access to formal education, while contemporary web-based activist organisations increasingly focus on consciousness raising in schools (see, for example, UK Feminista's recent 'Generation F' campaign).

## gender, education and international development

One of most powerful contemporary indicators of the economic, political and social significance placed upon gender equity in education is global activism for girls' equal access to schooling: consider, for example, the recent Nobel Peace Prize nomination given to Pakistani schoolgirl and equal education activist Malala Yousafzai. She came to international attention when she was shot and critically injured by Taliban gunmen while insisting on her right to attend school. She has since set up a foundation to support girls' education and empowerment worldwide.

Powerful organisations such as the World Bank and United Nations as well as charities such as Oxfam, Plan International and Action Aid have in recent decades devoted considerable attention and resources towards addressing this issue and girls' education has been prioritised by the international community as of critical importance in order to meet the United Nation's 2015 Millennium Development Goals (UNGEI, 2012). Economists and development practitioners argue that schooling for girls not only increases individuals' life chances and opportunities but also acts as a motor for national economic development and social progress. Widely cited benefits include: increased family income; improved health and nutrition of children; reduced fertility rates; reduced maternal and infant mortality; reduced rates of infection of HIV/AIDS and increased protection of women and girls from exploitation and abuse.

In many respects, progress in this area has been very encouraging. Thirty years ago, only 38 per cent of all children in primary schools in low-income countries were female but by 2005, the gender gap had narrowed to 48 per cent female, 52 per cent male (OECD/ UNESCO cited in Dolan, 2011). However, there is still considerable room for improvement as average figures mask wide variation in national contexts. Statistics reported by UNESCO in 2007 suggest that for every 100 boys out of education in India, there were 426 girls. In Iraq the comparative figure was 316 and in Yemen 270 (Dolan, ibid.). Girls are also more likely than boys to leave – or be removed from – school after primary level (UNESCO, 2012).

A recent research report by Plan International highlighted a variety of complex, cultural, political and economic factors that continue to act as significant barriers to girls' education in some of the world's poorest countries. These include: early and forced marriage; teenage pregnancy; prohibitive costs of uniforms, books and examination fees; girls' disproportionate burden of domestic labour; and the fear – and in too many cases reality – of violence and abuse that girls might experience while at school (Plan International, 2012).

# Addressing gender issues in UK education during the late twentieth century

Where social conservatives, or 'traditionalists', see the role of school as ensuring continuity with the past and maintaining the status quo, the British feminist movement of 1960s, 70s and 80s saw education as a critically important arena within which they could begin to effect significant change. Although, by the 1950s, girls throughout the country were officially entitled to primary and secondary education on the same basis as boys, in practice for much of the late twentieth century, schools tended to provide male and female students with a gender-differentiated curriculum. As early research by writers such as Sue Sharpe, Judith Whyte and

Rosemary Deem exposed, school curricula and teaching materials overwhelmingly served to reproduce very narrow and restrictive notions of femininity. Girls were commonly encouraged to see themselves in terms of limited domestic, secretarial or service sector roles and steered away from high-status subjects such as science or maths (Sharpe, 1976; Whyte et al., 1985). As well as critiquing gender stereotyping within the formal curriculum, researchers such as Dale Spender (1982) and Michelle Stanworth (1987) analysed typical classroom interactions between students and teachers to show how expectations of male power and superiority – in contrast to female submission and subservience – were regularly reinforced. One clear example was the consistently greater attention paid by teachers – and accepted by students – to assertive and demanding boys.

As a consequence, the first sustained gender interventions in education were primarily intended to improve the opportunities and attainment of girls. They aimed to do so by raising awareness of crude stereotyping, directly confronting student and teacher attitudes and challenging gendered expectations of aptitude and potential ability. Significant examples include the *Girls Into Science and Technology* (GIST), *Women Into Science and Engineering* (WISE), and *Girls Into Mathematics* (GAMMA) projects as well as cross-curricular initiatives such as *Genderwatch* (Myers, 1987).

The 1988 Education Reform Act (ERA) and introduction of a compulsory National Curriculum also had a significant impact upon the salience of gender in schools. It meant that all students now had to study the same core subjects. Girls were no longer able to opt-out of, or be discouraged from pursuing, those areas traditionally considered 'masculine' such as science or maths (Francis, 2000). The ERA also introduced standardised testing of English, maths and science for all students at each compulsory Key Stage, and in 1992, the creation of comparative league tables for GCSE and A level examinations brought the potential issue of girls' and boys' differential academic achievement into starker relief than had been possible before.

# The feminisation of education?

It was within this context that the sort of newspaper headlines that opened this chapter first began to appear. Throughout the 1990s, year on year examination data appeared to document that girls were outperforming boys in most curriculum areas and by the mid-1990s they had even caught up with and eventually overtaken boys in traditionally male-dominated science and maths (Francis, ibid.). This was quickly interpreted by the national media, politicians and many educational commentators as a very serious and problematic reversal of fortunes leading Her Majesty's Chief Inspector of Schools, Chris Woodhead, to suggest in 1996 that, *the failure of boys* was *one of the most disturbing problems* faced by the education system as a whole (cited in Foster et al., 2001, p.2).

In essence, Woodhead and others argued that boys were losing out in what they saw as an increasingly 'feminised' educational environment. To illustrate such 'feminisation', critics cited a number of factors including: policy shifts which placed greater emphasis on the completion of coursework (considered 'girl friendly' because it rewards the 'feminine' attributes which lead to conscientious hard work and diligence) over all-or-nothing end of year examinations (considered 'boy friendly' because they reward 'masculine' confidence, and innate ability); the under-representation of men among primary and secondary teaching staff (and thus the absence of suitable role models able to promote or appropriately respond to typical 'male values' such as risk-taking, competitiveness or boisterousness); and a curriculum which no longer adequately engaged 'boys' interests' or preferred learning styles.

Such arguments within the context of education reflected and related to wider concerns across society as a whole, that the feminist movement's successful campaign for improved equal opportunities provision had begun to turn the tide towards women's empowerment too far. The dramatic economic and industrial restructuring of the late twentieth century and the decimation of traditionally male manufacturing roles has exacerbated the sense that now is a particularly difficult and uncertain time to negotiate competing expectations of what it means to be a man (McDowell, 2003). Thus the notion of a 'crisis' in and of masculinity has been a regularly recurring feature of popular and political discussion across the United Kingdom for much of the last 20 years. Statistical evidence which alerts us to facts such as the much higher incidence of suicide, criminality, substance abuse and homelessness among men compared to women, for example, or the much higher rates of women than men who currently apply for and are accepted on university level courses certainly do suggest that there are significant socio-cultural issues worthy of further exploration here. However, crude arguments that girls are doing better *at the expense of boys* in education, as commonly played out in popular discourse and some academic discussion, require much closer critical scrutiny.

# Dismantling the 'problem' of boys' underachievement

As Gorard and Smith (2004) and Skelton (2001) urge us to consider, caution is required in terms of how we interpret any apparent statistical trend. Skelton has gone as far as to argue that our current concerns over boys' educational underachievement are *largely due to a superficial reading of the statistics* (2001, p.2). For a start, and as Skelton documents, girls doing better in school than boys is far from a recent phenomenon. Girls were in fact found to perform slightly better than male classmates at the 11 plus examination from as early as the 1940s and 50s. Thus a front-page story from a 1954 edition of *The Hunts Post* local newspaper ran under the headline, 'Girls Brainier than Boys'. The accompanying article explained that too many girls had been passing the examination and without the introduction of a quota system, girls would be over-represented in grammar schools. It is now estimated that had such quotas not been enacted, two-thirds of most mixed grammar school places would have been taken by girls (Chitty, 2001, pp.133–4). As has already been highlighted, what brought 'the gender gap' in educational achievement to widespread public attention was the introduction of nationally published league tables at a time when there were already mounting concerns within certain sectors of wider society that the established order of relations between men and women was increasingly under threat. One possible interpretation of the resulting outcry and political response is that they reflect a resilient androcentrism concerned to re-establish the rightful central position of boys and men through returning them as the focus of new interventionist measures in education policy (Younger and Warrington, 2007; Foster et al., 2001).

It is perhaps for this reason that concern over the gender gap in results between male and female pupils has become the focus of our newspaper stories and policy interventions rather than celebration at the parallel trend in improved performance for both girls and boys as indicated in Figure 13.1.

Why is the difference between male and female students a more interesting or important phenomena than the increased performance of both groups? Without recognition of this overall improvement, our analysis of 'the problem' is likely to be skewed. For all those factors in recent classroom and curricular policy and practice that are blamed for being too 'girl friendly' would also appear to be having a positive effect upon the exam achievement of many boys. Perhaps most importantly, the disproportionate focus on 'boys' underachievement' also obscures attention from statistically more significant barriers to equality in education such as ethnicity and social class (DCSF, 2009).

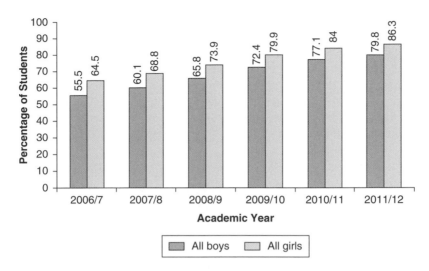

**Figure 13.1**   Graph showing comparison of achievement for boys and girls

All figures have been taken from the Department for Education website, **www.gov.uk/government/publications/ gcse-and-equivalent-attainment-by-pupil-characteristics-in-england**

The salient point to emphasise here is that the 'problem' of boys' educational underachievement is, in many respects, itself a social construction. This argument is made very clearly in a recent article by Moreau (2011) who uses data from France and England to demonstrate that both countries share very similar patterns of gendered attainment. However, it is only in England that male underachievement has become a high profile policy issue. In France, comparable debate and discussion simply does not exist. Moreau suggests that, rather than reflecting a grounded reality, discourses about boys' underachievement in schooling are largely created as a consequence of existing socio-cultural expectations and concerns.

# Revisiting gender theory: challenging the notions of 'girl friendly' or 'boy friendly' schools

If we return to the perspectives from gender theory which began this chapter, we discover that many of the explanations and 'solutions' offered to account for or address boys' underachievement can begin to sound rather problematic. For the notions of 'boy friendly' classrooms, teachers or learning styles all depend upon an essential concept of 'boy-ness' which, once again, is defined here in opposition to being, behaving, and *learning* 'like a girl'. In 2009, the then Department for Children, Schools and Families worked with respected educational researchers Gemma Moss, Becky Francis and Christine Skelton to confront and debunk some of the most commonly circulating gender and education myths. As their resulting publication instructively summarises, many of the most popular explanations and accompanying remedies for boys' underachievement are simply not supported by available research evidence. Arguably, many could in fact be seen to exacerbate existing problems by insisting upon a rather crude gender divide.

For example, it has regularly been argued that boys would benefit if there were more male teachers in both primary and secondary classrooms (as reported in Carrington and Skelton, 2003 and reflected in the 2005 policy position of the Teacher Development Agency (TDA)).

However, the weight of available research evidence indicates that matching the gender of students and teachers has no significant influence on either achievement or attitude towards school. On the contrary, numerous studies report that the majority of students prioritise a teacher's individual ability and the level of care they provide over whether or not they are a woman or man (DCSF, 2009). Perhaps just as importantly, the argument for gender matching depends upon and serves to reinforce clear binary thinking – that there is something essential and educationally important in 'maleness' that only men and boys can access and that makes them fundamentally and unalterably different to women and girls.

Likewise, the suggestion that schools need to reintroduce a more 'boy-friendly' curriculum to increase boys' motivation has proven similarly flawed. Again, the DCSF reports that *there is no evidence to show that where schools have designed or changed parts of their curriculum to be more appealing to boys that it improves boys' achievement* (2009, p.6). Moreover, and as the DCSF continues, *such changes may involve gender stereotyping which can lead teachers to ignore pupils' actual preferences and limit the choices that either boys or girls can make* (ibid.). Which boys are being appealed to within the notion of boys' interests and which boys excluded? Are an individual's interests really likely to be so predictably and conclusively deter-mined on the basis of whether that individual is a girl or a boy?

Nor does the argument that girls and boys have distinct preferred learning styles fare much better. The DCSF report describes the whole concept of 'learning styles' as highly contested with little evidence to support the argument that gender significantly determines the manner in which an individual is best able to learn. The authors conclude that even ostensibly gendered preferences, such as girls' apparent enthusiasm for group work, may in fact be largely due to established social norms. This would suggest there is a role to be played by schools in broadening rather than narrowing their repertoire of teaching and learning styles (2009, p.4).

In a recent interview for an online educational magazine, Christine Skelton concluded that, *the only convincing explanation for boys' underperformance in comparison to girls is to do with self-image.*

*Basically, boys are more concerned about measuring up as a 'proper boy' among their mates than getting good results. Showing you are a 'proper boy' means doing the opposite of everything female. If girls are valued for being conscientious, industrious and motivated at school, then boys are not going to demonstrate these characteristics.*

(Oates and Skelton, 2013)

But, as empirical research with young people can powerfully illustrate, there is nothing inevi-table about any of this. In their study of male students at secondary schools across London, Frosh et al. (2002) discovered that most boys did indeed recognise and respond to powerful peer group expectations of masculinity which were antithetical to doing well at school. However, during individual interview, many confessed to admiration of the conscientiousness and commitment to work that their female classmates displayed and expressed criticism of typically 'boyish' behaviours. As the researchers themselves conclude:

*All of this suggests that, given the right circumstances, boys can be very thoughtful about themselves and their predicament. Even at age 11, they are often capable of reflecting in a complex way on how their actual lives are at odds with what they would wish them to be, and even about how constraining certain aspects of masculine identity might be for them.*

(Frosh et al., 2002, p.256)

From this perspective, educational interventions – to help both male and female students – should focus on broadening rather than limiting expectations and understandings of both masculinity and femininity, resisting rather than reinforcing absolute and clear-cut binary gender divides. As the American neuroscientist Lise Eliot has similarly argued:

*Kids rise and fall according to what we believe about them, and the more we dwell on the differences between boys and girls, the likelier such stereotypes are to crystallize into children's self-perceptions and self-fulfilling prophecies.*

(Eliot, 2009, p.15)

Again, none of this is to deny the fact that there *are* significant differences in how girls and boys currently experience and perform in schools. To act as though gender never matters – in the classroom, or in wider society – would be to ignore the fact that gender has been *made to matter* in multiple ways and for several centuries. However, recognising difference is not the same as pre-empting or insisting upon the inevitability of such difference and it is critically important to remember that gender is only one dimension of our individual identities. Rather than unreflexively resorting to 'boy friendly' or 'girl friendly' strategies as an appropriate response to deal with male or female students, schools could become places in which both teachers and students are supported to openly explore the multiple possibilities of their own identities and critically consider exactly what the concepts of 'boy friendly' or 'girl friendly' have been made to mean.

> ### Pause for thought | sex, gender and relationship education in schools?
>
> As has been reflected throughout this chapter, to date, most of the attention paid to gender issues within education studies concerns the role of schools in reproducing dominant gendered expectations for behaviour and various forms of gendered educational inequality. Arguably, there is also an important role for schools to play in directly engaging students in critical reflection on the construction of their own gender identities and related societal and interpersonal relationships between women and men.
>
> In early 2013, the British government's Department for Education came under sustained criticism for its apparent reluctance to address a number of reported inadequacies in English schools' provision for sex and relationship education, most commonly addressed through the non-statutory subject Personal, Social and Health Education (PSHE). At present, schools are only required to teach young people the biological basics of reproduction, which can be delivered within the science curriculum. There is no duty placed upon schools to educate young people in such a manner as to promote the formation of healthy and mutually respectful interpersonal relationships, nor to confront issues of gender-based violence or domestic abuse. As a consequence, the authors of a severely critical report by the campaigning group *End Violence Against Women* argue that currently English schools can in fact serve to reproduce rather than challenge aggressive forms of masculinity and condone rather than condemn a culture of violence towards women and girls. They cite a recent YouGov poll which suggests that 71 per cent of 16–18 year olds report that they hear school-based sexual name-calling towards girls (such as 'slut' or 'slag') on a weekly if not daily basis while almost a third of girls within the same age group say they have experienced
>
> *(Continued)*

*(Continued)*

unwanted sexual touching while at school (EVAW, 2013, p.9). Meanwhile, research conducted with Scottish teenagers in 2005 found that *some young men and young women think that it is acceptable to be violent towards a woman under certain circumstances, or force her to have sex* (Burman and Cartmel, 2005, p.44, emphasis added) and within wider British society, 36 per cent of people asked within a 2009 Home Office Survey believed a woman should be held wholly or partially responsible for being raped or sexually assaulted if she was drunk at the time of the attack, and 26 per cent if she was in public wearing sexy or revealing clothes.

To what extent do you think that compulsory sex and relationship or gender education could be effective in addressing any of these issues or attitudes? Do you consider this an appropriate educational intervention? Why do you think the current government has rejected such a move in spite of widespread support from teaching unions and advocacy groups?

## Summary and conclusions

Throughout this chapter, we have adopted a perspective which understands gender to be a social construction rather than something which is fixed and firm in content, inevitable or innate. We have, however, also examined the historical argument that there are inherent biological differences between males and females which determine their aptitudes and behaviours and critically considered the most recent rearticulation of this position which draws upon neuroscientific research.

We then traced the changing focus of interest in issues of gender within education throughout the twentieth century, from equal opportunities interventions primarily targeted at girls, to a perceived crisis in male underachievement which continues to attract considerable media and policy-based attention in the present day. While recognising that gender can have very profound significance in educational spaces – as in all wider social contexts – the chapter highlighted the problems and limitations, for both male and female students, of thinking in reductionist and oppositional gender binary terms. Instead, we emphasised the importance of empirical research and educational perspectives which expand and complicate multiple rather than singular notions of masculinity and femininity.

## References

Baron Cohen, S (2003) *The Essential Difference: Men, women and the extreme male brain.* London: Allen Lane.
Bem, SL (1993) *The Lenses of Gender: Transforming the debate of sexual inequality.* London: Yale University Press.
Burman, M and Cartmel, F (2005) *Young People's Attitudes Towards Gendered Violence.* Edinburgh: NHS Scotland.
Carrington, B and Skelton, C (2003) Re-thinking 'role models': equal opportunities in teacher recruitment in England and Wales. *Journal of Education Policy*, 18(3): 1–13.
Chitty, C (2001) *Understanding Schools and Schooling.* London: RoutledgeFalmer.
Crompton, R (2006) *Employment and the Family: The reconfiguration of work and family life in contemporary societies.* Cambridge: Cambridge University Press.

DCSF (2009) *Gender and Education: Mythbusters*. Nottingham: Department for Children, Schools and Families Publications.

Dolan, J (2011) International education, in Walkup, V (ed) *Exploring Education Studies*. Harlow: Pearson Education Limited.

Durkheim, E (1956) *Education and Sociology*. New York: Free Press.

Eliot, L (2009) *Pink Brain, Blue Brain: How small differences grow into troublesome gaps and what we can do about It*. New York: Mariner Books.

End Violence Against Women Coalition (EVAW) (2013) *Deeds or Words? Analysis of Westminster Government action to prevent violence against women and girls*. London: End Violence Against Women.

Fausto-Sterling, A (2000) *Sexing the body: Gender politics and the construction of sexuality*. New York: Basic Books.

Fine, C (2010) *Delusions of Gender: The real science behind sex differences*. London: Icon Books.

Foster, V, Kimmer, M and Skelton, C (2001) 'What about the boys?' An overview of the debates, in Martino, W and Meyenn, B (eds) *What About the Boys? Issues of masculinity in schools*. Buckingham: Open University Press.

Francis, B (2000) *Boys, Girls and Achievement: Addressing the classroom issues*. London: Routledge.

Frosh, S, Phoenix, A and Pattman, R (2002) *Young Masculinities: Understanding boys in contemporary society*. Basingstoke: Palgrave.

Gorard, S and Smith, E (2004) What is 'underachievement' at school? *School Leadership and Management,* 24(2): 205–25.

Gove, J and Watt, S (2004) Identity and gender, in Woodward, K (ed) *Questioning Identity: Gender, class, ethnicity*. London: Routledge.

Gray, J (2008) *Why Mars and Venus Collide*. London: HarperElement.

Jordan-Young, R (2010) *Brainstorm: The flaws in the science of sex differences*. Harvard: Harvard University Press.

McDowell, L (2003) *Redundant Masculinities? Employment change and white working class youth*. Oxford: Blackwell Publishing Ltd.

Moreau, M-P (2011) The societal construction of 'boys' underachievement' in educational policies: a cross-national comparison. *Journal of Education Policy*, 26(2): 161–80.

Myers, K (1987) *Genderwatch: Self-assessment schedules for use in schools*. London: Schools Curriculum Development Council.

Oakley, A (1972) *Sex, Gender and Society*. London: Temple Smith.

Oates, T and Skelton, C (2013) The gender debate. *Independent School Parent*. [Online] 26 February. Available at: **www.independentschoolparent.com/education-news/the-gender-debate** (accessed 1 April 2013).

Paechter, C (1998) *Educating the Other: Gender, power and schooling*. Abingdon: RoutledgeFalmer.

Park, A, Clery, E, Curtice, J, Phillips, M and Utting, D (eds) (2012) *British Social Attitudes: the 29th Report*. London: NatCen Social Research.

Pease, A and Pease, B (2001) *Why Men Don't Listen and Women Can't Read Maps*. London: Orion.

Plan International (2012) *Because I am a Girl. The State of the World's Girls 2012: Learning for Life*. Oxford: New Internationalist Publications.

Raphael Reed, L (1999) Troubling boys and disturbing discourses on masculinity and schooling: A feminist exploration of current debates and interventions concerning boys in school. *Gender and Education,* 11(1): 93–110.

Sharpe, S (1976) *Just Like a Girl: How girls learn to be women*. Harmondsworth: Penguin.

Skelton, C (2001) *Schooling the Boys: Masculinities and primary education*. Buckingham: Open University Press.

Spender, D (1982) *Invisible Women: The schooling scandal*. London: Writers and Readers.

Stanworth, M (1987) Girls on the margins: A study of gender divisions in the classroom, in Weiner, G and Arnot, M (eds) *Gender Under Scrutiny*. London: Hutchinson.

UNESCO (2012) *World Atlas of Gender Equality in Education*. Paris: United Nations Educational, Scientific and Cultural Organisation.

UNGEI (2012) *Engendering Empowerment: Education and equality*. New York: United Nations Girls' Education Initiative.

Whyte, J, Deem, R, Kant, L and Cruickshank, M (eds) (1985) *Girl Friendly Schooling*. London: Methuen and Co. Ltd.

Younger, M and Warrington, M (2007) Closing the gender gap? Issues of gender equity in English secondary schools. *Discourse: Studies in the Cultural Politics of Education*, 28(22): 19–242.

## Further reading

The Gender and Education Association website **www.genderandeducation.com** is a very useful starting point for general information as is their international peer-reviewed journal, *Gender and Education.*

On young masculinities, femininities and gender's intersection with sexuality, ethnicity and social class: Nayak, A and Kehily, M (2013) *Gender, Youth and Culture: Young masculinities and femininities*. Basingstoke: Palgrave Macmillan.

For female education as an international issue, Plan International's *Because I am a Girl* campaign website houses several useful resources: **www.plan-international.org/girls/**

On education and gender-based violence: Womankind Worldwide (2010) *Freedom to Achieve. Preventing violence, promoting equality: A whole-school approach*. **www.womankind.org.uk/wpcontent/uploads/2011/02/WKREPORT_web-24-NOV-2010.pdf**

# Chapter 14

## Race and education

### Nasima Hassan

**Introduction**

This chapter addresses the issue of race in education through reference to historic and current research. It traces government initiatives from the 1960s to manage the post-war migration and the presence of black and minority (BME) pupils and to combat racism in schools. The political dimension to race in society and the current political response to migration from eastern Europe are considered. Wider issues associated with BME pupils in the classroom are reviewed through an exploration of race and identity. A discussion of race and achievement draws together conclusions as reflected in the experiences of black pupils in inner London schools, which are similar to other geographical locations in the UK.

## Educational initiatives to combat racism in education

Successive governments have proved unable to deliver a coherent philosophy and policy to combat racism in education and this has been at an undeniable cost to the nation, its education system and its fragile race relations. Critics argue that the very deracialisation of education policies has failed to address the growing cancer of low expectations of teachers, racist stereotyping and inadequate provisions for children learning English as a second language (Troyna and Williams, 1996). Indeed, the term 'learners of English as an *additional* language', for example, was not formally accepted in place of 'learners of English as a *second* language' by the Training and Development Agency for schools (TDA) until 2002. This can be taken to demonstrate the power of language to perpetuate low teacher expectations and implicitly devalue pupils' diverse skills. A series of reactive recommendations following several major high profile incidents might not have been necessary had diversity been embraced earlier (Macpherson, 1999; Cantle, 2001; Ousley, 2001).

This chapter addresses the issue of race in education through reference to historic and contemporary research and consequent initiatives. Some of the wider issues associated with black and minority ethnic pupils in the classroom are reviewed through an exploration of race and identity. Successive government initiatives to combat racism in schools in response to the socio-political conditions in Britain from the early 1960s onwards are considered. A discussion of the race and achievement nexus draws together conclusions as reflected in the experiences of black pupils in inner London schools, which might be considered representative of other geographical locations within the UK.

## Research box

### the roots of racism in the playground

The assumed innocence of children hinders informed debate about children's notion of 'race'. Many studies have identified awareness among even very young children of racial differences and therefore of different values placed upon different skin colour. In addition, the incidence of racial name-calling is an increasingly common feature of the primary school environment, more damaging perhaps than physical acts (Cohen, 1989; Wright, 1992). Swann (DES, 1985) has observed that racial abuse is referenced not only to the child but also by extension to their family and indeed more broadly to their ethnic community as a whole. Troyna and Hatcher (1992) have argued that children respond to specific situations more in anger at times than as 'racists'. Interestingly, their research along with that conducted by Gaine (1995) took place in predominantly white primary schools. The discussion therefore explores the socialisation processes on children in their understanding of 'race' and how this impacts on the friendships and relationships they form.

Historically, and in response to the need for successful integration of immigrant children, three policies that have received most criticism for their lack of thought and appropriateness include:

- assimilation;
- integration;
- cultural pluralism.

These policies were designed to make grassroots impact in textbooks and teaching strategies, as well as addressing the wider notions of race and equal opportunities characterised by legislation in their time. For example, the Race Relations Act 1976 has been heavily criticised for not going far enough to stamp out direct acts of racial discrimination in practice.

# Assimilation

To assimilate means to merge and become part of something. It is about the denial and rejection of individuality. The policy of assimilation, which lasted until the end of the 1960s, was more in reaction to a perceived problem rather than attempting to stabilise and strengthen race relations within the classroom environment. It was understood to calm the concerns of white parents alarmed at the presence of large numbers of immigrant children in their local schools, a state of affairs created by a system of dispersal designed to spread the problem of immigration throughout the country. The implementation of this dispersal policy required statistical data on immigrant pupils, such as their linguistic abilities and the socioeconomic status of their parents. This important information was used to secure access to additional funding via Section 11 of the Local Government Act 1966. Local education authorities (LEAs) could access this fund to aid their dispersal and assimilation work.

This assimilation phase existed against a background of the rise of the political far right and the growing strength of the National Front, now the British National Party (BNP). It proved a hopelessly problematic policy, however, almost impossible to implement, administer or measure in terms of success. It had been created on the very negative assumption that black pupils in the classroom were a problem to be dealt with through their inability to speak English.

Research has shown that bilingual and multilingual immigrant children in America, Canada and Britain opt for a 'silent period' when first exposed to a new language (Cummins, 2001). This silence can be understood in terms of response to a culture shock. However, in terms of language acquisition it marks a crucial listening period which varies in length, allowing children to learn at their own pace. Assimilation strategies actually pressurised immigrant children to learn English quickly in order to solve the problem of their very presence.

The view that immigrants are 'a problem' surfaced politically in Britain at the 2010 general election where the Labour Government was depicted as being too 'soft' on immigration, allowing in to Britain large numbers of people from new member states of the European Union (EU) in eastern Europe. While the UK economy was expanding during the early 2000s, the large numbers of Polish workers entering the country were swallowed up by the need for skilled labour. The banking crisis of 2008 brought about economic collapse and recession; unemployment rose, giving less need for migrant labour. Calls to limit immigration were strongly voiced by the Conservative members of the 2010 Coalition Government and in 2013 legislation was to be introduced that would bring *further reforms (to) Britain's immigration system …. (to) ensure that this country attracts people who will contribute and deters those who will not* (HMG, 2013). Anti-European and anti-immigration sentiments were reflected in the rise of the right-wing United Kingdom Independence Party (UKIP) during the 2013 local elections. UKIP campaigned for Britain's withdrawal from the EU, but it also attracted to it former members of the BNP whose policy is to campaign against *the immigration invasion of our country, the threat to our security posed by Islamism and the danger of the European Union to our sovereignty* (BNP, 2013). The three main political parties at the time were finding the need to respond to what seemed to be a dangerous phase of popular nationalism and xenophobia.

# Integration

The dawn of the 1970s, and of a new era of diversity, offered the policy of integration as a suitable replacement to assimilation. Quite simply, integration meant to become part of a bigger picture and to become fully absorbed into it (e.g. the American ideal of throwing everyone together in a melting pot to substitute a new identity of 'coffee coloured people' for the mishmash that had gone before). Integration introduced the first sighting of multiculturalism in education by way of an acknowledgement of cultural diversity (Parekh, 2000). Defining multiculturalism is no exact science. Literally, multiculturalism is about pluralism engaged in social theory. Alleyne (2002) concluded that multiculturalism celebrates difference as an end in itself. Powell and Schwartz (2003) opted for an unambiguous link to racism: *The notion of multicultural diversity entails exactly the same premise as racism – that one's ideas are determined by one's race and that a source of individual identity is [one's] ethnic heritage* (p.37). For some, there exists no incompatibility between multiculturalism and Britishness. For others, however, multiculturalism suggests 'separateness' and is often mistaken to mean that different cultural communities should live their own ways of life in a self-contained manner (Parekh, 2000).

The clear emphasis in developing integration policies was on absorption into the mainstream, while conceding that cultural differences could, when used selectively, be of interest to others. LEAs were expected to develop and implement multicultural strategies in schools to facilitate the process of integration. This was done through a 'bolt-on' approach, as something else to push some schools to implement. The anxiety felt by teachers forced into unfamiliar territory was in direct response to ill-considered multiculturalism, resulting in shallow, superficial and barely recognisable global education. This particular brand of multiculturalism had the aim of *institutional hybridity – a fusion of myriad cultures, Bhangra, Afro, Asian and South Indian with*

*Britishness … in order to ethnicise schools into integration* (Kundnani, 2001, p.14). In an attempt to redress the impact of racial stereotyping and growing prejudices based on ignorance, aspects of the immigrant life experience were to be shared.

These included food, music, costumes, rituals, faith practices, festivals and traditional ways of life. Critics summarised this approach as the '3 Ss' – saris, steel pans and samosas – as these were the least threatening elements of cultural diversity that might be shared. Exotica was the only way to go to integrate successfully, or so it seemed (Sarup, 1991). Swann (DES, 1985) was also openly and vehemently critical of integration and multiculturalism in this form. Although some initial barriers were overcome by this first phase of multiculturalism, the strategy was tokenistic and devalued the wealth of heritage that immigrants held so dear. Allowing British society to select elements of cultural diversity that they found particularly palatable, for example the curry, now as British as a bulldog or a pint of beer, could never facilitate social cohesion in the classroom or indeed anywhere.

# Cultural pluralism

The principle of cultural pluralism was introduced in the 1980s to find a resolution for the continuing dilemma of racism in education. Two ground-breaking government publications, *West Indian Children in Our Schools*, or the Rampton Report (DES, 1981), and *Education for All*, or the Swann Report (DES, 1985), left no doubt that the issues of underachievement as experienced by West Indian pupils in particular were now firmly included on the educational agenda. The Swann Report reflected a period of growing social unrest and signified a need to address deeply rooted ideologies of prejudice and discrimination, thus marking a transition. The title *Education for All* identified the intent to redress the balance, not only in education policy but in society as a whole. Swann was clear about how we had arrived at this important transition point:

*All in all, central government appears to have lacked a coherent strategy for fostering the development of multicultural education and thus to have been unable to play a leading role in coordinating or encouraging progress in this field. We regard both the assimilationist and integrationist educational responses to the needs of ethnic minority pupils as, in retrospect, misguided and ill founded.*

(1985, p.198)

Acknowledgement of recommendations made by Rampton and Swann was of foremost consideration, although traces of assimilation and integration still survived from the troubled 1960s and 1970s. The expectation that shared values and ideals should unite all citizens of the now multiracial, multiethnic Britain of the time was paramount. A sense of belonging was to be cultivated in the sharing of these values. Cultural pluralism rode on the wave of antiracism policies in all LEAs and schools. Funding from central government sought to employ bilingual support staff where possible. However, a controversial enforced ban on mother tongue in the classroom hindered linguistic progression. When coupled with advice to parents only to 'speak English with your children at home', this compounded the apparent value and status of mother tongues as worthless in the eyes of the education system. As with assimilation, all-white schools were not required to engage with such approaches and often remained oblivious to the need for them. This was no longer acceptable.

The Education Reform Act of 1988, which prepared the ground for the National Curriculum, promoted cultural pluralism through the buzzwords of 'choice and diversity', incorporating non-statutory guidance on multicultural education for all teachers. Despite the rhetoric of antiracism and equality of opportunity, strategies to combat racism in practice continued to prove inadequate. The foundations of successive policies were so deficient in structure and philosophy that they became a self-fulfilling prophecy by virtue of their inevitable failure.

Introduced in response to a perceived crisis in education – the presence of immigrant children in schools, the urban race riots in Liverpool and Birmingham, the underachievement of black boys as signalled by league tables – it is difficult to see how could they ever hope to impact positively. The National Curriculum, which made its first appearance in schools in 1989, provided direct strategic guidance to permeate all schools and provide *a broad and balanced curriculum ... an entitlement of all pupils* regardless of their catchments. In the spirit of shared values, the religious education syllabus was to dedicate 50 per cent study time to Christianity and 50 per cent to the main religions represented in Britain, namely Buddhism, Hinduism, Islam, Judaism and Sikhism. This measure was widely perceived as insufficiently progressive to offer a truly multicultural curriculum. The absence of black scientists, artists, poets and role models in general contributed to the mis-education of black pupils throughout the 1960s and 1970s, and it appeared that this institutional racism in education might continue. How could ideals such as the fostering of intelligence and mutual understanding take place within a blanketing white, western worldview? It became important to question the notion of tolerance, a word used happily in school mission statements the length and breadth of Britain. Tolerance means to put up with, perhaps reluctantly. It means to endure or permit grudgingly. It is not about acceptance, understanding and most significantly it is not about equality.

More recent government policy in the 1990s led to various initiatives championing equality of opportunity and high standards for all through parental choice, standards and diversity, bringing cultural pluralism into the political mainstream. Macpherson (1999) recommended Ethnic Minority Achievement Grants (EMAG) to replace Section 11 funding of the Local Government Act of the 1960s and all LEAs were directed to appoint EMAG co-ordinators and teams to make grassroots impact. These teams would be subject to the same accountability through inspection criteria as other sections of education. Macpherson emphasised the continued destructive impact of racism (endemic in the operations of the Metropolitan Police) and condemned *the collective failure of an organisation to provide a professional service to people because of their colour, culture or ethnic origin*. Racism can be seen in processes which discriminate through unwitting prejudice, ignorance, thoughtlessness and stereotyping.

The incorporation of citizenship as a compulsory secondary curriculum subject in the new millennium, supported by GCSE qualifications in citizenship studies, helped the 'inclusion' agenda, the replacement for cultural pluralism. A report on 'community cohesion' in the aftermath of race riots in Bradford, Oldham and Burnley was hailed as a race manifesto advising *black people to develop a greater acceptance of principal national institutions*, including citizenship (Cantle, 2001, p.8). Through the embedding of antiracist and multicultural elements into citizenship as a formally assessed and accredited discipline, a sea change has taken place which could be considered a start in the battle to combat racism in education (Kundnani, 2001).

# Race and achievement

Of the many powerful, commonplace generalisations about 'race' and achievement, those around African-Caribbean boys as the lowest-achieving group in comparison to their white and Asian peers, are the most tenacious (DES, 1981, 1985; Troyna, 1984; Gillborn and Mirza, 2000):

*West Indian children as a group are underachieving in our education system. There is no doubt that West Indian children as a group, and on average, are underachieving, both by comparison with their fellows in the white majority as well as in terms of their potential. The underachievement of West Indian children is a reinforcement of a stereotype that black people are academically challenged. Race, gender and class all impact on achievement. The lowest achieving ethnic groups (Bangladeshi, Pakistani and Caribbean) are disproportionately overrepresented in the lowest socio-economic groups.*

(Swann, 1985, p.10)

These comments reflect the complexity of the debate on race and underachievement, while at the same time reinforcing the central discourse that the underachievement of black pupils, in particular black boys, has continued to raise the greatest concerns. As with multiculturalism, underachievement has been defined in fluid terms depending on the subject (ethnic group) and context. The very use of the word 'underachievement' is synonymous with the many stereotypes associated with racial characteristics of black people: that they are lazy, lacking mental capacity, and inclined to challenging behaviours, conflict and aggression (particularly boys). However, in terms of educational achievement such powerful stereotypes have been applied both to black pupils and to their rates of learning.

Gillborn and Mirza (2000, p.56) have noted that:

*[i]t is vital to identify differences in attainment but we must be careful to avoid wider beliefs that reinforce wholly stereotypical perceptions that some ethnic groups are naturally talented in some areas or inherently culturally disposed to learning whilst others are not. Thus, simply replacing 'underachievement' with the more recent notions of 'difference' needs to be carefully considered.*

It is vital to point out that the underachievement of black boys is just one facet of the multiplicity of issues when the question of race and achievement is raised. One of the key factors in underachievement is poverty. Strand (2008), in a government-backed study, found that white working-class teenagers achieved less well than black and Asian pupils. Poverty and living in deprived neighbourhoods had a worse effect on white working-class results than it did on minority ethnic groups (Strand, 2008). It was also found by Mongon and Chapman (2008) that underachievement is endemic among white working-class pupils: white British boys entitled to free school meals were the male group with the lowest attainment and white British girls entitled to free school meals were the female group with the lowest attainment.

The all-encompassing nature of this debate has preoccupied politicians, journalists and educational professionals alike, with crime, gang culture, binge drinking, the wearing of hoodies, gun restrictions and sink schools all featuring prominently. Since the 1960s, when the education system was said to be responding to a crisis in relation to growing numbers of immigrant children in the classroom, institutional racism in its various forms has been blamed for the systematic and consistent failure of Britain's education provision to address the issue of underachievement. Activists within black communities became increasingly vocal in the 1970s, spurring the government to set up its inquiry chaired by Lord Rampton (DES, 1981), which noted that *whilst we cannot accept that racism alone accounts for the underachievement of West Indian children, we believe that taken together with negative teacher attitudes and an inappropriate curriculum, racism does play a major part in their underachievement.*

## black pupils' expectations and experiences of schooling

There are many factors that contribute to underachievement as experienced by black pupils. They include the lack of recreational options, high levels of unemployment in the family and poor housing (Modood and Berthoud, 1997), other material deprivation (Modood, 1994; Gillborn and Gipps, 1996), and experiences of racism in wider society (Maughan and Dunn, 1988). However, the mismatch between the expectations and experiences of black pupils compounds the entire underachievement debate. Parents from the Indian subcontinent who were educated in English, usually in larger teaching rooms and with the utmost respect for their teacher in a culture that valued discipline, found clear areas of difference in their children's schooling. The 'migrant effect' did not anticipate such lowering of expectations in terms of educational provision. Eade (1995) concluded that parental lack of knowledge about the systems in place might also be a factor in the mismatch experience. Among African-Caribbean pupils, the raising of aspirations aimed to combat notions of cultural inadequacy rooted in patterns of disaffection. Coard's (1971) report, *How the West Indian Child is Made Educationally Sub-normal in the British School System*, was endorsed by Swann (DES, 1985) who noted that *research evidence and our own findings have indicated that the stereotypes teachers tend to have of West Indian children are often particular with generally negative expectations of academic performance.*

African-Caribbean pupils continue to bear the brunt of concerns about underachievement. A review of inner London LEAs concluded that African-Caribbean pupils were the lowest-achieving ethnic group. In 2002, when the national average achieving five GCSEs grades A*–C was 51 per cent, African-Caribbean pupils were the lowest achieving ethnic group with 30 per cent. Follow-up inspection visits to the LEAs involved in the sample study uncovered a sense of helplessness regarding strategies to raise the achievement of black boys.

Sewell (1997) attempted to demystify the issue, reporting that *underachievement is strangely decontextualised from wider societal issues such as negative media representations and poverty*. Sewell explored many factors that have exacerbated the dilemma of underachievement, including violent and anti-school masculine culture, the absence of male role models in the classroom, challenging behaviour patterns and the mismatch of masculinity as a process of socialisation linked directly to academic underachievement. For some boys, masculinity means 'hardness', antagonism to school-based learning, sporting prowess and black pupils' expectations and experiences of schooling fashion. However, this cannot be interpreted as a standard for all, which is the immediate danger when considering the power of media stereotypes.

Successive studies have also noted *inter alia* low teacher expectations, inappropriate and inconsistent discipline systems leading to increased incidents of disruption and exclusion, misunderstanding about black identity and expressions of culture, lack of role models, the impact of institutional racism in society as a whole and the comprehensive failure of LEAs to embrace inclusion and diversity (Saunders, 1996).

Educationalists in America have reported a similar linked pattern of black boys and underachievement in external examinations, with higher exclusion rates and labelling as the lowest-achieving ethnic group, markedly in comparison with bilingual Latino students. Research has offered a range of possible explanations, including differences in cognitive abilities, aversion to intellectual competition, genetic difference, economic disadvantage and manifestations of racism in society. A comparative 'whiteness study' has had limited impact in Britain. 'Whiteness', it was argued, should be considered not as a biological fact but as a social construction, encouraging white teachers to explore how their ethnicity impacts on their work (Pearce, 2003). As with the American research into black underachievement, the ultimate aim of this study was to ensure equality of educational provision for all. Fundamentally, the impact of negative stereotyping and the lack of cultural identification with the system of schooling (and indeed the curriculum) are considered the most powerful of those socio-cultural factors that have contributed to the consistent disaffection and thus underachievement of black boys in American schools (Katz, 1993). American approaches include the successful mass recruitment of black teachers with international teaching qualifications and the delivery of training on black culture in all schools through two initiatives to attempt to understand the 'gangsta' street culture. Ethnic minority teachers make up only 7 per cent of London's teaching cohort, whereas ethnic minority pupils make up 44 per cent of the total school population. This has prompted some commentators to note that this is unacceptable in the twenty-first century school (Education Commission, 2004).

---

*Pause for thought* | cultural racism: a new phenomenon

Multicultural education policies combined with antiracist education policies are now charged with addressing an evolving phenomenon. Identified as 'cultural racism', the emergence of this development is illustrated in the rise of 'Islamophobia' since the Twin Towers disaster in New York in 2001. The classifying of such a cultural group prompted Gilroy (1992) to conclude that such a *form of cultural racism, which has taken a necessary distance from the crude ideas of biological inferiority now seeks to present an imaginary definition of the nation as a unified cultural community.*

Cultural racism may suggest that ethnic groups have a very defined culture that is distinct and easily identifiable. What evidence can you find to support cultural racism in the media? Which other groups are subject to this emerging racialised identification theory? Could it be argued that globalisation challenges such notions of ethnic identification? What should be the response of educationalists to the rise of Islamophobia? Consider the guidance given by the teaching unions, for example the National Union of Teachers (NUT) and the National Association of Schoolmasters and Union of Women Teachers (NASUWT), in response to incidents of Islamophobia in schools. Can multicultural and antiracist education policies have been effective in countering ethnic stereotyping?

---

## Summary and conclusions

This chapter has considered historic government strategies to embrace difference and has reviewed their relative success rates. The ways in which race impacts on language, deciding who belongs and who does not, has added to the notions of identity. In addition, the focus on achievement and attainment in this era of heightened concern around league tables has confirmed the need to celebrate diversity and acknowledge individual needs in order to promote high aspirations and challenge deeply held stereotypical assumptions.

The contemporary socio-political debate around 'race' and education attempts to address the historic 'island race' notion associated with being British. Not surprisingly, second- and third-generation immigrants are experiencing their own journeys of discovery, illustrating the complexity and at times controversy of the very nature of the debate. New ethnicities, identities and cultures are a common feature of every town and city, and education policy and governmental initiatives in education need continually to bear this firmly in mind.

## References

Alleyne, B (2002) An idea of community and its discontents: towards a more reflexive sense of belonging in multicultural Britain. *Ethnic and Racial Studies*, 25: 607–27.

British National Party (2013) *Manifesto*. London: British National Party. [Online] Available at: **www.bnp.org.uk/manifesto** (accessed 9 May 2013).

Cantle, E (2001) *Community Cohesion: a report of the Independent Review Team* (the Cantle Report). London: Home Office.

Coard, B (1971) *How the West Indian Child is Made Educationally Sub-normal in the British School System*. London: New Beacon Books.

Cohen, P (1989) *Tackling Common Sense Racism*. University of London: Institute of Education, Centre for Multicultural Education.

Cummins, J (2001) Cultural and linguistic diversity in education: a mainstream issue? *Educational Review*, 49(2): 105–14.

DES (1981) *West Indian Children in Our Schools* (the Rampton Report). London: HMSO/ Department of Education and Science.

DES (1985) *Education for All: Report of the Committee of Inquiry into the Education of Children from Ethnic Minority Groups* (the Swann Report). Cmnd 9453. London: HMSO/ Department of Education and Science.

Eade, J (1995) *Routes and Beyond: Voices from educationally successful Bangladeshis*. London: Centre for Bangladeshi Studies.

Education Commission (2004) *Educational Experiences and Achievements of Black Boys in London Schools, 2000–2003*. The London Development Agency. Available at: **www.lda.gov.uk** (accessed 18 April 2009).

Gaine, C (1995) *Still no Problem Here*. Stoke on Trent: Trentham.

Gillborn, D and Gipps, C (1996) *Recent Research on the Achievement of Ethnic Minority Pupils*. London: OFSTED/Institute of Education.

Gillborn, D and Mirza, HS (2000) *Inequality*. London: OFSTED.

Gilroy, P (1992) The end of anti-racism, in Donald, J and Rattansi, A (eds) *Race, Culture and Difference*. London: Sage.

HMG (2013) *The Queen's Speech 2013*. London: Her Majesty's Government.

Katz, M (1993) *The Urban Underclass*. Princeton, NJ: Princeton University Press.

Kundnani, A (2001) From Oldham to Bradford: the violence of the violated. *Race and Class*, 43(2): 105–31.

Macpherson, W (1999) *The Stephen Lawrence Inquiry*. Cm 4262-I. London: The Stationery Office.

Maughan, B and Dunn, G (1988) Black pupils' progress in secondary school, in Verma, G and Pumfrey, P (eds) *Educational Attainments: Issues and outcomes in multicultural education*. London: Falmer Press.

Modood, T (1994) *Not Easy Being British*. London: Runnymede Trust.

Modood, T and Berthoud, R (1997) *Ethnic Minorities in Britain*. London: Policy Studies Institute.

Mongon, D and Chapman, C (2008) *Successful Leadership for Promoting the Achievement of White Working Class Pupils – summary*. Nottingham: National College of School Leadership. [Online] Available at: **www.ncsl.org.uk/successful-leadership-for-promoting-full-report-4.pdf** (accessed 3 November 2008).

Ousley, H (2001) *The Bradford District Race Review*. Bradford: Bradford Vision.

Parekh, B (2000) *The Future of Multi-ethnic Britain – the Parekh Report*. London: Profile Books.

Pearce, S (2003) Compiling the white inventory: the practice of whiteness in a British primary school. *Cambridge Journal of Education*, 33(2): 62–9.

Powell, T and Schwartz, B (2003) The struggle to define academic multiculturalism. *Cultural Critique*, 55: 152–81.

Sarup, M (1991) *Education and the Ideologies of Racism*. Stoke on Trent: Trentham.

Saunders, P (1996) A British bell curve? *Sociology Review*, (6)2: 81–8.

Sewell, T (1997) *Black Masculinities and Schooling*. Stoke on Trent: Trentham.

Strand, S. (2008) *Minority Ethnic Pupils in the Longitudinal Study of Young People in England*, London: DCSF. [Online] Available at: **www.dcsf.gov.uk/research/data/uploadfiles/DCSF-RR029.pdf** (accessed 3 November, 2008).

Swann, M (1985) *Education for All*. London: HMSO.

Troyna, B (1984) Fact or artefact? The 'educational underachievement' of black pupils. *British Journal of Sociology of Education*, 5(2): 153–66.

Troyna, B and Hatcher, R (1992) *Racism in Children's Lives*. London: Routledge.

Troyna, B and Williams, J (1996) *Racism, Education and the State*. London: Croom Helm.

Wright, C (1992) *Race Relations in the Primary School*. London: David Fulton.

# Chapter 15

# SEN and the question of inclusive education

## Suanne Gibson

### Introduction

Special Educational Needs (SEN), 'inclusion' and/or 'inclusive education' refer to central aspects of education policy and practice. They are cited in national and local policy documents, research reports and papers, teaching guides and consultancy services. This chapter hopes to bring some clarity to them for the reader, in particular locating their origin, engaging in the key debates surrounding them and reflecting on related practices and research studies.

We will firstly look to define the terms: 'Special Educational Needs' and 'inclusion'. We will then consider where they have come from and look at the history of provision in relation to Special Educational Needs and significant developments regarding inclusion or inclusive education from the late 1990s to early 2000s. We will finally reflect on recent developments and revisions to policy. We will also address related research and education publications to provide additional critical insights into the field.

## Definitions and their location in time and policy terms

### SEN

The term 'Special Educational Needs' (SEN) has existed within the field of UK Education policy since 1978 (Warnock Report, 1978; Education Act, 1981). Mary Warnock's committee was set up in 1973 by Margaret Thatcher, then education minister in Edward Heath's Conservative government, to:

*review educational provision in England, Scotland and Wales for children and young people handicapped by disabilities of body or mind, taking account of the medical aspects of their needs, together with arrangements to prepare them for entry into employment; to consider the most effective use of resources for these purposes; and to make recommendations.*

(Warnock Report, 1978)

This report was seminal in the wording and content of the subsequent 1981 Education Act, which defined SEN as:

*For the purposes of this Act a child has 'special educational needs' if he has a learning difficulty which calls for special educational provision to be made for him.*

(DfE, 1981, Section 312)

Subsequent recommendations for education practices and funding provision for children with disabilities resulted in changes to local authorities and schools – both special and mainstream. Where appropriate, the integration of pupils with SEN into mainstream schools was encouraged. The following activity requires you to take on the role of a teacher in a mainstream school in the early 1980s and to consider the impact this legislation had on you and your school.

---

**Pause for thought** | group activity (for 3–5 people)

The year is 1982, you are a recently appointed primary school teacher and have been made aware of the 1978 Warnock Report and 1981 Education Act. You consider how this might impact on your class of 25 Year 3 children and have met with other teachers over break time to share thoughts. You each bring to the table one concern and a personal reflection on why you became involved in education. Having shared your inputs you then discuss who you believe has a right to access mainstream education and why, what values are informing this view, how language impacts on practices and what 'integration' might mean in a practical sense for you and your school. Consider issues like your professional training needs, school finance needs, community information needs, support for parents and pupils as well as what values inform your practice.

Recommended resources to draw on:

Runswick-Cole, K and Hodge, N. (2009) Needs or rights? A challenge to the discourse of special education. *British Journal of Special Education*, 36(4), 198–203.

The Warnock Report available at:

**www.educationengland.org.uk/documents/warnock/**

---

## 'Inclusion' and 'inclusive education'

The term 'inclusion' and related practices of 'inclusive education' signified a departure in government policy terms from the late 1990s and a new direction for mainstream education provision. Tony Blair's New Labour government of 1997 and its 'Education Education Education' manifesto were seminal to this departure. Defining 'inclusive education' as a dominant theme of policy and practice from that time, Armstrong (2005, p.135) summarises it clearly:

*New Labour has placed inclusion at the centre of its educational agenda. Its policies have been characterised by an attempt to include disabled children, together with others identified as having 'special educational needs', within the ordinary school system and the shifting of responsibility for meeting their needs to teachers in the ordinary classroom.*

'Inclusion' became a popular form of provision for learners who experienced exclusion from the mainstream or failure in education linked to matters of 'disability', 'gender', 'race' or 'ethnicity'

(DfEE, 1996, 1997, 1998; DfES, 2001). Policy and practice reflected on how causes of, or reasons for, student exclusion were linked to the culture and/or traditional forms of education practice and curriculum resulting in limited outcomes for diverse learners. On that basis 'Inclusion' became an ethical and political matter for policy makers, practitioners and, of course, recipients. The UN Salamanca statement (UNESCO, 1994) provided the foundation from which much education policy and connected political views on inclusion developed:

*Inclusion and participation are essential to human dignity and to the enjoyment and exercise of human rights. In the field of education this is reflected in bringing about a 'genuine equalisation of opportunity'. The fundamental principle of the inclusive school is that all children should learn together, where possible, and that ordinary schools must recognise and respond to the diverse needs of their students, while also having a continuum of support and services to match these needs.*

The terms 'Special Educational Needs' and 'inclusion' are critically dissected in academic research and certain versions promoted in linked practitioner publications. Current thinking and policy questions recent practices as well as the benefits and impact of significant government policy initiatives, in particular those stemming from the late 1990s (Armstrong, 2005; Hodkinson, 2011).

---

*Pause for thought* | three questions

Consider the following questions:

- What do you understand by the terms inclusion and Special Educational Needs?
- What teaching practices have you witnessed or been involved with in schools or youth centres that were linked to inclusive education?
- Reflecting on the views of Jonathon Bartley, how might his ideas be best applied in schools and whose views do we need to listen to when considering inclusive practice?

**www.youtube.com/watch?v=P38tJ1w-dRA&feature=player_embedded**

# Development of a separate 'Special Education' system

Forster's Education Act 1870 paved the way for compulsory education for children in England via the creation of a Schools' Boards system. Forster's Act emphasised the need for Britain to develop an educated workforce that could contribute to and ensure the country led the way in what was a growing international and industrial market. This was the first government legislation to impact upon the education of those with disabilities. Until 1870, education for children with disabilities was provided for by charities or hospitals and not taken account of in national policy or provision. The 1880 Education Act resulted in compulsory school attendance for those aged 5–10.

The first school in England for children with disabilities was the Liverpool Blind School (RSB, Liverpool). Founded in 1791, this school encouraged pupils who were deemed able to develop a trade; it did not aim to provide a broad education. The Egerton Committee was established in 1889 to address the issue of pupils deemed 'uneducable' by teachers in the mainstream. This committee report resulted in the 1893 Education Act which promoted the building of schools for children with sensory difficulties and contributed to the work of the 1898 Sharpe committee and subsequent 1899 Education Act. This resulted in the establishment of formal state special schools for children with other types of disabilities, from which a separate system of formal schooling, 'Special Education', evolved.

General education provision for children with disabilities from 1800s to mid-1900s was sporadic, inconsistent and segregated from the mainstream. Potts (1982) suggests that inadequate provision was due to the implementation of related education legislation being left to local authorities with no central power directing policy implementation or its evaluation. The 1921 Education Act led to five statutory categories for children with disabilities and made reference to the 'imbecile' (i.e. a child who was noted as having no potential to learn). The five categories for those children deemed to have a 'handicap' were as follows:

- blind;
- deaf;
- mentally defective;
- physically defective;
- epileptic.

This type of medicalised understanding and belief was reflected in the work of two prominent education psychologists, Burt (1935) and Schonell (1924). Their work suggested that on average 17 per cent of children had learning difficulties resulting in the need to be educated in separate classes, schools or in the case of the 'imbecile' and others classed as 'uneducable', institutionalised without any formal education provision.

These professional views contributed to policy formation that promoted a deficit model view of the learner with disability. Thomas and Vaughan (2004), reflecting on Goffman's 1961 work *Asylums*, link his critique of the purposes and impact of asylums to that of the special education system. They state (2004, p.31):

*Institutions [...] are constructed to serve the purpose of the wider system rather than the inhabitants of the institution, and one can draw from this insight the possibility that the special school system may exist primarily for the convenience of the mainstream system rather than for the purpose of helping or improving the lives of those who are directed to the special system.*

This critique of the special education system is linked with Armstrong (2003a), Goodley et al. (2004) and French et al. (2008). Their research and publications are about the question, purpose and impact of the institutionalisation of those with SEN in hospital settings or separate forms of special education provision. They argue such practices were not in keeping with the aims and objectives of 'education' as was then, or is now, commonly understood. Armstrong, engaging with the voices of those who experienced education in special schools, has a similar view to Thomas and Vaughan in his argument that separate special education is more to do with regulating difference and suppressing diversity than about education. He states:

*Although special education is a product of modernity, systems of care for the 'disabled', the 'ill' and the 'insane' did pre-date industrialised societies [...] the growth of special education is embedded in the rationalist ideology of modern society. Policy and practice interventions have been centred upon the management of difference, either through its eradication, as with the eugenics movement, or through its 'treatment' as with the policies of normalisation.*

(Armstrong, 2003a, pp.8–19)

Thus special education's existence as a separate area of education policy for those deemed 'unable' as learners in the mainstream, contributed to the stigma of disability, the pathologising of difference and from an inclusive educationalist point of view, inappropriate and ineffective forms of education for children with disabilities.

---

*Pause for thought* | thinking about the historical context and language

- What kinds of developments were taking place nationally and globally at the turn of the nineteenth century?
- What do you think was the rationale behind Forster's Act 1870?
- What kinds of assumptions might have been made by teachers at that time in relation to children with disabilities and why?

Think about some of the language used to label learners placed within the special school system, what do you think might be some of the issues and concerns regarding labelling in that way and its impact?

Sources to assist with this activity:

Armstrong, D (2003) 'The menace of the other within', in *Experiences of Special Education*. London: RoutledgeFalmer

Gibson S and Blandford, S (2005), 'Special Educational Needs', in *Managing Special Educational Needs – a practical guide for primary and secondary schools*. London: Sage.

---

# What do we mean by SEN? What is integration?

From the 1960s there were calls from practitioners, policy makers and parents, among others, for a change to the segregated system, arguably influenced by the post-Second World War development in public support for egalitarian philosophies (Tomlinson, 1982). In line with this, Mary Warnock and her committee were charged with assessing overall national education provision for children with disabilities across England, Scotland and Wales. The final report (Warnock, 1978) suggested that provision in local authorities and schools, mainstream and special, was inconsistent and in many cases inappropriate. In sum they made five recommendations which promoted significant change to the mainstream education system by encouraging the integration of children with disabilities.

## 1978 Warnock Report

The Warnock Report made the following key recommendations for changes to the education of pupils with disability:

1. The 1944 Education Act's statutory categories be removed and the concept of Special Educational Needs widened.
2. Children with Special Educational Needs should have their needs assessed.
3. These assessment procedures should involve five stages.
4. Parental involvement in the assessment procedure is encouraged.
5. There should be an expansion of LEA advisory and support services.

In line with this development, the 1981 Education Act encouraged integration of children with disabilities subject to the following four criteria (DfE, 1981, chapter 60):

1. *That this was in accordance with parental wishes.*
2. *That the child's educational needs could be met.*
3. *That it was consistent with the efficient use of resources.*
4. *That it would not detract from the education of the rest of the class.*

The Warnock Report recommended the removal of all categories of handicap by replacing these with the broader concept of 'Special Educational Needs'. In 1980 the Government produced a White Paper on Special Needs in Education. This formalised the use of the term 'Special Educational Needs' (SEN). The 1981 Education Act acknowledged that in certain cases the education of a child deemed to have a special need should take place within the mainstream setting. Furthermore it advocated that all statutory categories of 'handicap' were to be removed and in their place practitioners were to make use of the term 'Special Educational Needs' (SEN).

The result of the Warnock Report and 1981 Education Act were the development of Local Education Authority policies on integration and a formal system called 'statementing' to assess and provide, where necessary, additional funding to accommodate pupil need. A statement is a formal document produced after a statutory assessment has been carried out. The statutory assessment is usually conducted by a local authority education psychologist, who assesses the particular educational needs of a child and deduces what additional resources a mainstream school requires.

The statementing procedure that ensued resulted in a very bureaucratic process. This process was included in the 1988 Education Reform Act, thus institutionalising it and making it a significant and integral aspect of parental choice and devolved funding practices. The long-term impact was the significant growth of numbers in children with disabilities in mainstream education. The policy failed to provide for effective practice or the professional development needs of mainstream teachers and resultant provision was generally noted by practitioners as inappropriate. This was blamed partly on the lack of resources to support and encourage the professional development of mainstream teachers but also on the issue of culture. Deeply held beliefs and ideas on ability and disability continued to dominate practice and educator views regarding the education of children with disabilities. There was a continued cultural assumption by many educators that disability equals inability, children with disabilities are 'other' and 'unable', and so against a backdrop of policy for integration and the movement of many children out of hospitals and special schools into mainstream schools, the medicalised view of disability continued to dominate practitioner beliefs and opinion (Tomlinson, 1982).

It has been argued that the 1978 Warnock Report acted as a watershed in relation to education provision for children with disabilities, but interestingly Warnock herself has subsequently denounced the impact and changes the report encouraged. In relation to the statementing process she has stated (Shaw, 2008):

*It is the greatest obstacle to good provision, [...] There are far more children statemented than we ever envisaged. It has ceased to be about what the child needs and has just become a battle for resources.*

She went on to argue that recent moves towards full inclusion should be abandoned and the current system of education provision for pupils with disabilities overhauled.

---

*Pause for thought* | reflecting on Warnock's report

Our education world is, like our wider world, always changing. Depending on your values and point of view this can be for the good or for the bad. Take some time to reflect on Warnock's recent change of mind as cited above. What factors do you think she was taking into consideration? Why does she now maintain that the aims of her committee report of 1978 have not achieved positive outcomes? Do you agree with this or would you challenge this view?

Sources to assist:

Warnock M and Norwich, B (2010) *Special Educational Needs – a new look*. London: Continuum.

Runswick-Cole, K (2011) Time to end the bias towards inclusive education?, *British Journal Special Education*, 38(3), 112–119.

Hart, S, Dixon, A, Drummond, MJ and McIntyre, D (2004) *Learning Without Limits*. Berkshire: Open University Press.

---

# What is inclusion or inclusive education (IE)?

Subsequent to the push for integration in the 1980s came the drive for inclusion as promoted by the disability rights movement in the 1980s and 90s and subsequently targeted by the New Labour government of the late 1990s. Where there were barriers preventing integration of children with particular disabilities, inclusion – the ideals and policy – demanded that they be challenged thus upholding the human right of all children to a mainstream education. The theory and philosophy behind inclusive education is depicted clearly in the work of CSIE (2013) and the academic research of Allan (2010a, 2010b), Barnes (1996), and Barton (1998). These sources and their engagement with inclusion lay the matter squarely with that of human rights. See below for a series of definitions on inclusive education.

---

*Pause for thought* | definitions of and academic reflections on 'inclusive education'

Consider the following definitions:

- Barnes (1996, p.1)

*Disability is a complex form of social oppression or institutionalised discrimination ... theoretical analysis has shifted from individuals and their impairment to disabling environments and hostile attitudes.*

*(Continued)*

*(Continued)*

- Sebba and Sachdev (1997, p.75)

*The factor that has the greatest impact upon a school's ability to become inclusive are the expectations of the staff, parents and the pupils themselves.*

- Barton (1998, p.60):

*IE is about the education of all children, which necessitates serious change, in terms of society and its economic, social conditions and relations and in the schools of which they are a part.*

- Allan (2003, p.178)

*Becoming inclusive ... means becoming political; listening to what children and their parents say about what inclusion means to them and recognising the way in which we ourselves are implicated in practices that exclude.*

- Black-Hawkins, Florian and Rouse (2007, p.45)

*On the one hand legislation for special education has become increasingly enabling, inclusive and progressive, whilst on the other hand, raising achievement of all children as part of an ongoing standards agenda, continues to dominate educational debate.*

- Centre for Studies on Inclusive Education (2013)

*Arguments for inclusive education are well documented and rest on notions of equality and human rights. Much more than a policy requirement, inclusion is founded upon a moral position which values and respects every individual and which welcomes diversity as a rich learning resource.*

- Alliance for Inclusive Education (2013)

*Education should support the development of physical, vocational and academic abilities through mixed-ability tuition in mainstream schools so that all students have the opportunity to build relationships with one another. We believe that a fully inclusive education system will benefit everyone.*

In groups of two, identify similarities and differences between the above definitions. In particular, consider which one you find most persuasive and why.

In their reflections on inclusive education the above sources make no distinction between those with disabilities and those without. They do not advocate a special or distinct pedagogy to educate pupils with disabilities. They argue that good teaching is good teaching, that inclusion is political and that for effective inclusive education to happen a radical departure from previous, more traditional, ways of doing things in the classroom, school and community is needed. Education, from an inclusionist's view point, is about the human right to effective and mainstream education for all learners regardless or devoid of labels, be they medical or other. The above authors' research and publications engage with the complexities of inclusive education and furthermore they address where the term has been misused in both policy and practice terms. Inclusive education is a highly contested area full of debates and divisions; one key element of this is regarding 'voice'. The questions whose voice and what views are we listening to when we deliver on education are integral to both understanding and then providing effective forms of education for all learners. The processes of accessing, listening and responding to voices shared are problematic, fraught with cultural and bureaucratic hurdles (Armstrong, 2003a). As articulated by Gibson (2006, p.323):

*The aims and objectives of inclusive education, policy and research are caught up in political and cultural processes. There is a need [...] to genuinely listen to the voices of those currently being silenced in a way that acknowledges the tensions and complexities involved. Striking a balance between empathy and analysis may work some way in overcoming these difficulties.*

So one might summarise by saying, inclusive education is about the ideal of social justice for all, political in its formation, structure and impact. It sets out to deconstruct the status quo and reconstruct a very different form of education system (CSIE, 2013; ALLFIE, 2013) but to date a fully inclusive education system has not emerged.

---

### *Pause for thought* | integration versus inclusion?

- How does integration differ from inclusion?
- What are the different values informing them?
- Can you provide a practical example of integration and one of inclusion?
- What experiences in education have you had or what teaching approaches/provision have you observed that reflect inclusion?

Sources to draw on:

Richards, G and Armstrong, F (2011) *Teaching and Learning in Diverse and Inclusive Classrooms*. London: Routledge.

Thomas, G and Vaughan, M (2004) *Inclusive Education: Readings and Reflections*. Berkshire: Open University Press.

Miles, S and Ainscow, M (2011) *Responding to Diversity in Schools*. London: Routledge.

---

# Our current situation: a time of change and regression versus opportunity to reassert IE values?

There are tensions in current education policy (Gibson, 2006, 2012) and concerns regarding misinterpretation of inclusion in relation to learners with SEN (Gibson 2009). There is also a current academic view that we need to revisit original aspects of IE theory, e.g. Vygotsky on the socio–cultural, and to remind educators of the original rationale for inclusive education with its need to be political, if indeed one is aiming to be inclusive in their practice (Allan, 2010a, 2010b; Gibson, 2012; Runswick-Cole, 2011).

Inclusion has arguably become lost in various bodies of evidence, schools of thought and linked education policies. It seems at present to mean many things to many people. There are some who confuse it with integration and forms of exclusion within mainstream schools. There are others who misunderstand it as a bureaucratic exercise, a managerial role that increasing numbers of mainstream schools have taken on since the 1990s in order to cut government spending. However, in essence it is political, a movement originating from the Disability Rights discourse of the 1980s, demanding change within society and its institutions on the basis of civil rights and equal opportunities. Its agenda stems from and is articulated by the voices of those who have been, and in many cases continue to be, silenced. Inclusion calls for radical change, a change of culture in order to bring about sustainable changes in practice. Strogilos identifies a key barrier as the slow pace of system reform (2012, p.1241):

*Inclusive education involves changes on many levels – from policy and structural levels, teacher training, family, to the level of schooling – through changes to the curriculum and teaching strategies. Research has shown that system reform is a major challenge.*

'Inclusion', far from being a lost cause or a negative legacy, has become a victim of misinterpretation, misapplication and generally abandoned by an increasingly neoliberal age, conservative governments and overly stretched, excessively assessed practitioners. This is further heightened by limitations of practitioner vision secured by a background of austerity and global economic retrenchment.

## The neoliberal diversion

Some maintain IE has failed and this can be linked to hierarchical approaches of policy development and implementation alongside ineffective resource allocation and inappropriate forms of practitioner preparedness (Mittler, 2000; Kershner, 2007). Others, refuting the claims and statements of Warnock on the 'problem of inclusion' (Warnock, 2005), lay the blame with regressive statements and publications. While the aforementioned variables have contributed toward IE's current malaise there is also the argument that dominant western culture, the impact of late capitalism or the diversion created by popular neoliberal value systems, has also taken a toll. 'Neoliberal' or 'neoliberalism' is a complex term but one that is necessary to grasp to engage with the complexities of inclusive education and consider the question why this ideal seems ever to be out of reach. Larner (2000, p.5) provides a comprehensive definition of the term:

*The term 'neo-liberalism' denotes new forms of political-economic governance premised on the extension of market relationships [...] neo-liberalism is associated with the preference for a minimalist state. Markets are understood to be a better way of organizing economic activity because they are associated with competition, economic efficiency and choice.*

Neoliberalism's developing strength and dominance since the 1980s challenges professional discourse engagement with 'inclusion' as a valid political aim, (Apple, 2001; Runswick-Cole, 2011). Apple (2001, p.410), writing about the convergence and alliance of 'conservative' groupings in society since the turn of the century, the rationale for their convergence and the marginalisation and silencing of minority groupings which present a threat to its hegemony, explains further:

*While there are clear tensions and conflicts within this alliance, in general its overall aims are in providing the educational conditions believed necessary for increasing international competitiveness, profit and discipline and for returning us to a romanticised past of the 'ideal' home, family, and school.*

The alliance he writes about comes from various sections of capital; social and economic groupings that merge over a common ideology; aims, objectives and outcomes, where a successful future is located in the furtherance and resurgence of a strong global capitalist market, where right-wing religious zeal is the order of the day and accountability alongside 'scientific' forms of measurement and assessment of effectiveness are applied to societal institutions. Hierarchical forms of management are legitimised, thus furthered, and notions of 'holistic' and 'diverse' thinking or challenges to the norm as defined from above do not have a place. In sum he refers to neoliberalism as a disease originating in the 1980s which over the past 30 years has become a global epidemic. It has been argued that notions of diversity, enabling education for all, responding to varied 'voices' and promoting a politics of IE do not fit in such a world (Davies and Bansel, 2007). Arguably this is why the UK coalition government recently took a clear view against inclusion which, from within the kind of right-wing hegemonic alliance depicted by Apple, legitimises such views. DfE (2011, p.29) says:

*We believe the most vulnerable children deserve the very highest quality of care. We will improve diagnostic assessment for schoolchildren, prevent the unnecessary closure of special schools, and remove the bias towards inclusion.*

The response of many academics and progressive thinkers in the field of education and sociology was one of concern and fear regarding this legitimising of regression from the IE political agenda (Apple, 2001; Runswick-Cole, 2011). The words of Giroux (2010, p.185) provide much to reflect on:

*With the advent of neoliberalism, or what some call free-market fundamentalism, in the last 30 years, we have witnessed the production and widespread adoption within educational theory and practice of what I call, borrowing from the work of Giorgio Agamben (1998), bare pedagogy.*

The thesis on 'bare pedagogy' suggests a form of education where the main and only purpose is regarding self benefit, the promotion of individualism and the furtherance of capital with little thought given to ethical considerations (Giroux, 2010). While Giroux's work is focused primarily within HE, the arguments developed and points raised are generic in scope and thus applicable throughout the education sector. They connect with the 'efficiency' ethos, consumer choice and promotion of entrepreneurialism in current UK government thinking and education policy.

Neoliberalism's rise and dominance in contemporary society promotes tension and confusion regarding definitions and applications of inclusion. Arguably we have lost a sense of the liberal rationale for education, particularly as linked to those who are deemed 'Other'.

Robertson (2012) reflects on the changing role of the Special Educational Needs Co-ordinator (SENCO) in schools and how, under the SEND green paper, there may be *policies that could lead to the needs of some pupils being unmet, and others being marginalised through an expansion of separate forms of provision* (p.77). His work predicts worrying times, fears that not only is IE in the dustbin, but established forms of progressive practice are moving backwards.

Research box

## WeCan2

In the project 'WeCan2', Professor Kellet and her contributors looked at questions of democracy and empowerment. The research was conducted *by a group of young people with learning disabilities exploring their experiences of youth democracy and meaningful participation in decision-making forums* (2010, p.31).

The project looked at key aspects in the debate regarding voice, power and democracy for those marginalised within our society. The work is linked to three key areas of research on the topic of 'Social and Political Inclusion':

1. The question of children and young people as 'participants' in academic research, in particular tensions between active versus passive forms.
2. The issues regarding children and young people's voice, in particular matters of power and adult mediation.
3. The driver of young researchers as protagonists, in particular questions regarding emancipation and ownership of research.

On reading this paper we see links to some of the earlier questions raised when trying to define and then 'do inclusion' in our education world, be that in a school, community centre, youth club, family home or other residential setting. On the basis of Kellet et al.'s arguments and the story of their work together please consider the following questions:

- How might inclusive methods of education be promoted and carried out successfully?
- What stakeholders should be involved in related discussions?
- How might a process of community involvement, to develop ideas and practices of inclusion, take place without members becoming disempowered by bureaucracy or centre-led policy?

Resources for this exercise:

Kellet, M. with original research contributions by young people with a learning disability: Allan Aoslin, Ross Baines, Alice Clancy, Lizzie Jewiss-Hayden, Ryan Singh and Josh Strudgwick (2010) 'WeCan2: exploring the implications of young people with learning disabilities engaging in their own research', *European Journal of Special Needs Education* 25(1): 31–44.

Ledwith, M (2005) *Community Development: A critical approach*. Bristol: The Policy Press.

# What next? Relationship for inclusive education

In problematising government policy on inclusion and linked practices, Alexander (1998) suggests the problem is society's lack of critical citizens. A critical citizen (Alexander, 1998, p.122) *must hold values of impartiality, truth, fairness, equality and freedom.* Such an individual connects to the model of political educator as articulated by Allan (2010a), to enable educators to *play seriously* (p.411) with inclusion. This is also connected to her work calling on academics to re-engage with the 'other' and remember their political commitments (Allan, 2010a, 2010b). Where are genuine inclusive-orientated educators to look if they believe there is hope and they have an ethical responsibility to the 'other'? What needs to take precedence to re-establish a movement for IE?

Research, recently undertaken by the author, attempted to establish the positive and negative aspects of learning for students with disabilities and from this deduce best education practices for inclusive universities. The project was a qualitative study which entailed two researchers working closely from 2009–11 with five undergraduate students who had disclosed disabilities. Researchers made use of 'participatory' methodology to engage with and understand, from students' perspectives, inclusive and non-inclusive experiences of education.

## Research box

### positive relationships

In this project, a recurring theme emerged of the importance of positive relationships in the learning environment. Students spoke of the need to have this with their tutor, student colleagues and the educational institution itself. Participants expressed desire for tutors and other students to show a genuine interest to know and understand them; to engage with their situation as linked to their disability and the barriers this created for them.

Recommendations for inclusive practices as linked to the research findings:

- The importance and significance of students with disability having a named contact/personal tutor whom they trust and can turn to with questions/concerns as and when they arise.
- The need to ensure that other lecturers/tutors are clear on the particular learning needs of all students and that this information is relayed in confidence and in advance of the students' attendance.
- Tutor awareness of possible student self-esteem issues.
- The need for disability assist services at university having a high profile.
- The importance that students meet with course representatives from other year groups in their induction week.
- The need for a Virtual Learning Environment (VLE) where lecturers ensure that teaching materials are posted in advance or straight after lectures/seminars.
- The importance of faculties/universities ensuring information regarding their disability assist services and contacts is provided to students with disabilities in advance of induction week/registration.

The research suggested participants were disillusioned with inclusion, the majority being of the view that inclusive education had failed them. From listening to students it seems the colonisation of inclusion by policy makers, its fragmentation and inefficient provision, led to an 'emperor's new clothes' scenario or as Ahmed and Swain (2006) have argued in relation to the matter of 'race' and 'doing diversity', it was a case of 'doing inclusion' – without fully understanding the 'other'. In relation to the matter of schools, it seems that there are similar issues here. Porter et al. (2011) in their research addressing the challenges of categorising and keeping up-to-date records of pupils with disabilities in schools, note the complexities regarding disability and the negative perception placed on such data collection in schools.

*(Continued)*

*(Continued)*

Their findings have noted that, similar to Gibson and Kendall (2010), there is a real need to get under the surface and to understand the situation from the prespective of the individual and her or his family. To fully enable equality of opportunity in education they argue for:

*a robust system of data collection which allows professionals to gather and understand parents' and children's accounts of their experiences of impairments and the barriers and supports to progress.*

(Porter et al., 2011, p.122)

Resource:

Gibson, S, and Kendall, L (2010) Stories from school: Dyslexia and learners' voices on factors impacting on achievement. *Support for Learning*, 25(4): 187–93.

SENDA and linked institution policies may exist in the UK's mainstream education, further and higher education sectors; however, this has not managed to achieve inclusive education. Perhaps the final barrier is that of understanding and knowing our diverse learners and their stories.

## Summary and conclusions

The history regarding SEN, related education policy, inclusive education and the various debates that have evolved over the past 30 years are enough to leave the reader's head spinning. Allan writes clearly and is engaging regarding the 'what next?' question for inclusive education, stating (2010a, p.416):

*There is a need to refuse some of the closure in thinking that surrounds inclusion and education – literally by refusing the texts and preventing students engaging with them – to begin to do justice to the complexity and messiness of the processes of inclusion and exclusion.*

She follows this with a call for educationalists to remember their political role, to engage with open hands in their work, using forms of critical pedagogy rather than aiming to apply a 'one size fits all' model of education. Thus IE becomes more than ensuring learners with dyslexia have access to voice recognition technology or those with visual needs have access to enablers. IE is a political process, one which needs to start from an engagement in the politics of relationship, where understanding of the 'other' provides a foundation from which to move forward and make changes to ways of doing things. This links back to Alexander's definition of the critical citizen (1998) and the importance of learning from stories as articulated by Armstrong (2003a).

The future lies with all of us in education and you, as a student of education and possibly a volunteer or support assistant in a youth centre, school, community group or hospital setting. The key when it comes to inclusive education or practice is the ability to listen, understand and respond in a way that links to policies of equality, human rights and dignity; remembering that, as reflected in Kellet's work, inclusion is about meaningful participation by *all* involved.

# References

Ahmed, S and Swain, E (2006) Doing diversity. *Policy Futures in Education*, 4(2): 96–100.

Alexander, D (1998) I am us and we are you. *Discourse: Studies in the Cultural Politics of Education*, 19(1): 121–25.

Allan, J (2003) Productive pedagogies and the challenge of inclusion. *British Journal of Special Education*, 30(4): 175–79.

Allan, J (2010a) The inclusive teacher educator: spaces for civic engagement. *Discourse: Studies in the Cultural Politics of Education*, 31(4): 411–22.

Allan, J (2010b) The sociology of disability and the struggle for inclusive education. *British Journal of Sociology of Education*, 31(5): 603–19.

Alliance for Inclusive Education [Online] Available at: **www.allfie.org.uk/** (accessed 24 May 2013).

Apple, M (2001) Comparing neo-liberal projects and inequality in education. *Comparative Education*, 37(4): 409–23.

Armstrong, D (2003a) *Experiences of Special Education. Re-evaluating policy and practice through life stories.* London: RoutledgeFalmer.

Armstrong, D (2003b) The menace of the other within, in *Experiences of Special Education.* London: RoutledgeFalmer.

Armstrong, D (2005) Reinventing inclusion: New Labour and the cultural politics of special education. *Oxford Review of Education*, 31(1): 135–51.

Arnot, M (2012) (ed) *Sociology of Disability and Inclusive Education: A Tribute to Len Barton.* London: Routledge.

Barnes, C (1996) *Disabling Imagery and the Media.* Leeds: Disability Press.

Barton, L (1998) Sociology, disability studies and education, in Shakespeare, T. (ed). *The Disability Reader: Social science perspectives.* London: Cassell.

Black-Hawkins, K, Florian, L and Rouse, M (2007) *Achievement and Inclusion in Schools.* London: Routledge.

Burt, C (1935) *The Subnormal Mind.* Oxford: Oxford University Press.

Centre for Studies on Inclusive Education (2013). [Online] Available at: **www.csie.org.uk/inclusion/** (accessed 24 May 2013).

Davies, B and Bansel, P (2007) Neoliberalism and education. *International Journal of Qualitative Studies in Education*, 20(3): 247–59.

Department for Education (1981) *The Education Act.* [Online] Available at: **www.legislation.gov.uk/ukpga/1981/60/crossheading/preliminary/enacted** (accessed 5 March 2013).

Department for Education (DfE) (2011) *Support and Aspiration: A new approach to SEN and disability.* London: DfE.

Department for Education and Employment (DfEE) (1996) *The Senco Guide.* London: DfEE.

Department for Education and Employment (DfEE) (1997) *Excellence for all Children. Meeting Special Educational Needs.* London: HMSO.

Department for Education and Employment (DfEE) (1998) *Meeting Special Educational Needs: A Programme of Action.* London: HMSO.

Department for Education and Skills (DfES) (2001) *The Code of Practice for Special Educational Needs.* London: HMSO.

Elkins, A (2012) *The Changing Face of Special Educational Needs.* London: Routledge.

French, S, Swain, J, Atkinson, D and Moore, M (2008) *An Oral History of the Education of Visually Impaired People: Telling stories for inclusive futures.* New York: Edwin Mellen Press.

Gibson, S (2006) Beyond a 'culture of silence': Inclusive education and the liberation of 'voice'. *Disability and Society,* 21(4): 315–29.

Gibson, S (2009) Inclusion versus neo-liberalism: Empowering the 'other', in Gibson, S and Haynes, J (eds) *Perspectives on Participation and Inclusion: Engaging education.* London: Continuum, pp.11–26.

Gibson, S (2012) Narrative accounts of university education: socio-cultural perspectives of students with disabilities. *Disability and Society*, 27(3): 353–69.

Gibson, S and Blandford, S (2005) Special educational needs, in *Managing Special Educational Needs – a practical guide for primary and secondary schools*. London: Sage.

Gibson, S and Kendall, L (2010) Stories from school: Dyslexia and learners' voices on factors impacting on achievement. *Support for Learning,* 25(4): 187–93.

Giroux, H (2010) Bare pedagogy and the scourge of neoliberalism: Rethinking higher education as a democratic public sphere. *The Educational Forum*, 74: 184–96.

Goodley, D, Lawthom, R, Cough, P and Moore, M (2004) *Researching Life Stories*. London: RoutledgeFalmer.

Hart, S, Dixon, A, Drummond, MJ and McIntyre, D (2004) *Learning Without Limits*. Maidenhead: Open University Press.

Hodkinson, A (2011) Illusionary inclusion – what went wrong with New Labour's landmark educational policy? *British Journal Special Education*, 28(1): 4–11.

Kellet, M with original research contributions by young people with a learning disability: Allan Aoslin, Ross Baines, Alice Clancy, Lizzie Jewiss-Hayden, Ryan Singh and Josh Strudgwick (2010) WeCan2: exploring the implications of young people with learning disabilities engaging in their own research. *European Journal of Special Needs Education*, 25(1): 31–44.

Kershner, R (2007) What do teachers need to know about meeting SEN? in Florian, L (ed) *The Sage Handbook of Special Education*. London: Sage.

Larner, W (2000) Neo-liberalism: policy, ideology, governmentality. *Studies in Political Economy,* 63, Autumn 2000, 5–25.

Ledwith, M (2005) *Community Development: A critical approach*. Bristol: The Policy Press.

Liasidou, A (2012) *Inclusive Education, Politics and Policymaking*. London: Continuum.

Miles, S and Ainscow, M (2011) *Responding to Diversity in Schools*. London: Routledge.

Mittler, P (2000) *Working Towards Inclusive Education: Social contexts*. London: David Fulton Press.

Porter, J, Daniels, H, Feiler, A and Georgeson, J (2011) Recognising the needs of every disabled child: the development of tools for a disability census. *British Journal of Special Education*, 38(3): 120–25.

Potts, P (1982) *Special Needs in Education*. Milton Keynes: Open University Press.

Richards, G and Armstrong, F (2011) *Teaching and Learning in Diverse and Inclusive Classrooms*. London: Routledge.

Robertson, C (2012) Special educational needs and disability co-ordination in a changing policy landscape: making sense of policy from a SENCO's perspective. *Support for Learning,* 27(2): 77–83.

Royal School for the Blind Liverpool. [Online] Available at: **www.rsblind.com/#/history/ 4559365884** (accessed 3 April 2013).

Runswick-Cole, K (2011) Time to end the bias towards inclusive education? *British Journal Special Education*, 38(3): 112–19.

Runswick-Cole, K and Hodge, N (2009), Needs or rights? A challenge to the discourse of special education. *British Journal of Special Education*, 36(4): 198–203.

Schonell, F (1924) *Backwardness in the Basic Subjects*. London: Oliver and Boyd.

Sebba, J and Sachdev, D (1997) *What works in Inclusive Education?* Ilford: Barnardo.

Shaw, M (2008) Warnock calls for a rethink. *Times Education Supplement* [Online]. Available at: **www.tes.co.uk/article.aspx?storycode=384105** (accessed 10 March 2013).

Strogilos, V (2012) The cultural understandings of inclusion and its development within a centralised system. *International Journal of Inclusive Education,* 16(12): 1241–58.

Thomas, G and Vaughan, M (2004) *Inclusive Education: Readings and reflections*. Maidenhead: Open University Press.

Tomlinson, S (1982) *A Sociology of Special Education*. London: Routledge.

United Nations Education Science and Cultural Organisation (UNESCO) (1994) *World Conference on Special Needs Education: Access and Quality*. Paris: UNESCO.

Warnock, M (1978) *Report of the Committee of Enquiry into the Education of Handicapped Children and Young People*. London: Her Majesty's Stationery Office.

Warnock, M (2005) *Special Educational Needs – a new look*. London: PESGB, Impact Series N.11.

Warnock, M and Norwich, B (2010) *Special Educational Needs – a new look*. London: Continuum.

## Further reading

Arnot, M (2012) (ed) *Sociology of Disability and Inclusive Education: A Tribute to Len Barton*. London: Routledge.

Elkins, A (2012) *The Changing Face of Special Educational Needs*. London: Routledge.

Liasidou, A (2012) *Inclusive Education, Politics and Policymaking*. London: Continuum.

Richards, G and Armstrong, F (2011) *Teaching and Learning in Diverse and Inclusive Classrooms*. London: Routledge.

# Chapter 16

# Faith in education

## Kate Adams and Mark Chater

### Introduction

The education system in the UK has a long established, but rapidly changing, presence of faith communities in schools, manifested in multi-faith classrooms as well as publicly funded schools with a faith foundation. This chapter enables readers to pose and explore questions about that presence and how it impacts on pupils, teachers and other educational professionals. The chapter explores: the role of Religious Education (RE) in the curriculum, the growth of faith schools and the implications of their aims and the legal requirement to promote children's spiritual development across the curriculum. It considers possible ways to secure an appropriate place for the presence of faith in education.

## Religious Education: a British export

Nearly unique among the educational jurisdictions of the world, the UK offers a model of Religious Education that embraces religious and philosophical diversity and promotes positive attitudes and skills. RE has evolved into an academic subject with its own educational justification and is protected by legislation that pre-dates the national curriculum (DCSF, 2010). The main features of RE are that it:

- should be taught by all state schools, whether academies, local authority schools or faith schools;
- should be taught to all year groups and pupils from age 5 to 18, except those whose parents wish to withdraw them;
- sits outside the national curriculum, allowing local authorities and faith school authorities to devise their own syllabus;
- can be inspected by Ofsted, although different arrangements pertain for faith schools.

Beneath these arrangements there lies considerable diversity of rationale and method. RE is understood differently, depending on school context. It might be a form of faith nurture, or an objective study of beliefs and practices, or a vehicle for promoting social harmony, or a context for exploring spirituality, meaning and values. The failure to make clear choices between these competing rationales is noted as a weakness in inspections (Ofsted, 2010), leading to muddled teacher understanding, compromised planning and low standards in a significant number of lessons. Inside this 'big tent' of RE is an assumption that the subject needs to hang together and to fudge or hide its internal differences. It has also been argued that RE has a major identity problem and will only raise its game if it clarifies its educational purposes (Chater and Erricker, 2013).

The dominant model of RE is expressed in two government documents for England: the national framework (QCA/DfES, 2004) and the guidance (DCSF, 2010). Between them, these documents advocate an open, critical approach that explores principal religions (Buddhism, Christianity, Hinduism, Islam, Judaism and Sikhism) as well as smaller religious communities (Baha'i, Jain and Zoroastrian) and secular world views such as humanism. This breadth of study is widely taken up in resources (Culham St Gabriel's, 2013) and, when taught well, is a popular subject for pupils, who recognise its capacity to raise challenging questions for debate and to promote positive attitudes to diversity (NATRE, 2011). This type of RE is also of growing interest in several European countries where pupil feedback strongly underlines the importance to young people of having forums in which beliefs can be explored with respect, and post-9/11 attitudes or stereotypes can be critically addressed (Jackson, 2011). The model of England and Wales, though not without flaws, has been imitated in different jurisdictions with considerable success. The flaws lie in the relationship between law, curriculum design and classroom practice.

# Faith schools

The place of religion in the public sphere is currently a subject of widespread and vigorous debate in the UK and other western developed nations. From the BBC's *Thought for the Day* to the right of nurses to wear religious symbols at work, and other instances, lively questioning about the public role of religious commitment and the place of religious organisations in the constitution or the public sector is evident. There are some who argue that the long-term tide of secularisation is continuing, that Britain is becoming less and less religious and that the privileged place accorded to religion should be questioned. On the other hand, there are arguments that Britain is less secular than it seems, that forms of profound religious belief continue under the surface, and therefore that religious discourse and reasoning ought to have its place, visible in public, and not relegated to private piety.

In the context of this ongoing debate, the place of religion in education is similarly discussed, ranging over wide territory but usually settling on three specific contested items:

- whether churches and other religious groups should have the right to run schools and academies in the state sector, and if so, how their admissions policies should be framed to ensure fairness;
- whether religious state schools should be exempt from discrimination legislation, e.g. in relation to religion or to sexual orientation;
- whether collective worship, as currently prescribed in law, has a place in state schools.

'Faith schools' – a shorthand term for state schools which are recognised in law as having a religious ethos – have grown proportionately over the last decade. Among the 20,000 maintained schools other than academies and free schools, there are 7,000 faith schools. Among academics (counted in 2011 – anecdotally the figure has grown since then) faith schools total 91 out of 629 (DfE, 2013). Among applicants to start up a free school, one quarter were religious organisations (BBC, 2013). The largest provider of faith schools is the Church of England, with 4,677 schools in England (Church of England, 2013). The rapid growth of the faith school sector in state-provided education has proved controversial. Some opponents have raised concerns about segregation and have argued that separate faith schools hold back efforts at community cohesion. A Home Office report argued that faith schools contribute significantly to divisions within communities, where people live parallel lives (Cantle, 2001). Barry Sheerman MP, when Chair of the Commons Education Select Committee, gave voice to this view just as the rapid expansion was beginning:

*Do we want a ghettoised education system? Schools play a crucial role in integrating different communities, and the growth of faith schools poses a real threat to this.*

(Taylor, 2005)

Others have seen faith schools as an expression of choice, a positive commitment to diversity and (in the case of Church of England schools, which form by far the largest group) an expression of the Church's commitment to a diverse society. In its latest thinking, the Church of England reaffirms its commitment to admissions policies that serve *the local community as well as Christian families* (Chadwick, 2012, p.16) and to providing excellent and effective schools *not merely because the government says so [but also because] the enabling of every child to flourish in their potential as a child of God ... is at the heart of the Church's distinctive mission* (op. cit., p.3).

The Runnymede Trust's extensive research into the impact of faith schools led it to recommend that, while they should not be abolished, selection on the basis of faith was problematic and in too many schools was a surrogate for other factors such as class, ethnicity or educational success:

*At the moment, faith can be used by parents as a means of ensuring exclusivity within a school ... cohesion was not considered to be important ... Too often, there remains a resistance to learning about other faiths.*

(Berkeley, 2008, p.4)

Berkeley suggested that faith schools should be opened up to the whole community. He concluded that *faith should continue to play an important role in our education system, offering diversity ... as a means of improving standards, offering choice to parents and developing effective responses to local, national and global challenges in education* (op. cit., p.68).

The term 'faith schools', while convenient, obscures the reality that there are at least three different types. First, those that cater for their own faith; an Islamic school, for example, is a school mostly for Muslims. Second, those schools, mostly Church of England, that cater for the whole community as an expression of a church's national role. A third is a more recent type of school, with a religious ethos but with a completely open admissions policy. It is a model taken by some new Church of England academies and the Oasis Academies, for example.

In the English system, parental choice is an additional, complicating factor. In the marketisation of education, all mainstream political parties have prioritised parental choice and diversification among schools, which in practice has made school ethos a political issue. Choice in relation to the curriculum has led to increasing expectation that any aspect of school life with the potential to give offence, or to compromise the right of an individual or group to express their beliefs, can and should be optional. Human rights case law and the Toledo Principles (OSCE, 2007) have reinforced the assumption that schools ought to respect the religious identities and preferences of all pupils, even when that means being flexible over some compulsory elements of the curriculum such as sex education.

Although the Toledo Principles have no force of law in the UK or any other jurisdiction, they are an authoritative interpretation of case law and are gaining recognition as a model of good practice. Coupled with them is the force of arguments: for example, Cooling (2011) defends the rationality of religious belief and discourse, and suggests the irrationality of outlawing them from educational settings. Cooling approaches this defence from a Christian starting point, but attends with seriousness to the problem of how all religious and non-religious beliefs can work alongside each other in education. His appeal is to a specifically Christian 'anthropology' (op. cit., p.11), which offers legitimate principles underpinning teaching and learning.

However, in some cases the expectations of religious groups have outstripped the state's power or willingness to accommodate them. In its guidance for schools, the Muslim Council of Britain (2007) underscores the legal right of parents to withdraw their child from RE or collective worship, but also heightens expectations that schools can and will have, for example, a uniform policy that *includes the particular dress requirements of Muslim pupils* (op.cit. p.22). The guidance also suggests that Muslim parents can negotiate favourable conditions for swimming, drama and some other curriculum areas: *Provided these guidelines are adhered to, there should be no reason why Muslim children should be withdrawn* (op. cit., p.38). The implication of these expectations is that school curriculum and pedagogical provision should be almost limitlessly flexible in response to the preferences of religious groups, including minorities.

If the education system and its political leaders are ambivalent and divided about faith schools, it is also fair to say that religions are ambivalent and divided about education. In the west, the commitment of the various churches to education dates back to the earliest times of the historical development of Christianity, and includes the early development of pedagogical and child development perspectives. In all three western majority faiths, Judaism, Christianity and Islam, a strong commitment to intellectual enquiry is evident through works of philosophy, jurisprudence, economics, technology and ethics, all inspired by theology in the earliest universities of Baghdad, Bologna, Paris and Oxford. The same commitment led churches in nineteenth-century England to open schools for the poor as an expression of their sense of mission in response to the industrial revolution. With the schools came church teacher training colleges, many of them now universities with a Christian foundation and a particular commitment to education.

However, faith-based critiques of education voice concern that national education systems have lost sight of their spiritual and moral goals in a preoccupation with skills, employability, functional outcomes and learning for its own sake. In the case of minority religious communities, a fear of absorption and loss of identity has been a factor in their ambivalence towards schools and the curriculum. The impulse to conserve traditional cultures and values can be observed in strategies such as separate religious and moral teaching or distant and suspicious attitudes to the local state community school. However, it would be a mistake to conclude that all minority communities wish to separate themselves and their children from state education. The reality is more complex. For example, Muslims have both praise and criticism for British education and the society that evolved it, and they have differing response strategies in education, family life and politics. For example, Maurice Irfan Coles, a British Muslim, challenges his fellow Muslims to engage positively with the outcomes of Every Child Matters, particularly concerning health, educational progress and making a positive contribution (Coles, 2008).

Another cause of religion's ambivalence toward western education lies in the religious extremism and fundamentalism that exists on the margins of every major religion. Several characteristics of global fundamentalism set it in direct conflict with the aims of western education. Belief in the literal truth of sacred texts, even when they clash with scientific evidence, has led some groups to question the science national curriculum and to teach creationism or intelligent design. An appeal to total faith in one unquestionable leader or text sits awkwardly with education's interest in critical enquiry and independent thinking skills.

Historically and still today, principal religions balance their commitment to education with their need to conserve their identities and beliefs. While this conservation is evident through ethos and Religious Education, identities and beliefs are also a component of another aspect of the curriculum: spiritual development.

# The spiritual development of children

As well as the obligation to teach Religious Education, all schools are required by law to promote the spiritual, moral, social and cultural (SMSC) development of children throughout the curriculum. Schools were first obliged to promote spiritual development by the Education Reform Act 1988, and shortly after, in 1992, it became a focus for inspection by the Office for Standards in Education (Ofsted). Recently, Ofsted (2011) reaffirmed that schools' provision of SMSC will be a focus in inspections of all maintained schools and academies. However, while the requirements to promote spiritual development are clear, there are significant conceptual and practical difficulties which make this component of SMSC particularly complex. In this section we explore some of the issues which make spirituality the least well understood of the four components, and we encourage you to begin to formulate your own views on this important cross-curricular theme.

One of the most fundamental complexities of promoting spiritual development is confusion over the definition of spirituality itself. Academics have long debated its meaning with reference to education and continue to do so. While the definition of many aspects of wider curriculum topics and concepts is relatively straightforward, this is not the case with the spiritual. For example, Brown and Furlong (1996, p.4) described spirituality as a *weasel word … a convenient catch-all, suitably vague and elusive of definition*. Best (2000, p.10) goes further to suggest that the greater the attempts to define spirituality, the more elusive a definition becomes. These authors' comments are particularly pertinent, but may offer little comfort for teachers faced with their obligation to address it in the classroom. Before considering the possible meaning of the spiritual in more depth, it is worth exploring your own definitions of spirituality.

---

***Pause for thought*** | what is spirituality?

Consider answers to the following questions, ideally with colleagues: Would you describe yourself as a spiritual person? If not, who do you know of who could be described in this way? How can the spiritual dimension of the person be described to a Martian who has landed on Earth? Discuss these issues with your colleagues and consider the variety of answers that you have collected. Are there common themes? Are there significant differences? How can those differences be accounted for?

Many people throughout history have claimed to have had a spiritual experience. Have you? If so, how would you describe it? What was it that made the experience a *spiritual* one, rather than one which might be described as purely emotional or psychological?

---

It is likely that differences in opinions among you and your colleagues have arisen, potentially making consensus difficult. For example, did religion enter into the discussion? In an earlier document, Ofsted (1994) stated that, for the purposes of education, religion and spirituality were not synonymous. Later, they noted that any definition of spiritual had *to be acceptable to people of faith, people of no faith, and people of different faiths* (Ofsted, 2004, p.4). Similarly, other authors including Hart (2003), Hay and Nye (2006) and Hyde (2008) argue that spirituality is innate and thus not dependent upon a faith stance. However, such a view is contested, with others arguing that spirituality can only be taught in the context of a faith tradition (e.g. Thatcher, 1999).

As Castelli and Trevathan (2005) observe, many argue that it is unrealistic to expect schools to ensure children's spiritual development when there is no consensus over its definition. In order to assist teachers, Ofsted published further guidance in order to clarify the position for schools. In their most recent publication, Ofsted (2011, p.23) states that pupils' spiritual development is shown by their:

- beliefs, religious or otherwise, which inform their perspective on life and their interest in and respect for different people's feelings and values;
- sense of enjoyment and fascination in learning about themselves, others and the world around them, including the intangible;
- use of imagination and creativity in their learning;
- willingness to reflect on their experiences.

Further elucidation for teachers also comes from academics who discuss the characteristics of spirituality, which offers a more rounded overview of what spirituality may be and how it may be described, rather than trying to achieve a hard and fast, inclusive definition. For example, a common theme arising is the centrality of relationships (Champagne, 2001; Hay and Nye, 2006). Authors tend to categorise these in different ways but often refer to relationships with the self, with others, with the transcendent and/or with the world. Linked to the notion of relationships is identity, as children come to learn who they are and understand and negotiate their place in the world (Scott, 2004; Adams et al., 2008). 'Awe and wonder' is a common example of spirituality expressed in the classroom as children make new discoveries through their learning (Hart, 2003).

### Research box

## children's spirituality

Research into children's accounts of their spirituality suggests that spiritual experiences can play an important role in their lives, helping to shape their ideas and beliefs. For example, Scott (2004) gathered adults' recollections of spiritual experiences from childhood, demonstrating that some make a life-long impact. Such experiences may or may not have a religious element. Children have, for example, reported: seeing angels; seeing deceased friends, relatives or pets; seeing auras around people; and experiencing intense feelings of 'being at one' with nature (Hart, 2003). In other studies, children have reported dreams which had a spiritual impact (Adams, 2010), and finding comfort after the death of a much loved dog in the belief that the pet had been reincarnated into a neighbour's new puppy (Hyde, 2008). While some experiences are likely to be dismissed by many as children's imagination, it is important to bear in mind that what is meaningful to one person, often confirming, shaping or altering their worldviews, would be meaningless to another. A key conclusion arising from these studies is that it is essential that school staff are respectful of children's interpretations and meaning-making, even if the children's views contradict their own.

Importantly, spirituality is not simply about the positive aspects of human flourishing. It is also about the challenging and difficult times which children encounter in their lives, times which can frighten and shake worldviews, all of which children need to make sense of (Adams, 2010).

# Faith in education: new paradigms for an old relationship

Whether or not faith schools are justifiable is not the issue under discussion here. This is a major debate which is dealt with elsewhere. (See Gardner et al., 2004, for arguments both for and against faith schools.) Rather, this chapter's conclusions work on the basis that faith schools exist, and that there are increasing numbers of multi-faith communities within non-denominational schools and other educational settings.

In all schools, the coverage of religions must go beyond Christianity. In addition, the five other main religions which are represented in Great Britain must also be covered across the key stages. As noted above, these are:

- Islam;
- Judaism;
- Buddhism;
- Sikhism;
- Hinduism.

For some pupils, teachers and parents, particularly those with a strongly exclusive commitment to a faith, this may pose difficulties. Naturally, for some (though not all) devout religious people, the process of engaging with different religious beliefs may pose difficulties. Learning about different points of view can be uncomfortable, even painful, perhaps leading to reflection on one's own beliefs which may have been held for a lifetime.

However, the process of becoming a reflective practitioner is fundamental to an educator's job. As Pollard (2002) writes, it is essential that teachers are fully aware of their own identity. He encourages teachers to reflect upon different aspects of themselves, including how they appear to others, their values, aims and commitments, and their perceptions of pupils. Given that religious beliefs – in addition to atheistic or agnostic views – form part of a person's identity, it is inevitable that teachers will have to confront other people's views. This can occur in the course of either teaching about religions and beliefs in a variety of educational settings or in conversations with members of faith communities in other contexts.

Most teachers would agree that children should be encouraged to:

- listen to others' views;
- reflect on their own views;
- engage in debate with others;
- respect others' views.

This cannot happen by accident, and happens most effectively when *teachers* model an openness to diversity, an enquiring approach, willingness to ask critical or empathetic questions and respect for identity and experience. Where teachers feel insecure, for example in their knowledge of religious beliefs and practices, they can seek professional development. It may be helpful to realise that, while striving to be objective is praiseworthy, in fact no one can be objective about the world of religions and beliefs in which they themselves live: even the recounting of simple 'facts' can be open to question.

Enquiry into a range of opinions and beliefs, conducted with integrity and in an environment of respect, probably offers the best chance to protect young people from extremism and prepare them for adult life in a diverse and surprising world.

**Summary and conclusions**

The place of faith communities in the education system, particularly through the contested notion of faith schools, is an ongoing issue which requires recognition of the complexities inherent in it. Likewise, the legal obligations to teach Religious Education and to promote children's spiritual development are not necessarily straightforward. However, through an appropriate education which actively encourages open enquiry into the nature and impact of religion and belief, children and young people can be supported in becoming critically reflective thinkers who can make informed judgements about such matters. All pupils can then be given the opportunity to raise views about faith in an ethos of open enquiry.

# *References*

Adams, K (2010) *Unseen Worlds: Looking through the lens of childhood*. London: Jessica Kingsley.

Adams, K, Hyde, B and Woolley, R (2008) *The Spiritual Dimension of Childhood*. London: Jessica Kingsley.

BBC (2013) Free school applicants' religious affiliation revealed. London: BBC, 21 February 2013. Available at: **www.bbc.co.uk/news/education-2152016** (accessed 8 March 2013).

Berkeley, R (2008) *Right to Divide? Faith Schools and community cohesion*. London: Runnymede Trust.

Best, R (2000) (ed) *Education for Spiritual, Moral, Social and Cultural Development*. London: Continuum.

Brown, A and Furlong, J (1996) *Spiritual Development in Schools*. London: The National Society.

Cantle, T (2001) *Community Cohesion: A report of the independent review team*. London: Home Office.

Castelli, M and Trevathan, A (2005) The English public space: developing spirituality in English Muslim schools. *The International Journal of Children's Spirituality,* 10(2): 123–31.

Chadwick, P (2012) *The Church School of the Future*. London: Archbishops' Council Education Division.

Champagne, E (2001) Listening to…listening for…: A theological reflection on spirituality in early childhood, in Erricker, J, Ota, C and Erricker, C (eds) *Spiritual Education. Cultural, Religious and Social Differences, New Perspectives for the 21st Century*. Brighton: Sussex Academic.

Chater, M and Erricker, C (2013) *Does Religious Education have a Future?* Abingdon: Routledge.

Church of England (2013) *The National Society*. London: Church House. Available at: **www.churchofengland.org/education/national-society.aspx** (accessed 8 March 2013).

Coles, M (2008) *Every Muslim Child Matters*. Stoke on Trent: Trentham Books.

Cooling, T (2011) *Is God Redundant in the Classroom?* Canterbury: Canterbury Christ Church University.

Culham St Gabriel's (2013) *RE: ONLINE*. Available at: **www.reonline.org.uk** (accessed 24 March 2013).

DCSF (2010) *Religious Education in English schools: Non-statutory guidance*. London: DCSF. Available at: **www.education.gov.uk/schools/teachingandlearning/curriculum/a0064886/religious-education-in-english-schools-non-statutory-guidance-2010** (accessed 8 March 2013).

DfE (2013) *Faith Schools*. London: DfE. Available at: **www.education.gov.uk/schools/leadership/typesofschools/b0066996/faith-schools** (accessed 8 March 2013).

Gardner, R, Cairns, J and Lawton, D (2004) *Faith Schools: Consensus or conflict*. London: Routledge.

Hart, T (2003) *The Secret Spiritual World of Children*. Maui: Inner Ocean.

Hay, D and Nye, R (2006) *The Spirit of the Child*. London: Fount.

Hyde, B (2008) *Children and Spirituality, Searching for Meaning and Connectedness*. London: Jessica Kingsley.

Jackson, R (2011) (ed) *Religion, Education, Dialogue and Conflict: Perspectives on Religious Education research*. Abingdon: Routledge.

Muslim Council of Britain (2007) *Meeting the Needs of Muslim Pupils in State Schools: Information and guidance for schools*. London: MCB.

NATRE (2011) *What do you know about RE?* Available at: **www.natre.org.uk/explore/video. php?id=48** (accessed 24 March 2013).

Ofsted (1994) *Spiritual, Moral, Social and Cultural Development: An Ofsted discussion paper*. London: Ofsted.

Ofsted (2004) *Promoting and Evaluating Pupils' Spiritual, Moral, Social and Cultural Development*. London: Ofsted.

Ofsted (2010) *Transforming Religious Education*. London: Ofsted.

Ofsted (2011) *Subsidiary Guidance: Supporting the inspection of maintained schools and academies from January 2012*. London: Ofsted.

OSCE (2007) *Toledo Guiding Principles on Teaching about Religions and Beliefs in Public Schools*. Warsaw: OSCE Office for Democratic Institutions and Human Rights. Available at: **www.osce.org/odihr/29154** (accessed 8 March 2013).

Pollard, A (2002) *Reflective Teaching*. London: Continuum.

QCA/DfES (2004) *Religious Education: The non-statutory national framework*. London: QCA and DfES.

Scott, D (2004) Retrospective spiritual narratives: exploring recalled childhood and adolescent spiritual experiences. *International Journal of Children's Spirituality*, 9(1): 67–79.

Taylor, M (2005) Two thirds oppose state aided faith schools. The *Guardian,* 23 August 2005. Available at: **www.guardian.co.uk/uk/2005/aug/23/schools.faithschools** (accessed 8 March 2013).

Thatcher, A (1999) (ed) *Spirituality and the Curriculum*. London: Cassell.

# Chapter 17

# Education for citizenship and democracy

## Howard Gibson

### Introduction

In 1998, under the guidance of Professor Bernard Crick, an Advisory Group on Citizenship issued its report on *Education for Citizenship and the Teaching of Democracy in Schools* (QCA, 1998). The outcome of this report was the introduction of citizenship education to primary-aged pupils from September 2000, and to secondary pupils from September 2002. Crick had concluded that there were three principal strands of the citizenship curriculum: social and moral responsibility, community involvement, and political literacy. The third of these, political literacy or education for democracy, has had less attention than other aspects of citizenship education and Crick later acknowledged that his committee's recommendations for teaching politics were limited. This chapter looks at different issues associated with democracy and examines the causes of political apathy in young people. There is a critique of the assumptions made by the Crick Report, which fail to recognise the power and influence of the media and the diminished role of the state in the global economy. An alternative curriculum is suggested which, through such areas as media studies, would make pupils aware of the constructed nature of political discourse and encourage them to engage in political action.

## What does democracy mean?

The origin of the word democracy lies in the Greek *demos*, meaning 'people in a community'. The ending '...ocracy', from the Greek *kratos*, meaning 'power' or 'strength', implies rule. So democracy is about the rule of the people. However, going to a dictionary to find an authentic definition doesn't always work, for in so doing meaning is invariably compressed and practical complexities sequestered. For example, some might say that democracy should involve having a parliament. But while the United States of America claims to be democratic, for example, it has no parliament (although it does have two elected legislative assemblies). Perhaps democracy has nothing to do with an institutional name but with having the right to vote for who represents you in that institution, in which case a more direct form of democracy might be appropriate, such as voting via the web. It might be argued that, instead of representative parliamentary democracy, where a party is elected for a period of time to make decisions, there should be a referendum where citizens vote on all the big issues as they come along. There are also worries about democracy when it can allow minority racist parties, such as that of Le Pen in France, to gain representation and influence.

There are also problems with how democracy is implemented. General Pervez Musharraf, who carried out a military coup in Pakistan in October 1999, declared he was instituting:

*... not martial law, only another path to democracy. The armed forces have no intention to stay in charge any longer than is absolutely necessary to pave the way for true democracy to flourish in Pakistan ... what Pakistan has experienced in recent years has merely been a label of democracy, not the essence of it ... I shall not allow the people to be taken back to the era of sham democracy but to a true one.*

(Goldenberg, 1999)

It might be argued that states with military rulers are more effective than democratically elected governments. There is also a question as to whether we have a true democracy when members of the public have the right to participate in an election but do not bother to vote.

In 1997, for example, Labour was elected by only 31 per cent of those qualified to vote. In 1932, Hitler's Nazi Party came to power in Germany with 37 per cent support among the democratic electorate. In 2010 Britain's first coalition government since the Second World War came to power. If this is indicative of the effects of the rise of smaller third parties, then it could destabilise the tradition of two-party contests and lead to more hung parliaments or coalition governments in the future. The problem for democracy is that while coalitions may be legal, and common in countries like Italy, they leave worries about their legitimacy when policies promised by parties before elections are ignored when in office. Nick Clegg, for example, the leader of the Liberal Democrats and currently Deputy Prime Minister, pledged that his party would not raise university students' fees before the election, but as part of the Coalition government performed a *volte-face* and eventually apologised to the electorate for his change of mind: *We made a pledge, we did not stick to it, and for that I am sorry* (Clegg, 2010). For these reasons, some question whether democracy is always a good thing. It is not easy to talk about democracy with clarity, let alone define it. Saward (2003) has summed up the issue well when he suggests that it is *an enormously rich, suggestive, evocative political term, and it is partly this fact that makes it such a potential political weapon* (p.9).

# Democracy and the curriculum

While a clear definition of democracy is not easy to give, from the Crick Report (QCA, 1998) and the curriculum documentation for citizenship education we get glimpses of how it is represented.

- *Participation*. There is a concern for the problem of apathy and dwindling commitment of young people in political life and the need to reverse this lack of interest and engagement. These worrying levels of apathy, ignorance and cynicism about public life need to be tackled at every level.
- *Communication*. There is a need to communicate views and opinions and engage in open discussion with others. Talk or discourse is obviously fundamental to active citizenship. Thus, to the need for pupils to participate in their community and become active in politics, we can now add the important skill of learning how to debate and engage with others.
- *Rule of law*. There is the requirement for members of a democratic community to obey the law. The assumption is that once debate has progressed sufficiently and decisions reached, however unpopular they may be with some individuals, the rule of law should apply. Respect for the rule of law is a necessary condition of social order and a necessary component of education.

But this apparently self-evident account of what democracy is, and how schools should prepare pupils for it, is both questionable and contentious.

> **Pause for thought** | political apathy
>
> Political apathy is said to be a key problem for democracies and one of the reasons for citizenship becoming mandatory in primary and secondary schools in England. However, while the government's response has been to emphasise the need to increase participation by encouraging the democratic involvement of pupils in school councils and the like, an alternative could have been to investigate why British democracy might be producing apathetic citizens and what consequences this might have for the teaching of citizenship in schools. Discuss political apathy with friends and colleagues. Do you think it really exists? Do you vote yourself, or take an active part in politics at any level? Why are governments interested in the political views of a nation's youth?

# Participation

The claim about the need for more commitment and participation is unconvincing because, although it rails against the problem of apathy, it fails to examine the historical decline of political commitment and ignores the huge changes to the nation state in recent years. These have come primarily from the effects of globalisation.

- The idea of national autonomy, which used to define the democratic state, can no longer be assumed.
- Cultural pluralism and multiple identities in societies present complex challenges for national governments.
- The inability of states to deal with global problems, such as the environment, inequality and poverty makes them appear ineffective and powerless.

These are some of the issues that affect modern democracies and which may account for apathy. James Anderson (2002) has described the stark effects of globalisation on national democracies:

*Globalisation is putting democracy in question and is itself being questioned as undemocratic. Its border crossings are undermining the traditional territorial basis of democracy and creating new political spaces which need democratising. 'Global forces' are disrupting the supposedly independent, sovereign states and national communities which have provided democracy's main framework. And these 'global forces' are apparently beyond control or, more specifically, beyond democratic control. The political implications are wide reaching and far from clear ... National democracy's problems are experienced most immediately in perception that the national state is losing its sovereignty to 'outside' bodies and is being infiltrated by them. Actions taken in or by other states are having increasing impact on supposedly 'sovereign' neighbours. State electorates are more directly affected by decisions made in other jurisdictions, including supra-state bodies like the EU. Private multinational corporations have become more powerful, and foreign-owned ones may determine the success or otherwise of national economies. States are losing some of their autonomy, as power 'goes upwards' to other, supra-state, political institutions, 'sideways' to privatised operations, or in some respects 'goes nowhere' or just 'evaporates', as economics outruns politics and political control is simply lost to the global market.*

(pp.6–9)

By putting much of the decision-making processes beyond the borders of individual countries, there has been a decline in the economic, political and social effectiveness of the national state. As private multinational corporations have become more powerful they have affected the success or otherwise of national economies. Hertz (2001) went so far as to suggest that modern democracies are now resigned to the fact that multinationals are taking the place of elected governments and that shopping may be now more effective than voting: *This is the world of the Silent Takeover … Governments' hands are tied and we are increasingly dependent on corporations* (p.7). Since the Thatcher era of government in the 1980s, 'rolling back the state' has been policy in the UK, relaxing regulation on business and encouraging private health care and education. Bottery (2003) has argued that a consequence is the undermining of loyalty to the state. Put another way, as the nation state's influence on its citizens withers, so does their allegiance to it.

Democratic theory, from Locke to Rousseau and Bentham to Mill, has always been vigilant in separating the public from the private realm, and liberal democracies have tended to preserve free market economies. Within the walls of a factory or beyond a nation's borders can be found the economic freedoms for individuals to innovate, produce, market and sell.

The point for democracies is this, while those economic freedoms that accompany capitalism whet consumers' appetites for more products, dealing with the less pleasant by-products, such as global warming, becomes problematic. To reduce global warming, for example, it might be considered sensible to reduce dramatically the use of private motor vehicles (though the link remains subject to intense scientific debate), but a government which does this will probably not be elected the next time round. A democratically elected government finds it difficult to limit the freedom of its voters.

### Research box

### market sovereignty or democracy?

The historian Eric Hobsbawm (2001) has argued that *democracy can be bad for you* and that the market and democracy are mutually exclusive. Is he right?

*Market sovereignty is not a complement to liberal democracy; it is an alternative to it. Indeed, it is an alternative to any kind of politics, as it denies the need for political decisions, which are precisely decisions about common or group interests as distinct from the sum of choices, rational or otherwise, of individuals pursuing private preferences. Participation in the market replaces participation in politics. The consumer takes the place of the citizen … [We] face an age when the impact of human action on nature and the globe has become a force of geological proportions. Their solution, or mitigation, will require measures for which, almost certainly, no support will be found by counting votes or measuring consumer preferences. This is not encouraging for the long-term prospects of either democracy or the globe.*

(p.26)

Because of colonisation, globalisation and increasing mobility, many citizens within national states now have multiple identities. One can, for example, be a UK citizen, British, a Muslim, a member of the EU, have a commitment to another country by birth or marriage, and so on. The state today is plural and diverse and no longer consists of a single people. In consequence, according to Parekh (2002), the state *cannot claim to embody and legitimate itself in terms of [its inhabitants'] sense of collective identity either, both because many of them no longer place much emphasis on their national identity or privilege it over their other identities, and because some of them increasingly cherish trans-national ties and identities*. The publication of Salman Rushdie's *Satanic Verses* in 1988, for example, produced a strong reaction from some members of the Muslim community and led to a conflict which lies at the heart of modern democracies: freedom of speech versus blasphemy.

Such issues as these place great pressure on democratic governments. It was suggested earlier that the citizenship education curriculum (QCA, 1998) recognises the need to engender participation and commitment to counter the alienation and cynicism of the young, but it skirts around the causes. To say that 'trust in society's core institutions has been falling steadily' does not explain the phenomenon. Given the complexity of issues attending globalisation, including the expansion of corporate capitalism, the withering power of the nation state, the proximity within single nations of people with diverse and sometimes conflicting identities, it seems reasonable to explain dwindling participation not simply in terms of individual apathy but in recognition of the challenges that face modern, complex democracies.

---

***Pause for thought*** | spin, sleaze and political apathy

It is sometimes argued that voter apathy is the consequence of spin and the so-called 'dumbing-down' of modern political life. In Britain, examples of political sleaze are easy to come by and you can use the internet to remind yourself. You might research the questions that arose about the legality of the 2003 war with Iraq. Allegations about lies in political life and the spoon-feeding of the public with sound bites all perhaps contribute to political apathy. Pupils' trust in politics and politicians remains constantly at 'low levels' according to attitude surveys (Cleaver et al., 2005). Furedi (2004) has suggested that the government's response to such claims has only reduced its credibility:

*Apathy and disengagement breed both anti-political and apolitical reactions. The political class is aware of this: but instead of attempting to address the underlying malaise and disillusionment through developing challenging political ideals that could inspire the electorate to vote, its response has been to acquiesce in dumbing down.*

(p.80)

It might be argued that rather than instead of merely reminding young citizens of their duty to participate in their local community or to become more charitable (QCA, 1998), there should be a curriculum that attempts to explain the complex causes of apathy and the actions of government. What do you think?

---

# Communication skills

Earlier it was suggested that political literacy or the education for democracy component of the citizenship education curriculum emphasises debate and discussion: *Talk or discourse is obviously fundamental to active citizenship ... [because] open and informed debate is vital for a healthy democracy*. For some, echoing John Stuart Mill (1806–73), free communication is one of the central pillars of liberal democracy. For Mill (1969) there was no test for the adequacy of a claim to a good idea or 'truth' other than the force of better public argument: put your idea on the table, await critical scrutiny, argue your case when challenged, but be prepared to accede to new and better ideas.

However, while Mill's rationale for open and free communication seems convincing in theory, in practice it is a different matter because powers of communication are not equally distributed. In the real world, media-moguls have the power to persuade and to influence the views of others. As Karl Marx argued, the free exchange of ideas may be good in principle but, when tied to the market and the free exchange of commodities, the reality of freedom becomes illusory for the majority of ordinary people. Habermas (1972) similarly warned against *the fiction that Socratic dialogue is possible everywhere and at any time*. To put it simply, liberal democratic philosophy presupposes the existence of the very sense of community that dialogue is intended to develop and, in so doing, overlooks the reality that debate rarely takes place on a level playing field.

In the citizenship education curriculum, discussion is not problematised and the term 'communication' is preferred, portraying debate as if it were a content-free skill (see Cameron, 2000). It presents classroom discourse as if it should mimic the procedures of debates that go on outside – in Parliament, in town councils, between parties and the electorate, and so on. This failure to acknowledge the power structures that determine or distort free communication has two main consequences for citizenship and democracy.

- Political activity is always 'mediated'. Political issues are most often communicated to us via television, radio or newspaper and so we need to understand how media discourses are constructed. Understanding the media is fundamental to an understanding of politics, as the Leveson Report (2012) has shown.
- Because teachers largely mediate what pupils can or cannot say in school, there needs to be more clarity regarding the power structures that determine, restrict or enable 'open' discussion. In other words, we need to be clear about where the boundaries lie if our aim is to democratise schools through school councils and pupil involvement.

These two points are addressed in turn. First, there is inadequate theory or critique of the link between the media and modern democracy. This link is crucial in understanding democracy:

*So-called 'spin' originates in a bottom-line desire to look good. So it's essential to assert you are right, providing explanations and then reasons for why it has to be as you've presented it. If all else fails … everything becomes a question of opinion … Most people find this process unedifying. It is certainly deeply damaging to democracy.*

(Brighouse, 2004, pp.18–19)

An important area of late has been the behaviour of newspapers, like Rupert Murdoch's *News of the World*, that were found to have hacked into the mobile phones of celebrities, including Hugh Grant and that of a murdered 13-year-old school girl, Milly Dowler. The outrage that resulted prompted an Inquiry in 2011 led by Lord Justice Leveson with the remit to *inquire into the culture, practices, and ethics of the press, including … contacts and the relationships between national newspapers and politicians* (Leveson Inquiry, 2011). What followed were lengthy public hearings concerning the ethics of the media and the eventual recommendation to abolish the Press Complaints Commission and replace it with a statutory regulating body (Leveson, 2012). The problem for democracy is that tying the press closer to regulation could lead to political interference insofar as the separation of the media from political intrusion is said to keep it courageous and free to carry out investigative journalism. On the other hand, some have argued that 'freedom of the press' beyond the remit of political interference has become merely a smoke screen of late for prurient, unethical and unaccountable behaviour. The solution varies from politician to politician and at the time of writing there has been no agreed outcome, with the prime minister, David Cameron, arguing against the interference of politicians in the regulation of the press while the victims' group *Hacked Off* are determined to see it become more accountable (Hacked Off, 2013). The point for schools is that while 'communication' or 'mediation' between politicians and the press may be vital to an understanding of how democracy works, this complex relationship is not reflected in either the current or proposed National Curriculum (DfE, 2013, p.150).

A curriculum designed to prepare pupils for the realities of debate in a modern democracy might, therefore, include a variety of media themes.

- It could explain the links between media ownership and political discourses (e.g. between the newspaper and publishing magnate Rupert Murdoch and the Prime Minister's office).
- It might examine work that has helped our understanding of the way the rhetorical styles of politicians are constructed (e.g. Margaret Thatcher was taught to lower her voice to sound more authoritative).
- It might grapple with democratically complex issues concerning the control of information during periods of international conflict (e.g. the Falklands, Afghanistan or Gulf wars).
- It could attempt to account for the rise and effect of 'synthetic conversation' in the tabloid press in the presentation of public policy.
- It could provide an understanding of the symbiosis between politicians and the media and how each exploits the other.

In short, while the citizenship curriculum makes a passing reference to media education, there is little hint about how pupils might develop an awareness of the constructedness of political discourses. Debate is not problematised and the political structures within modern democracy that obfuscate or enable genuine encounter are not explained.

The second point is that, within the school environment, the issue of free communication remains unproblematised. Education for democracy says it wishes to establish *a classroom climate in which all pupils are free from any fear of expressing reasonable points of view which contradict those held either by their class teacher or by their peers* (QCA, 1998). But the notion that teachers are responsible for what is reasonable classroom discourse glosses over complex and questionable areas. To illustrate the effect of the embedded nature of communication within the socio-cultural practices of the school as an institution, consider the effect that market-funding mechanisms might have on open debate in schools like city academies which are owned by private corporations. If the governing body has welcomed sponsorship of the school's computer suite by, say, Nescafé, Burger King or Nike, it could be difficult to hold a critical discussion of the use of child labour, or the merchandising policies of the companies that help augment the excesses of western consumption.

## Research box

### school councils

The Crick Report (QCA, 1998) recommended the formation of school councils, although it did not suggest making them compulsory. There seems to be a consensus regarding the value of their consultative nature insofar as they give pupils responsibility and enable them

*(Continued)*

*(Continued)*

to experience democracy first hand in a way that mimics the parliamentary process (Print et al., 2002; Hannam, 2003). Others have their doubts. Control of the agenda or topic, for example, is a major way of limiting such debate. Rudduck and Flutter (2000) have suggested that school council discussions often revolve around *the charmed circle of lockers, dinners and uniform*. For Fielding (2001) debate and discussion is often tokenistic:

*How many school councils can we all think of that have flourished for a while but have subsequently declined from their former vibrancy and engagement with real issues into a mechanistic and largely tokenistic set of procedures for recycling the minimum and redictable minutiae of the status quo?*

(p.105)

The suggestion here is that the liberal philosophy of discussion and debate always needs to be grounded in social, political and educational contexts where it then becomes a much more complex notion than the education for democracy curriculum seems to acknowledge. There is inadequate coverage about how pupils might become aware of the constructedness of media discourses, and debate. Discussion is presented in an unproblematic way that prevents understanding of how social and political power limits the ability of some groups to engage, both within and outside the school.

# The rule of law

The third element of education for democracy is that it should foster *respect for law, justice, democracy* (QCA, 1998). Because of the difficulty with words like 'justice' we need to approach this issue with care, just as we should the rather provocative suggestion that young citizens should be helped to *distinguish between law and justice*. This appears to suggest that democratic citizens could, under certain circumstances, move their political ambitions outside the law and is perhaps not what a recent Chief Inspector of Schools had in mind when he insisted that citizenship education should lead to 'genuine action' (Bell, 2005). Democratic theorists have often accepted the possibility of unlawful dissent. They distinguish between principled unlawful dissent and other unlawful practices, like theft, which do not aim to change the law. The examples the curriculum documents give of illegal acts, like theft and glue-sniffing, are thus not politically disobedient for they imply no desire to engage in issues of social justice. The second point theorists frequently make is that there has been a long history of unlawful dissent within liberal democracies which has not toppled them. Healthy democracies, some say, can and should absorb these challenges.

*Pause for thought* | law or justice?

What is 'law' and what is 'just' are not synonymous in democracies. Think of the illegal acts performed by the women's suffragette movement; of Gandhi's peaceful march to take salt from the Indian Ocean in defiance of the colonial law that raised tax by selling it; or the occupation of woods around airports and supermarkets in protest at environmental degradation. Consider also how a senior Vatican official insisted that good Catholics should oppose Spain's law permitting marriage between gay couples since *a law as profoundly iniquitous as this one is not an obligation, it cannot be an obligation. One cannot say that a law is right simply because it is a law* (cited in Gledhill, 2005). Where do you stand on the issue of law and justice?

It is possible to imagine a classroom scenario in which the disparity between law and justice could be open and flourish. Reaction in schools to the 2003 Iraq war is an example, with UK pupils taking illegal action to join street protests against the threatened war – illegal in that it was school truancy. The issue is not whether their action was appropriate and just, or simply naïve and ineffective. The point is whether this type of action is an appropriate activity in an education for democracy curriculum. We need to be clear that the stated aim of education for democracy is not just to *know* about politics but to take action: pupils should be encouraged *to recognise, reflect upon and act upon these values and dispositions … this is vital in developing pupils into* active *citizens* (QCA, 1998; see also Bell, 2005).

Over a period of study about the war in Iraq these pupils could be shown to have demonstrated many of the skills and qualities valued by the citizenship curriculum. They have shown:

- a sense of commitment to the issue;
- they are able to communicate well and counter alternative views in a reasonable and responsible manner;
- they have developed a caring attitude to both their local and global community;
- they understand how liberal democracies work, as well as some of their limitations, such as governments refusing to change direction despite huge opposition by the public; or that in the past some, particularly colonial, wars have been fought to secure natural resources and not for reasons of justice;
- they have learnt about the media and about 'camera consciousness' and how politicians and members of the public use it to gain mainstream attention and maximum publicity for their cause.

In short, these hypothetical pupils are far from apathetic, have a good understanding of the issues and, as responsible citizens and as the recipients of a lively curriculum, have come to the point of conviction about their moral duty to take political action.

There are different ways of managing pupil action. The first is containment, where the citizenship education and education for democracy curriculum is akin to dramatic role-play, possibly enjoyable and active, but consequence-free and devoid of 'genuine action' (Bell, 2005). This would quite possibly reinforce pupils' cynicism and increase their apathy.

A second scenario is that political action would be permitted but only if closely controlled and monitored by what the Crick Report (QCA, 1998) calls 'those in authority'. Action would be legitimated, but only when the topics under discussion involved recycling or fundraising for charities, or where it addressed problems such as street litter. In this scenario, the school would permit action to raise money for new playground equipment for the local primary school, but forbid a demonstration against insufficient public funding in state schools.

A third scenario would be the fragmentation of views into what the curriculum calls 'personal opinions' (DfEE/QCA, 2000). Here a pupil would be permitted to write to a councillor or to the Prime Minister with an argument about the war, but only in a personal capacity and not as the representative of the class or school. This is to 'personalise' the opinion – to diminish it as simply the view of an individual – and to remove its public legitimacy. The tag (merely) 'personal' can be applied to those who are recalcitrant, intractable or intolerable, and serves to de-activate them. If teachers are 'in authority' to decide who is or is not a responsible student, or what or what is not a responsible personal opinion, the rules for deciding whether pupils' views and actions should remain personal or become public rests squarely with them.

---

## Summary and conclusions

It has been suggested that defining a citizen involves understanding democracy and it has been shown that the problematic nature of what a modern democracy might be is not evident in the curriculum for citizenship. There needs to be a debate about what it is and what it could become in the light of the threats to the nation state today. Pupils should be part of this. The power structures underlying debate and discussion need to be clearer and media studies should become a much more important and integral aspect of citizenship education and education for democracy. Teachers are a relatively powerless group required to teach about citizenship and democracy. They need to see beyond a curriculum that bores pupils with the facts of government and to raise the stakes by looking very carefully at where their energised and enlightened pupils may roam.

Unfortunately, much of what is shortly to become the new National Curriculum for citizenship in 2014 seems to look back to a time when teaching pupils about the facts of government and the nature of the British Constitution was preferred. Michael Gove the Education Secretary has confirmed: 'I'm not going to be coming up with any prescriptive lists, I just think there should be facts' (BBC, 2011). The new curriculum for citizenship seems to elevate this preference – 'the role of the monarchy', 'the development of our constitution and Parliament', 'the nature of rules and laws', 'the difference between criminal and civil law', 'the roles of the executive, legislature and judiciary' and so on (DfE, 2013) – rather than problematise, as this chapter has tried to do, some of the more complex issues that underpin the meaning of democracy that inform what an active citizen might become.

---

## References

Anderson, J (2002) Questions of democracy, territoriality and globalisation, in Anderson, J (ed) *Transnational Democracy: Political spaces and border crossings*. London: Routledge.

BBC (2011) Gove stresses 'facts' in school curriculum revamp. Available at: **www.bbc.co.uk/news/education-12227491** (accessed 17 April 2013).

Bell, D (2005) *Education for Democratic Citizenship*. Roscoe Lecture by Her Majesty's Chief Inspector of Schools, Liverpool, 2 November. Available at: **www.ofsted.gov.uk/publications/** (accessed 18 April 2009).

Bottery, M (2003) The end of citizenship? The nation state, threats to its legitimacy, and citizenship education in the twenty-first century. *Cambridge Journal of Education*, 33(1): 101–22.

Brighouse, T (2004) Tough on the causes of Tony. *The Times Educational Supplement*, 29 October.

Cameron, D (2000) *Good to Talk? Living and Working in a Communication Culture*. London: Sage.

Cleaver, E, Ireland, E, Kerr, D and Lopes, E (2005) *Citizenship Education Longitudinal Study: Second cross-sectional survey 2004. Listening to young people: citizenship education in England*. Slough: National Foundation for Education Research.

Clegg, N (2010) Nick Clegg says 'sorry' for making tuition fees promise, *The Telegraph*. Available at: **www.telegraph.co.uk/news/politics/nick-clegg/9554391/Nick-Clegg-says-sorry-for-making-tuition-fees-promise.html** (accessed 17 April 2013).

DfE (2013) *The National Curriculum in England: Framework document for consultation.* London: Crown copyright.

DfEE/QCA (2000) *National Curriculum – Citizenship*. London: Department for Education and Employment/Qualifications and Curriculum Authority.

Fielding, M (2001) Beyond the rhetoric of student voice: new departures and new constraints in the transformation of twenty-first century schooling? *Forum*, 43(2): 100–10.

Furedi, F (2004) *Where Have all the Intellectuals Gone? Confronting 21st century Philistinism.* London: Continuum.

Gledhill, R (2005) Vatican attack on Spain's gay marriage law. Available at: **www.thetimes.co.uk/tto/news/world/article1974366.ece** (accessed 18 April 2009).

Goldenberg, S (1999) Coup to 'save Pakistan from ruin'. *Guardian*, 18 October. Available at: **www.theguardian.com/world/1999/Oct/18/pakistan.suzannegoldenberg1** (accessed 22 September 2013).

Habermas, J (1972) *Knowledge and Human Interests*. London: Heinemann.

Hacked Off (2013) *Campaign for a free and accountable press*. Available at: **http://hackinginquiry.org/** (accessed 17 April 2013).

Hannam, D (2003) Participation and responsible action for all students: the critical ingredient for success. *Teaching Citizenship*, 5: 24–33.

Hertz, N (2001) *The Silent Takeover: Global capitalism and the death of democracy*. London: Heinemann.

Hobsbawm, E (2001) Democracy can be bad for you. *New Statesman*, 5 March, pp. 25–7.

Leveson Inquiry (2011) *Culture, Practice and Ethics of the Press*. Available at: **www.levesoninquiry.org.uk/** (accessed 17 April 2013).

Leveson Report (2012) *An Inquiry into the Culture, Practices and Ethics of the Press: Report*. London: The Stationery Office. Available at: **www.official-documents.gov.uk/document/hc1213/hc07/0780/0780.pdf** (accessed 21 April 2013).

Mill, JS (1969) On the liberty of thought and discussion, in Warnock, M (ed) *Utilitarianism*. London: Fontana.

Parekh, B (2002) Reconstituting the modern state, in Anderson, J (ed) *Transnational Democracy: Political spaces and border crossings*. London: Routledge.

Print, M, Ornstrom, S and Skovgaard, N (2002) Education for democratic processes in schools and classrooms. *European Journal of Education*, 37(2): 193–210.

QCA (1998) *Education for Citizenship and the Teaching of Democracy in Schools: Final report of the Advisory Group on Citizenship* (the Crick Report). London: Qualifications and Curriculum Authority.

Rudduck, J and Flutter, J (2000) Pupil participation and pupil perspective: carving a new order of experience. *Cambridge Journal of Education*, 30(1): 75–89.

Rushdie, S (1988) *The Satanic Verses*. London: Penguin.

Saward, M (2003) *Democracy*. Cambridge: Polity Press.

# Chapter 18

# The impact of New Media technologies on children's learning and well-being

## Elizabeth Hopkins

### Introduction

Today's children are surrounded by New Media such as television, video, computer games and the internet. It would seem to be important, therefore, for those interested in children and their well-being to consider the impact such new technologies may have on children's learning. This chapter considers both the positive and negative impact of New Media technology.

# Educational technology versus entertainment technology

Traditionally young people have been characterised either as the victims of New Media technology, encouraged to indulge in violent computer games, helpless to the hypnotic power of the screen, or as canny 'cyber citizens', the digital generation. Prensky (2001) names them as 'digital natives', empowered by technology to discover and even create new worlds of communication and learning.

Historically adults have made a distinction between 'education' and 'entertainment'. The 'educational' promise of New Media technology is seen by some as beneficial, but the 'entertainment' such technologies can provide is condemned by others as culturally worthless and even morally damaging (Sigman, 2007). Young people today, however, appear not to differentiate between these two positions. The distinction is not as clear cut as historically it has seemed to be. 'Education' taught well can indeed be entertaining and likewise much quality 'entertainment' can inform and educate. Furthermore, what young people perceive to be educational or even entertaining may be different from adults.

What is certain is that New Media technology is here to stay, and with that comes the need for those involved in children's learning and well-being to embrace the potential benefits of such technology, to create new opportunities for using it for learning and to reflect on some of the negative impacts New Media technology may have in order to prepare those in their charge to become critically aware of what New Media technology can offer.

# The positive impact of New Media technology

## Learning the e-way and a virtual school for children in care

Many young people are now part of online communities, downloading latest installments from websites of their favourite authors and belonging to a virtual community of 'flash' animators who post their efforts onto community websites. They critique their work and rate others' contributions, offering advice and sharing with authors they have never met. In this they are independent learners, demonstrating many of the skills that formal education tries to cultivate. Many young people are now armed with the know-how that makes better learning possible. The 'Learners and Technology: 7–11' report (Condie and Munro, 2007, p.1) on primary children's use of ICT found that,

*The most engaging and most desirable use of ICT was reported by pupils to be 'games'. Conversely the least exciting and most objectionable uses of ICT were reported to be related to school 'work'. As such there was little sense of ICT leading children to be more engaged with school-related learning as is often claimed by education technology commentators.*

However, the gap between New Media technology used outside and inside school is closing. The government's e-strategy (DfES, 2005, p.13) stated that by *spring 2008 every pupil should have access to a personalised online learning space with the potential to support an e-portfolio*; this is some way away from being realised. There appears to be a drive to keep the curriculum moving, to take advantage of new methods in all subject areas, and to keep demanding a better response from the technology in order to engage all learners, even the 'hard to reach', with more motivating ways of learning, and more choice about how and where to learn.

The updated National Curriculum Guidance (QCA, 2008) allowed for greater flexibility and schools exploring new ways of organising learning using technology, often blurring the boundaries between formal and informal learning. Some schools are e-twinned with schools across Europe to exchange ideas, solve mathematical puzzles and learn about each other's culture. Other schools use technology to work with businesses so that the application of the curriculum has a real purpose and application. Online Learning Communities for pupils, parents and teachers are being developed. These tools are often referred to as Virtual Learning Environments (VLEs) or Learning Platforms (LPs).

The *Care Matters* White Paper (DCSF, 2007) outlined the government's strategy for supporting children in care. As a result of the publication 11 virtual schools were opened in England. By 2010, under The Children and Young Person's Bill (DCSF, 2008) every local authority was to be required to have a virtual school to make sure that education is kept to the forefront of any decisions made about children in care. In 2006, only 12 per cent of children in care achieved five A* to C GCSEs, compared to 59 per cent per cent of their age group nationally (DCSF 2007). Children in care attend school but are also registered at a virtual school. They have access to technology such as laptops to use at home as well as access to online examination revision tools to use anywhere they can log on. As well as hardware, pupils in care also have access to a 'virtual' tutor to teach and mentor them as well as providing support and encouragement. The Global Education Trust (Gannon-Leary and Fontainha, 2006) piloted a two-year study of New Media technology virtual support, which showed that the examination success of children in care is being raised.

> **Pause for thought** | potential benefits of a virtual learning environment
>
> Virtual learning environments open the doors to personalised 24/7 learning. This brings potential benefits. Construct two lists of the potential benefits of a virtual learning environment, one for learners and one for educators.

# Children's television and language development

For many, the idea of children watching television as a positive occupation is unconvincing; however, Davies (1989, p.84) states that *there is no evidence … that watching television is a mindless activity – for children or for anybody else.* When under the control of the viewer television may have the potential to be an entertaining, informative educator.

Children view television primarily as a source for entertainment, while their parents and carers see it as a useful educational tool for intellectual development (Rideout et al., 2003). In order to be able to consider the impact of television on learning it is useful to understand how children acquire skills that help them to make sense of television. Children develop their understanding of television alongside their cognitive development. They do not see television in the same way as an adult, but by the age of 12 it is assumed that children can understand television in a similar way to adults. Research undertaken by the Literacy Trust (Close, 2004) found that parents and carers who share the experience of television-viewing with their children can assist both cognitive and language development:

*Attention and comprehension, receptive vocabulary, some expressive language, letter-sound knowledge, and knowledge of storytelling all benefit from high quality and age-appropriate educational programming … co-viewing with parents aids oral ability and comprehension.*

(p.15)

> ## Research box
>
> ### television and language development
>
> Language acquisition seems to be related to age-appropriate programmes with specific educational purposes (Lemish, 2007). In Marsh et al.'s (2005) research into the positive benefits of high quality children's television 79 per cent of parents and carers believed that their children's language development was assisted. Children were *actively engaged with television content for some of their viewing time, with singing, dancing and copying characters* (Marsh et al., 2005, p.27). Marsh et al.'s research indicates that, when used in a measured way, New Media technology can be an extremely useful tool.
>
> When considering the positive links between television, language development and the curriculum for the Foundation Stage in England, Marsh et al. (2005) found that television viewing, in the right circumstances, can help pre-school children to:
>
> - use words, gestures, simple questions, statements;
> - listen to nursery rhymes, stories and songs, joining in with repeated refrains;

- enjoy listening to and using spoken language;
- sustain attentive listening;
- respond to extended vocabulary;
- explore the meaning and sounds of new words;
- use language to recreate experiences;
- use talk to clarify thinking, ideas, feelings and events;
- link sounds to letters;
- begin to be aware of the way stories are structured.

Research undertaken by Bazalgette (2003) for the British Film Institute found that children who watched television understood image sequences as well as combinations of images and sounds. This understanding of media could be transferred to the written word. Bazalgette suggests that children in their first year of school are *in a sense, bilingual, because they are already readers of television and film* (p.5). Earlier, Kremer et al. (2002) looked at six-year-old children's comprehension of non-written texts (the television cartoon *Rugrats* and the audio tape of *The Cat's Purr*). Children's recall of plot, character motivation and causal connectives were tested. The research found that these skills were a more significant indicator of reading ability at age eight than were the basic reading assessments of six year olds. This research suggests that there may be 'text level' concepts, for example genre and narrative structure, which are not restricted to print literacy, which can be developed through the engagement with quality screen viewing, these skills being transferable to print literacy.

Can media literacy help writing? Parker (1999) looked at the relationship between creative work with moving images and children's writing in two primary classes. The children looked at Roald Dahl's story *Fantastic Mr. Fox*. One class created simple animations of the story the other class read the story. The writing produced by the children demonstrated that the children who had worked with animations produced written work that contained more detail and depth. The children who used animation produced written work that showed character empathy; they understood that by repositioning, the reader could get inside the character. Having to select a camera position appeared to be the key for the children to be able to develop their writing. From this research it appears that teachers can encourage children to be actively engaged in media content without fear.

There has been little research undertaken into older children's learning from television. This could be because educational television has less of an impact on children once they have started school and due to the decline of children's late afternoon television programming from the terrestrial channels. Older children prefer drama, verbal humour and relationships.

## How gaming can develop cognitive thinking skills

The early work of Greenwood (1984) found that computer game-playing required a range of cognitive skills, including problem solving, memory, inductive thinking, parallel processing, spatial awareness as well as the more obvious hand-eye coordination. Much of the research into the cognitive benefits of computer gaming identifies short-term effects, which are transferable. Flynn (1994) suggested that the development of representational skills acquired through gaming may be responsible for the rise in American children's IQ scores. According to Williamson and Facer (2005), computer games aid learning and promote motivation more than formal education does. Their research identified a growing interest in the potential application of [computer and video game] environments for formal educational objectives and focused on children's gaming habits rather than the software used to provide an insight into the relevance of formal educational settings. The findings highlighted the importance of playing games in peer groups and the social contexts required for gaming online and concluded that the social practices to which games-play provide young people with access are equally, if not more, motivating than the actual games themselves.

This New Media gaming culture appears to provide an innovative resource for the kinds of learning which are often not present in a traditional school setting. So, as with learning to play games, children need to be introduced to systematic ways of solving problems, the social networking offered by on-line gaming, or as Gee (2004) describes, 'affinity spaces' can provide for this.

## Research box

### the educational value of New Media technologies

There have been contrasting assessments of the educational value of these new media technologies. Papert's (1996) research described children's' 'love affair' with computers, arguing that they provide a more creative and spontaneous form of learning that can improve family relationships. Sceptics like Healy (1998) argue that such learning is superficial and trivial and that claims about computers' educational potential are highly overstated. According to research by Livingstone and Bovill (2002), children choose computer games when they want to 'stop being bored'. Favourite computer games are those which focus on sports and adventure, boys preferring sports and fighting games, girls favouring adventure quest, although these are also enjoyed by boys. Gee (2004) found that harnessing video games as a teaching medium was a powerful tool, but found that *most schools seek to avoid invoking feelings of both pleasure and frustration, blind to the fact that these emotions can be extremely useful when it comes to teaching kids*. (ibid, p.2).

If we want our children to benefit from technological innovations and to avoid the harm that some games may pose, educators need to embrace the potential benefits and incorporate the technology into their delivery.

## A 'tablet' to cure reluctant readers

Almost ten years ago Leu et al. (2004) reported how new technologies were beginning to redefine literacy in school, work and home. Today, information and communication technologies (ICTs) have become everyday tools for teachers. Larson's (2010) research on the use of the Kindle in schools found that children's engagement with and comprehension of text improved. The digital reading device allowed pupils to customise their reading experience in several ways, notably through changing the font size, making notes on the text as they read and using the audio dictionary. Being able to curl up rather than sit facing a desk computer or a laptop appeared to result in longer reading sessions.

The invention of the tablet computer or iPad in 2010 has perhaps even more educational potential. Some educators, notably Ludlow (2010), Ferriter (2010) and Allen (2011), have even claimed the iPad as the future of one-to-one educational delivery, particularly for children who require intervention strategies to improve their literacy skills. In 2012 McClanahan, an American university professor working with pre-service teachers (trainee teachers) on a reading course for children with Attention Deficit Hyperactivity Disorder (ADHD), found that during a six-week reading recovery course using iPads children gained one year in their reading age. They also gained confidence and a greater sense of being in control of their own learning. McClanahan identified some aspects of the iPad, which may have contributed to the success of the reading course. The manipulative touch screen promoted the use of several modalities, especially visual and tactile, and being able to record their own reading and play it back to hear their mistakes while looking at the text allowed for the integration of aural modality effectively. The higher levels of sensory stimulation using the iPad may also have contributed to the ADHD children's increased engagement.

In addition to supporting reluctant readers the iPad may also provide a solution to two whole-school practical concerns about ICT use: the limitations of hardware and software, and teacher expertise. Tablet computers are relatively inexpensive and very little training is required in order to make an iPad a valuable addition to a teacher's toolkit.

## Research box

### the iPad as a tool for education

Longfield Academy in Kent, England is a recently built school covering Years 7 through 13 (ages 11 to 18). At Longfield, they strive to provide a cutting-edge learning experience incorporating a high level of technology integration in the curriculum. In 2011 over 800 students were issued iPads, across the full spectrum of grade levels. The study used surveys to assess the impact of iPad use on motivation, quality of work, achievement, collaboration and other factors.

Among the findings:

- 77 per cent of faculty respondents felt that student achievement appeared to have risen since the introduction of the iPad;
- 73 per cent of students and 67 per cent of staff felt that the iPad helped students improve the quality of their work;
- 69 per cent of students who completed the survey felt that using the iPad was motivating and that they worked better with it than without it;
- 60 per cent of faculty thought that students were more motivated by lessons that incorporated the iPad than those that did not.

Students wanted to make more use of their iPads and suggested a variety of activities that they felt should be further incorporated into their academic studies including:

- photography editing and animations;
- making videos/movies;
- word games to help teach spelling;
- use of the iPad in place of pen and paper;
- more writing assignments on the iPad;
- taking tests on the tablet;
- replacing text books with ebooks;
- designing games;
- more science Apps.

(Heinrich, 2012)

# The negative impact of New Media technology

## Early-years language development and screen viewing

Recent studies into the time spent reading before and after the advent of television suggest that the time children spend reading has remained relatively stable through the years. Children spent little time reading before the invention of television and they spend little time reading now.

Four significant stages which need to be in place before reading can be mastered are:

- phonological awareness (sounds);
- memory;
- co-ordination of perception with smaller motor movement;
- operation of symbols (letters).

Most children by the age of three today recognise the golden arches M of McDonald's, but this does not mean that they can decode complex symbols. Children have to learn how symbols work, that numbers, for example, can be represented by their Arabic symbols or spelled alphabetically and above all that letters stand for sounds that can be combined. Metacognition is crucial in the early stages of reading: children need to grasp that language itself must be thought about and considered from different perspectives. Playing games with sounds, rhyming and discovering onomatopoeia are all aspects of metacognition that help a child to begin to read. Critics have long suspected that television viewing is negatively associated with reading. Singer and Singer (1990) point out the fallacy of assuming that television viewing has a negative effect on reading. When children's television is removed or decreased, reading increases; so it is tempting to conclude that television viewing detracts from reading. However, studies by Snow et al. (1998) show that it is the amount of television viewed at critical developmental stages which is significant.

Television may influence the type of reading that children prefer, not merely the amount. Morgan (1980) found that teenagers who were heavy television viewers preferred to read material that resembled television content. Likewise, younger children enjoy written stories about television characters. Reading had positive effects on oral and written expression, as well as creative imagination. Educators have long observed that the presentation of a story on television causes curiosity about and demand for the book. This curiosity applies to both children and adults alike; one only has to think of the effect on book purchase of TV adaptations of classic stories by Charles Dickens and Jane Austen.

According to some research the potential of television to aid a young child's linguistic development is limited. Too much early television viewing may hinder 'self identity', as this is developed through real people rather than the screen. Light viewers of television have a better-developed language shown in their use of more adjectives, adverbs and linguistic complexity than heavy television viewers (Singer and Singer, 1990).

> **Pause for thought** | visualisation and imagination
>
> The development of the imagination appears to be supported through reading (Singer and Singer, 1990). Another aspect from which to assess the impact of TV is to ask what the effect might be of too many messages and the degree to which children have become saturated by communication including TV. Gardner (1982) found little evidence that TV had a stimulating effect on the imagination. Interestingly, people denied perceptual stimulation

like TV, music and radio – for example, those taken hostage (Horowitz 1976), reported an increase in frequency and vividness of imagery. Could it be, then, that saturation with sights and sounds reduces the capacity to visualise, to generate mental images?

Together with a group of friends or colleagues explore how your own capacity to visualise and be imaginative is linked with perceptual stimulation. For example, what might a school look like in 2050? Where do the images that you bring to mind come from? To what extent are the sources of these images helpful or limiting? Is it possible to be imaginative without a bank of mental pictures?

It has been found that children who listened to an incomplete story produced more imaginative story endings than children who saw the same incomplete story on TV. In an experiment by Greenfield and Beagles (1988) two groups of 192 socially mixed children were asked to tell a story about what would happen next. One group watched an animated TV cartoon the other group listened to an audio version. Those who had watched the story used more words and ideas from the story. The group who had listened produced far more creative and imaginative endings. Belton (2001) found that reading and writing ability and creative writing ability in children correlated positively with the number of books read, the level of parental education and paramount interest (including restriction of quality and type of viewing, watching TV together and discussing it, reading aloud when the child was small) and negatively to the number of viewing hours. In fact, the amount of viewing emerged as the single most significant factor in predicting writing ability.

Watkins in 1988 asked children to write two stories – one for television and one for 'real life'. Children used different contexts for the two genres irrespective of how much TV they viewed. BUT those who were low viewers wrote more complex stories for both genres, while the high viewers' stories were less developed, the TV story being more complex than the real life story.

So, TV images are widely seen and can create a collective memory, which may limit the possibilities for original thinking and images. Books allow the mind to paint its own pictures. Children's ability to create visual, fluid 'dreamlike' images could be hindered by over exposure to hard-edged, detailed finished pictures.

## New Media, aggressive behaviour and educational attainment

Concern about children and popular media has a long history. Plato proposed to ban poets from his ideal republic, because he feared their stories about immoral behaviour would corrupt young minds. In modern times 'moral' pressure groups have tried to protect children from:

- popular literature;
- the music hall;
- the cinema;
- comics;
- television;
- 'video nasties'.

TV does portray violence, but there are broader social, cultural and historical factors which also influence. What did children do before the invention of television? Studies (Buckingham, 1996; Davies, 1997) show that when television sets are removed for a while children find other things to do. The romantic nostalgic image of childhood 50 years ago which offered little in the way of TV viewing conveys images of children running freely in fields and kicking footballs about in the street outside their homes. Now only one in five of today's children play outside in the street or local parks (Farmer, 2007). A fear of traffic accidents, paedophiles or bullies and the growth of home electronic entertainment have meant a whole generation is growing up without the joys of playing freely in their own neighbourhood. Research into the 'effects' of TV violence on children has focused on single cause and direct effect, putting the research into the behaviourist tradition.

### Research box

## television viewing and aggressive behaviour

Liebert and Baron (1972) looked at how willing children were to hurt other children. They found that children who had watched violent programmes were more prepared to hurt another child. Boys appeared to be able to inflict pain on others more than the girls studied. These findings may appear shocking, but the research did not take into account that the programmes used in the research were not typical of these children's usual viewing, and that most children do not usually watch television alone. The children also watched the violent programmes in an artificial situation, which could have affected their responses. However, Rosenkoetter (2006) demonstrated that children understood moral lessons contained in situation comedy shows.

Berkowitz (1993) suggests that people are naturally aggressive, but that normally this is repressed. Heavy violent television viewing it seems may weaken these inhibitions and lead them to feel that aggression is acceptable. The conditions of ordinary television viewing may encourage viewers to relax, accept and possibly enjoy violent images. Drabman and Thomas (1984) found that children between the ages of eight and ten who were shown a video of aggressive behaviour took longer to intervene in apparently real life violence between two younger children they were left in charge of than children who had not seen the video.

Television programmes perceived by children as realistic are watched with more involvement, more emotion and less detachment than those programmes which seem fantastic, e.g. cartoons. Adults clearly have a role to play in monitoring children's access to violent television programmes. As violence sells, so violent television programmes will inevitably continue to be made. This makes the monitoring and censoring role of the parent or other adult critical.

### *Pause for thought* | television viewing and academic performance

Research into the effects of television and other screen viewing on academic performance shows that children who view heavily experience difficulties with impulse control, task performance and delay of gratification. Smith (1986) and McIlwraith (1990) in America also found that children who watched a lot of television had significantly more trouble with mind wandering, distractibility, boredom and unfocused daydreaming. Based on your own experience, what factors might account for a link between television viewing and poor academic performance?

# The effects of New Media technology on children's physical development and health

The increase in the number of obese people not only in the United Kingdom but in the developed world generally is of growing concern. Much research into the causes of obesity has identified excessive screen viewing as one of the contributing factors. A study by Robinson (1999) for the Kaiser Family Foundation found that the average American child between the ages of 8 and 18 spent over six hours a day with media technology. This is more time than is spent in school, with parents or involved in any other activity other than sleep. In their research Cooper et al. (2006) found that as viewing time increased the resting metabolic rate of television viewers decreased. A number of studies have identified a correlation between weight gain and screen media usage, including television, video and electronic games.

Watching screen media frequently displaces other activities, such as sports and playing outside and also appears to lead to a greater consumption of calories; both children and adults eating more, even when not actually hungry. Early childhood is a time of rapid physical growth; research on pre-school children by Janz (2001) found that girls who watched a lot of screen media had bone density that was lower than that of light viewers. In 2007 Sigman reported that 75 per cent of all meals are eaten in front of a screen.

In 2008 the Office of Communications (Ofcom) implemented TV advertising restrictions on 'junk food' during programmes of particular appeal to children. The earlier *Which* Report, 'Cartoon Heroes and Villains', had found that nearly one in three children in England alone were overweight or obese, a trend reflected across the UK and stressed the need for the government to restrict the advertising of foods high in fat, sugar and salt before 9 p.m. The National Opinion Poll by the Children's Society (2008) found that 66 per cent of children felt that computer and television viewing prevented active pursuits, 88 per cent of them wanted more educational advice about healthy eating and 95 per cent stated that physical health promoted mental health.

A growing body of evidence suggests that excessive viewing can lead to poor health and changes in cognitive development. While there are many factors which contribute to poor health, these studies indicate that children's engagement with new technology media is an important piece of the puzzle. It may well be worth reducing young children's exposure to screen viewing, particularly to advertising, and to increasing the number of media messages which can promote fitness and sound nutrition.

# Virtual violence: the fight against cyber bullying

The phenomenal expansion of social networking sites and their use by children under 13 (Ofcom, 2011) brings a new range of risks, one of the most worrying being cyber bullying. In addition to the victimisation of young people by their peers there has been an increase in the electronic harassment of teachers by pupils and parents. The current DfE guidance on this topic (DfE, 2011) references cyber bullying as a specific area of bullying, and notes that it is an illegal activity under the Protection from Harassment Act of 1997.

Cyber bullying generally has a negative impact on victims. However, some groups are more vulnerable and targeted more often than others. Research undertaken by Cross et al. (2012) identified four at-risk categories of children: those whose parents are less educated; those whose parents do not use the internet; disabled children; and those from minority ethnic groups. These groups are also less likely to have access to support and guidance. Teachers too are at increasing risk of being harassed, rating platforms such as RateMyTeacher.com, Facebook and YouTube being popular sites on which to post abusive comments, photographs and video clips. A study by the Association of Teachers and Lecturers (ATL) in 2010 surveyed 630 teachers and found that 15 per cent had been harassed online. Abuse came from pupils, former pupils, parents of pupils and, perhaps surprisingly, other teachers. Research clearly shows that bullying and abuse are devastating at any age and schools have a responsibility to ensure that e-safety measures are in place to protect everyone.

In Ofsted's (2012) school inspection handbook e-safety is included as an important part of the inspection process. Included are a range of indicators that evaluate the breadth of a school's safeguarding strategy to include the online environment in which staff, pupils and their families can learn and communicate. E-safety and cyber bullying are highlighted in two of the four key Ofsted judgements: *the behaviour and safety of pupils in school* and *the quality of leadership and management*.

---

### Research box

## inspecting e-safety briefing for inspectors 2012

Common risks inspectors are likely to encounter. (Please note that this is not an exhaustive list.)

Content

- exposure to inappropriate content, including online pornography, ignoring age ratings in games (exposure to violence associated with often racist language), substance abuse;
- lifestyle websites, for example pro-anorexia/self-harm/suicide sites;
- hate sites;
- content validation: how to check authenticity and accuracy of online content.

Contact

- grooming;
- cyber-bullying in all forms;
- identity theft (including 'frape' (hacking Facebook profiles) and sharing passwords).

Conduct

- privacy issues, including disclosure of personal information;
- digital footprint and online reputation;
- health and well-being (amount of time spent online (internet or gaming));
- sexting (sending and receiving of personally intimate images);
- copyright (little care or consideration for intellectual property and ownership (for example music and film)).

(Ofsted, 2012, p.5)

# Shut down or re-boot? The role of Computer Science

Increasing concern has been expressed by academics, teachers, business and industry about the current provision of education in computing in UK schools. There is no doubt that there is a need to improve the nature and scope of computing and recognition of Computer Science as a rigorous academic discipline of importance to the future careers of many pupils.

The Royal Society's report (Furber, 2012) into computing in UK schools makes 11 recommendations which include the abandonment of the term ICT, targets for the recruitment of specialist Computer Science and Information Technology teachers, pupil-friendly programming environments, improved schemes of work, and a national qualification in Computer Science at Key Stage 4 (KS4). These proposals form the basis for a national curriculum in Computer Science. Children will learn to write computer programs from the age of seven in this first step to revolutionise the way that schools teach technology. Learning to code will be taught in primary school alongside history and science. Children will not simply learn how to use technology; instead they will learn how to create technology. The success of the reforms should move the United Kingdom from a digitally literate population to a nation of technology creators.

---

### *Pause for thought* | what every child should know

What do you think of the Computer Science curriculum recommendations from the BCS Academy of Computing 2012 listed here?

Age 5–7

Use knowledge of algorithms to write simple programs; store and retrieve data; know ways in which information is represented digitally.

Age 7–11

Write programs to accomplish goals; detect and fix errors in algorithms and programs; use variables and tables to store, retrieve and manipulate data; analyse and evaluate digital content.

Age 11–14

Represent aspects of a problem as abstractions that can be described within a program; generate, develop and implement creative programmatic solutions to a range of computational problems; explain how and why an algorithm works; know the hardware components of a computer system.

Age 14–16

Develop understanding of digital technologies, including managing online identity and participating in communities; develop and apply computational thinking skills.

## Summary and conclusions

This chapter has considered positive and negative aspects of New Media technology. Such technologies, television, computer games and the internet are permanent resources for education, entertainment and play. They are part of children's everyday lives and their relationship with them is complex. It may be shocking that children spend many hours engaged in screen viewing, but is this necessarily a bad thing? While being able to read and write have become accepted as essential skills to the processes of mental development, there appears to be every possibility that young children's access to New Media technology may also develop children's minds. What is far from clear is how educators can prevent children from being exposed to harmful aspects, while simultaneously encouraging them to make the most of the educational and cultural potential which New Media technology has to offer.

## *References*

Allen, R (2011) Can mobile devises transform education? *Education Update,* 53(2) 2: 6–7.

Bazalgette, C (2003) *The Children are Watching.* London: British Film Institute.

BCS Academy of Computing (2012) [Online] Available at: **http://academy.bcs.org/** (accessed 6 December 2012).

Belton, T (2001) Television and imagination: an investigation of the medium's influence on children's story making. *Media, Culture and Society,* 23(6): 799–820.

Berkowitz, L (1993) *Aggression: its causes, consequences and control.* New York: McGraw-Hill.

Buckingham, D (1996) *Making Images Understanding Children's emotional reponses to television.* Manschester: Manschester University Press.

Children's Society (2008) *UK failing to meet children's mental health and well-being needs.* GfK, National Opinion Poll.

Cooper, TV, Klesges, LM, DeBon, M, Klesges, RC and Shelton, ML (2006) An assessment of obese and non-obese girls' metabolic rate during television viewing, reading and resting. *Eating Behaviours,* 7(2): 105–14.

Close, R (2004) *Television and Language Development in Early Years.* London: National Literacy Trust.

Condie, R and Munro, B (2007) *The impact of ICT in Schools–A Landscape Review.* London: BECTA Research.

Cross, E-J, Piggin, R, Douglas, T and Vonkaenel-Flatt, J (2012) *Beat Bullying Virtual Violence 11 Progress and challenges in the fight against cyberbullying.* Oxford: Nominet Trust/ NAHT.

Davies, MM (1989) *Television is Good for Your Kids.* London: Hilary Shipman.

Davies, MM (1997) *Fake, Fact and Fantasy: Children's interpretations of television reality.* New Jersey: Erbaum.

DCSF (2007) *Care Matters: Time for Change.* London: HMSO.

DCSF (2008) *Children and Young Person's Bill.* London: HMSO.

DfE (2011) *Preventing and Tackling Bullying: Advice for head teachers, staff and governing bodies.* London: HMSO.

DfES (2005) *Harnessing Technology: Transforming learning in children's services.* London: HMSO.

Drabman, PS and Thomas, MH (1984) Does media violence increase children's toleration of real-life aggression? *Developmental Psychology,* 10: 418–21.

Farmer, TW (2007) The developmental dynamics of aggression and the prevention of school violence. *Journal of Emotional and Behavioural Disorders,* 15(4): 197–208.

Ferriter, W (2010) E-Readers: get ready for a revolution. *Educational Leadership,* 68(3): 84–5.

Flynn, JR (1994) IQ gains over time, in Sternberg, RJ (ed) *Encyclopaedia of Human Intelligence.* New York: Macmillan.

Furber, S (2012) *Shut Down or Restart? The way forward for computing in UK schools.* London: The Royal Society.

Gannon-Leary, P and Fontainha, E (2006) *Communities of Practice and Virtual Learning Communities: Benefits barriers and success factors.* London: HSBC.

Gardner, H (1982) *Art, Mind and Brain: A cognitive approach to creativity.* New York: Basic Books.

Gee, J (2004) *Situated Language and Learning: a critique of traditional schooling.* New York: Routledge.

Greenfield, PM and Beagles, J (1988) Radio and television: Their cognitive impact on children of different socio economic and ethnic groups. *Journal of Communication,* 38(2): 71–92.

Greenwood, PM (1984) *Mind and Media: The effects of television, computers and video games.* London: Fontana.

Healy, JM (1998) *Failure to Connect: How computers affect our children's minds – for better or worse.* New York: Simon and Schuster.

Horowitz, MJ (1976) *Stress Response Syndromes.* New York: J Aronso.

Janz, KF (2001) Physical activity and bone measures in young children: The Iowa bone development study. *Pediatrics,* 107, 1387–93.

Kremer, KE, Lynch, JS, Kendeou, P, Butler, J and Van Der Broek, P (2002) *Role of Narrative Understanding in Predicting Future Reading Comprehension.* Universities of Minesota and Kentucky paper presented at AERA conference. [Online] Available at: **www.clera.org** (accessed 20 October 2008).

Larson, IC (2010) Digital Readers: the next chapter in eBook reading and response. *The Reading Teacher,* 64, 15–22. Doi: 10. 1598/RT.64.1.2.

Lemish, D (2007) *Children and Television: A global perspective.* Oxford: Blackwell.

Leu, DJ, Kinzer, CK, Coiro, JL and Cammack, DW (2004) Towards a theory of new literacies emerging from the internet and other information and communication technologies, in Ruddell, RB and Unrau, N (eds) *Theoretical Models and Processes of Reading* (5th edn). Newark, DE: International Reading Association.

Liebert, R and Baron, R (1972) Some immediate effects of televisual violence on children's behavior. *Developmental Psychology,* 6: 469–75.

Livingstone, S and Bovill, M (2002) *Young People and New Media.* London: Sage.

Ludlow, B (2010) The future of reading. *Teaching Exceptional Children,* 43(1): 4.

Marsh, J, Brookes, G, Hughes, J, Ritchie, R, Roberts, S and Wright, K (2005) *Digital Beginnings: Young children's use of popular culture, media and new technologies.* Sheffield: Literacy Research Centre: University of Sheffield.

McClanahan, B (2012) How use of an ipad facilitated reading improvement. *TechTrends,* 56(3).

McIlwraith, RD (1990) *Theories of Television Addiction.* Boston: American Psychological Association.

Morgan, M (1980) Television and reading: Does more equal better? *Journal of Communication,* 30(3): 159–65.

Ofcom (2011) *Children and Parents; media use and attitudes report.* London: Ofcom.

Ofsted (2012) Inspecting e-Safety Briefing for Inspectors. Manchester: Ofsted.

Papert, S (1996) *The Connected Family: Bridging the digital generation gap.* Atlanta, CA: Longstreet Press.

Paker, D (1999) *Moving Image, Media, Print Literacy and Narrative.* London: British Film Institute.

QCA (2008) *National Curriculum Guidance.* London: Stationery Office.

Rideout, V, Vandewater, E, and Wartella, A (2003) *Zero to Six*, in Kaiser Family Foundation Report. California: The Henry J Kaiser Family Foundation.

Robinson, TN (1999) *Kids and Media in the New Millennium: A comprehensive national analysis of children's media use*. Washington: The Henry J Kaiser Family Foundation.

Rosenkoetter, L (2006) The television situation comedy and children's prosocial behavior. *Journal of Applied Social Psychology*, 29(5): 979–93.

Sigman, A (2007) *Remotely Controlled: How television is damaging our lives*. London: Vermillion.

Singer, DG and Singer, JL (1990) *The House of Make-believe: Children's play and the developing imagination*. Cambridge, MA: Harvard University Press.

Smith, R (1986) Television addiction, in Bryant, J and Zillman, D (eds) *Perspectives on Media Effects*. Hillsdale, NJ: Lawrence Erlbaum.

Snow, C, Burns, M and Griffin, P (eds) (1998) *Preventing Reading Difficulties in Young Children*. Washington, DC: National Research Council.

Watkins, B (1988) Children's representations of television and real life stories. *Communication Research*, 15: 59–184.

Williamson, B and Facer, K (2005) More than 'just a game': The implications for schools of children's computer games communities. *Education, Communication and Information*, 4(2 and 3): 255–70.

# Chapter 19

## Comparative education

## Namrata Rao and Anesa Hosein

### Introduction

Comparison is a natural intellectual inquiry which we pursue all the time when making judgements and during decision-making. You would have made such comparisons when deciding which university to pursue your undergraduate studies. Increasing globalisation and international mobility has increased the need to do studies that tend to be drawn towards comparisons between local, regional and national education systems due to their increasing interdependence. As students of education, you would engage in such comparisons all the time to judge the effectiveness of an educational system, policy or practice. However, these comparisons may not be as simplistic as they appear, as the educational system of a country is influenced by a multitude of factors often unique to that country. Further, to be able to compare, you need to have a deep understanding of your own education system and cultural background so that you can recognise your own biases and prejudices. This has led to the emergence of a field of academic study, 'comparative education'. This chapter focuses on developing your understanding of this area of study, the use and potential misuse of comparative studies and finally the issues faced by comparativists in the pursuit of such studies.

## Defining comparative education

According to Noah (1984, p.551), *comparative education can help us understand better our own past, locate ourselves more exactly in the present, and discern a little more clearly what our educational future may be.* Comparative education involves the comparisons of the education processes and practices within and between countries. Mallinson (1975) emphasised that it is a systematic examination of other cultures and other systems of education deriving from those cultures in order to discover resemblances and differences. More recently, Clarkson (2009) defined comparative education as that strand of the theory of education, which is concerned with the analysis and interpretation of educational practices and policies in different countries and cultures.

*Pause for thought* | stakeholders of comparative education

According to Bray (2007, p.15), the categories of people/stakeholders who undertake comparative studies of education are:

- parents who commonly compare schools and systems of education in search of the institutions which will serve their children's needs most effectively;
- practitioners including school principals and teachers, make comparisons in order to improve the operation of their institutions;

*(Continued)*

*(Continued)*

- policy makers to identify ways to achieve social, political and other objectives in their own settings;
- international agencies to compare patterns in different countries to improve the advice they give to national governments and others;
- academics to improve understandings of the forces which shape education systems and processes in different settings and of the impact of education systems and processes on social and other development.

Take one or two of these categories and think about at least three areas the stakeholders might want to compare?

An attempt to define comparative education itself can prove to be problematic considering its amorphous nature, i.e. no pattern or structure. While some consider it to be a discipline in its own right, others consider it to be an interdisciplinary field of study, which draws on the knowledge of several disciplines. The other issue when defining comparative education lies in the fact that it often overlaps with another area of study called 'international education'. In the following section, we attempt to establish whether comparative education is a discipline in its own right or whether it is an interdisciplinary field. It might also be worth considering whether comparative and international education are separate fields of study or are the two so closely entwined that this demarcation has blurred?

## Is comparative education a discipline in its own right or is it a cross-discipline?

Halls (1990) and Epstein (1994) consider comparative education as a cross-disciplinary activity, which draws on the knowledge, theories and methods of several disciplines for example sociology, psychology, politics, history and philosophy. Lê Thành Khôi (quoted by Eliou, 1997, p.113) concurs, suggesting that comparative education *is not strictly a discipline, but a field of study covering all the disciplines which serve to understand and explain education*. However, Phillips and Schweisfurth (2008, p.13) recognise it as a 'quasi-discipline' as they argue that although it is not a discipline in its own right it has many characteristics of a discipline. Some writers (for example, Chabbott, 2003; Higginson, 1999; Kerawalla, 1995) have described comparative education as a discipline.

## International education?

While comparative education has a relatively long history, international education is considered to be a recent emergence. The fields of comparative and international education often overlap and it is difficult to distinguish one from the other. Bray (2010) suggested that such an overlap and ambiguity could lead to conceptual dilemmas. The two fields are somewhat complementary but are considered to have different foundations and purposes. Wilson (1994, p.450) used the analogy 'Siamese twins' to symbolise the similarities and differences between the two fields. To gain an understanding of the two and to appreciate the distinction it might be appropriate to define these. Watson (1996) considered comparative education to be theoretical and research based and international education as that which makes practical use of the data generated by comparative education.

Phillips and Schweisfurth (2008) stated that *a comparative study is usually international in nature and an international study is often comparative* (p.7), suggesting the two are equal in status. However, Halls (1990) considered international education as a subset of comparative education. Further, contrary to Halls, Bunnell (2008, p.415) proclaimed that comparative education was a subset of international education suggesting that *international education involves a dichotomy of study between the largely theoretical discipline of comparative education, and the still relatively under-researched body of international schools.* Some have emphasised comparative and international education to be one comprehensive field of study. For example, Crossley (1999) suggested that the theoretical knowledge from comparative education and applied research from international education go hand in hand and the two constitute one comprehensive multidisciplinary field rather than being two separate fields of study.

There are differences in the roles of those engaged in the study of comparative and international education as suggested by Epstein (1994, p.918) who described comparativists as *primarily scholars interested in explaining why educational systems and processes vary and how education relates to wider social factors and forces*. In contrast, he described international educators as those who *use findings derived from comparative education to understand better their ability to make policy relating to programmes such as those associated with international exchange and understanding.* To conclude, there are differences in comparative and international education that pervade through the differing role of the practitioners engaged in the study of these.

In spite of the complexities in defining the very nature of comparative education one cannot deny the importance of this field of study in the increasingly globalised world where boundaries between countries are vanishing. The next section explores what the purpose of undertaking such comparative studies is and what could be the potential misuses.

# Purpose of comparative education

According to Sir Michael Sadler (1900 reprinted 1964, p.310), *the practical value of studying, in a right spirit and with scholarly accuracy, the working of foreign systems of education is that it will result in our being fitted to study and understand our own*. Comparative education provides cross-national data about the relationship between education and the factors that might influence the same. It considers the implications of the research outcomes in influencing the educational policy and practice at both national and international levels. According to Broadfoot (2000), *comparative education has always been explicitly or implicitly reformative* (p.366) with the intention of not typically being a simple scholarly pursuit but to find out what works and to use such insights for educational reforms.

---

*Pause for thought* | purpose and reasons for comparative and international education

Based on a literature review, the purpose and reasons of comparative and international education as identified by Crossley and Watson (2003, p.19) are to:

- gain a better understanding of one's own educational system;
- satisfy intellectual and theoretical curiosity about other cultures and their education systems; and better understand the relationship between education and wider society;

*(Continued)*

*(Continued)*

- identify similarities and differences in educational systems, processes and outcomes as a way of documenting and understanding problems in education, and contributing to the improvement of educational policy and practice;

- promote improved international understanding and co-operation through increased sensitivity to differing worldviews and cultures.

Can you think of any others?

# Key uses of comparative educational research

We have now discussed some of the important aspects of the uses of comparative education including views of some of the leaders in this field. A comprehensive discussion around the use of comparative education is beyond the scope of this chapter. However, we will focus on some of the key uses of comparative educational research and further discuss some of the potential misuses.

## Decision-making

A description of what other countries are doing, have done and what lessons they have learnt, can be of value to the other countries. The knowledge and understanding of such descriptions in cognate situations can be of value to other countries seeking solutions for their own problems. For example, the inconsistencies in the educational provision across England led to the birth of the National Curriculum in England in 1989. This response to disparities in the educational provision was informed by the implementation of a similar standardised national education provision in other European countries. However, 'adoption without adaptation' is not recommended. Often in an attempt to find a 'quick-fix' solution countries tend to adopt practices which have been successful elsewhere without critically analysing the contextual aspects which may play a crucial role in the success of these practices elsewhere. It is important to note that an approach which might appear successful in one context might not be successful in another. Therefore, the success of an approach in dealing with a problem cannot be generalised in all contexts. For example, a study by Moin et al. (2011) explored how kindergartens in Germany and Israel dealt with supporting the development of bilingualism where one of the languages was Russian in both countries. One of the approaches used in Germany was recruitment of teachers from East Germany as many of them have a Russian lineage. However, this approach might not be appropriate for Israel as for them it might be more practical to employ immigrant teachers from Russia. Therefore, an approach for addressing the issue in Germany cannot be successful in Israel due to the lack of the resource – an indigenously trained Russian teacher.

***Pause for thought*** | educational transfer or educational borrowing: what is it?

Transfer of a successful educational practice/idea from one context to another with the view to reform a current practice is referred to as educational transfer or educational borrowing. Kendal (1936, p.404) warned against adopting the theories and practices of other countries directly *without the necessary safeguards of modification*. Such transfers are not straightforward as they might require recognition of ancillary factors, which might have contributed to the success. Reasonable adjustments may be required so that such copying and emulation meets success.

According to Sadler (1900 reprinted in 1964, p.331):

*We cannot wander at pleasure among the educational systems of the world, like a child strolling through a garden, and pick off a flower from one bush and some leaves from another, and then expect that if we stick what we have gathered into the soil at home, we shall have a living plant.*

What according to you should be some of the factors that one needs to be mindful of when considering such an educational transfer or educational borrowing?

# Benchmarking

Descriptive studies can be of value in judging the effectiveness of the current educational provision of a country and identifying areas of improvement. For example, the three-yearly Programme for International Student Assessment (PISA) published by the Organisation for Economic Co-operation and Development (OECD) provides valuable comparative data of parallel education systems across the world. PISA and similar international league tables not only are important for benchmarking but also help in identifying areas which need improvement. For example, after the poor performance of Germany in the 2000 PISA results, the importance of early years education came to light, which compelled Germany to revamp its early years education, which previously was left to families to sort out. Following this, early years education became central to any educational policy in Germany. However, it is important that it is recognised that such data sets do not always acknowledge the reasons for these differences, which are often embedded in the society. This may therefore make the use of such data for any accurate and meaningful comparison difficult. For example, in India and England children enrol for primary school at the age of 5 years but OECD take primary school enrolments as running from ages 6–12 years.

## Research box

### global education rankings can be misleading

According to a report published by Sutton Trust (Smithers, 2013), the performance of England in three different international league tables indicated discrepancies and therefore can be misleading. While PISA seemed to suggest that England performed poorly, the Pearson Global Index 2012 suggested England was a leader and in Trends in International Mathematics and Science Study (TIMSS) 2011, England sat somewhere in the middle of the table. The report further points out differences in the mathematics performance of secondary pupils, with students being ranked 27th out of 65 for their performance in PISA 2009 and 10th out of 42 in TIMSS 2011. Therefore, international comparisons provide invaluable comparative performance data but they need to be interpreted with caution.

# Addressing misconceptions

These studies can also be of value in addressing misconceptions. For example, there is a great debate in western universities which have a high influx of international students that Indian students appear to lack critical thinking skills.

To address this debate, Mazuro and Rao (2011) surveyed undergraduate students in both a British and an Indian university to determine their beliefs and approaches to education. A perceptions inventory questionnaire was administered to these students which included sections that looked at critical skills, beliefs and values, and role of the tutor. The study revealed there were more similarities than differences in terms of beliefs and approaches to education among these students. In particular, it was found that both sets of students felt they had similar levels of critical thinking skills. This finding may suggest that the students view critical skills in different ways. In particular, there might be cultural differences in the way these skills are communicated and conceptualised in the western and non-western parts of the world. Perhaps, students in India may not feel comfortable to criticise established theories and concepts rather than lacking the ability to do so. Therefore, comparative research of this type may be helpful in determining where misconceptions may be arising and putting together action plans to address them.

---

***Pause for thought*** | approaches towards comparative educational research

A typical approach to comparative studies involves comparing the educational processes and practices across two systems or countries. This has been typical of most of the comparative studies that have been undertaken since the early nineteenth century (Adamson, 2012). Another approach involves placing education in one location at the centre of analysis and then making comparisons as appropriate with other locations where the detail to which these locations may be examined is not equal (ibid). A third approach involves comparisons between several locations all being given equal status and examined in equal detail (Bray et al., 2007).

According to Carnoy (2006) there can be four ways of engaging in comparative educational research:

1. By pursuing a research programme involving study of one country or region at a time and comparing it with a similar study done at a later time or at a different space.
2. By undertaking a study that builds on others' studies of the same issue, with the intent of constructing a larger, comparative study on that theme.
3. By studying various countries or regions using the same methods of data collection and analysis.
4. By using large international data sets already available or creating an international data set from national data sources, and then analysing the data comparatively.

What do you think might be the most relevant approach for different international educational issues? Justify your answer.

---

Comparative education is an area of study worth pursuing for several reasons – some of which have been outlined above. However, considering the complex nature of comparative education, which draws on the theory and methods of several disciplines, the job of comparativists is not an easy one. In the following section we explore the challenges faced by those engaged in the study of comparative education.

Research box

## the ideal student: perspectives of five countries

Harkness, S et al. (2007) Teachers' ethnotheories of the 'ideal student' in five western cultures, *Comparative Education*, 43(1), 113–35.

Before this article was published, research suggested that there was variability in how a child's intelligence and competence is viewed depending on the country/culture. Based on that research, the researchers wanted to know whether primary and kindergarten teachers had different views on what an ideal student was, i.e. was it a student who was intelligent, or well-mannered, etc. depending on their culture. The focus therefore was on teachers' cultural ideas or what is sometimes called 'ethnotheories'. The researchers chose to investigate this research problem in five western societies (Italy, the Netherlands, Poland, Spain and USA) to represent various cultural, religious and geographic dimensions of western societies.

The data used in their research was drawn from a larger project called the 'International Study of Parents, Children and Schools' (ISPCS) of mainly middle-class families. The researchers used a mixed methods approach and collected both quantitative and qualitative data. Eighty-nine teachers were interviewed in their native language to ensure that cultural concepts and language expressions were captured. From the transcribed interviews, a list of words and phrases were created that captured the quality and behaviour of the ideal students. In a few cases, it was difficult to translate some words to an English equivalent. Using a qualitative data analysis software, NVivo, the words were coded into themes/categories which allowed numerical analysis. Following this, a statistical data analysis software (SAS) was used on these words to do a statistical analysis called *discriminant analysis* to segregate which words were more common in each country. They found that all of the countries had different views of an ideal student:

1. Italy: the creative scientist – children who were curious and had an enthusiastic attitude towards learning.
2. Netherlands: the cheerful diplomat – children who were happy, stable, well-regulated and 'comfortable in their skin' i.e. children who come to school with pleasure.
3. Poland: the socialist entrepreneur – children who are well-balanced, autonomous and self-regulated.
4. Spain: the social academic – children who have social skills, are motivated, focused and intelligent.
5. USA: the 'Wild West adventurer' – children who had high motivation and were willing to put in the effort and take risks.

This research thus shows that intelligence is not the main focus of an ideal student and that the qualities and behaviour of students, which may be promoted/praised are influenced by their culture.

# Challenges of comparative educational research

Research in the field of comparative education is complicated due to the problems stemming from the complexity in defining the very nature of comparative education. These difficulties are also mirrored in the decisions regarding identification of an appropriate research process. Thus, the nature of this area of study generates a variety of perspectives, which makes it complex to research in this field. We have identified seven challenges that are described in more detail below.

## 1. Knowledge of various disciplines

The educational system, policy and practice, of a region/nation are influenced by a plethora of factors. To understand the influence of the political will, the religion, the economic condition of a country and several such complex issues on the education of a region or country requires an understanding of several disciplines such as sociology, politics, and history to name a few. It would be unrealistic to expect this from a single individual. This would be an unrealistic expectation from a single individual. The only way to deal with this issue is to undertake collaborative comparative educational research involving specialists across various disciplines but such collaborative studies have their own limitations in trying to coordinate the activities.

## 2. Methodological approach

The argument around whether it is a discipline in its own right or a cross-disciplinary field creates complications for deciding an appropriate methodological approach. Further complications may arise from the discussion around its identity as a science or a social science as these follow different methodological approaches. On one hand, Noah and Eckstein (1969) consider comparative education as a science, on the other, Alexander (2001) considers it as a social science. Therefore, should we be using the methodological approaches appropriate for science or social science? A study currently being undertaken by one of the authors of this chapter, headed by Mooney et al. (2013), involves investigating the effect of the nutritional status of middle school children on their academic achievement. For identifying the nutritional status, methods of science might be more appropriate (such as using laboratory analysis of nutritional content of food) but for analysing the academic achievement, a social science approach might be more apt (such as observing students' engagement at school). Therefore, a specific focus on the purpose and the intended outcome of the comparative study is essential when deciding the methodological approach.

## 3. Incompatibility of comparison units

In comparative education, sometimes we need to compare education systems based on the same things such as the ways of teaching or assessment – these are called the units of analysis. Comparisons can be made across various units of analysis. However, such comparisons are meaningful only if the units are comparable. The identification of the similarities and differences of the units being compared is important. For example, a comparison between the education systems of the UK and USA can be problematic due to the intra-national diversity in their educational systems. In the UK alone, the educational system differs between Scotland, Northern Ireland, England and Wales and makes it difficult for the researcher to determine what can be compared with the US at the same level. In a study conducted by Vidovich (2004), the comparison of the curricula between Singapore and Australia overlooked the significant differences in the size and population of these countries that subsequently led to erroneous inferences.

*Pause for thought* | units of analysis

Traditionally, comparative educational research has focused on cross-national comparisons. However, a strong case has now been made for many other units of comparison (see for example Bray and Thomas, 1995; Wolhuter, 2008).

According to Adamson (2012, p.642) some of the main units of analysis covered by the field of comparative education are as follows:

- locations;
- systems;
- policies and policy making processes;
- times;
- cultures;
- values, conflict resolution and citizenship;
- curricula;
- educational organisations, governance and accountability;
- ways of knowing and learning;
- ways of teaching;
- economics of education;
- assessment;
- teacher education and professionalism;
- ideologies, goals and purposes of education;
- social equity and access to education;
- educational achievements, international indicators and student performance;
- language in education.

If you were going to compare two countries' educational systems, and could only choose three units of comparison, which would you use, and why? How do you think these choices will affect the type of data you collect and what conclusions you can make about these countries?

## 4. Linguistic issues

The knowledge of language has a considerable impact both during field work and when communicating the research outcomes of any research and here we look at two different impacts.

**i. Lack of linguistic equivalence:** Lack of a standard name/taxonomy causes problems for comparativists. For example, 'college' in the UK often refers to sixth form colleges whereas in India and USA it is often used for institutions for degree level study. Often every country has a different range of meanings for educational terms. According to Crossley and Watson (2003), the lack of linguistic equivalence could be of enduring significance when international educational organisations like UNESCO make global recommendations for education. These recommendations and the terminologies used are often informed by western contexts.

**ii. Lack of knowledge of foreign languages:** One of the prime aims of comparative education is to develop a deep understanding of education systems. In order to develop an understanding of the systems, one could read literature. However, there is paucity of such literature for some countries and, where available, the literature's credibility is questionable. A more reliable approach could be to gain first-hand information by actually researching the system such as through interviewing citizens. However, this can be problematic as according to Bereday (1964), it is an expectation that the comparative researchers should have certain levels of competency in the language of the countries they choose to investigate. This however can sometimes be an unrealistic expectation. Thus, this lack of knowledge of the local language can seriously handicap data collection as the researcher would either need to spend a considerable amount of time gaining proficiency in the local language or will have to rely on others to do the data collection. Here there is a serious risk of some vital information being 'lost in translation'. The problems may be compounded further in multi-lingual nation states like India and Switzerland. Even within a nation there could be different languages spoken in different parts of the country, which can complicate these issues further. India has 25 official languages; Hindi, the national language, is spoken in less than 50 per cent of the country. Where do we start?

## 5. Funding issues

It is widely recognised that the funding sources for research are sparse. Most researchers need someone to fund their research, i.e. a funding sponsor, otherwise they would not be able to afford it. Lack of sufficient funding, as well as the type of funding sponsor, can have serious implications for data collection and sometimes implicitly may influence the research outcome. For example, if someone from the UK wishes to undertake a comparative study on the impact of social class on the educational outcomes of primary-aged children in another country, an understanding of the other country's social structure is crucial. While the researcher may have an apparent understanding of their own social structure, to develop a similar level of understanding of the foreign system requires spending prolonged periods of time within the local population in addition to the theoretical knowledge one might have. Such transnational studies would therefore require a significant amount of funding to facilitate such a prolonged stay, which is a luxury that only a few can afford.

Furthermore, the influence of funding on the likely research outcomes is a delicate issue. The researchers may find themselves under pressure to appease their sponsors such as government agencies, private charities or international organisations. This can bring the credibility of such studies, which may be doctored to suit the agenda of these funding sponsors, under the scanner.

## 6. Decontextualised approach

When providing policy/practical suggestions based on research, the recommendations have to be made within the context of the education systems for them to be meaningful. They may need to take into account, for example, culture, attitudes or religion – this is called contextualisation. For example, when comparing the adult education provision in India and England, it is important to understand that the very purpose of adult education in India and England may be different. In India, adult education programmes are geared more towards the rural population and focus on dealing with illiteracy among adults. However, in England, adult education is not exclusively for people living in the countryside and does not deal with literacy issues; it may focus on vocational/professional aspects of learning. It is crucial that the understanding of the local context in transnational comparative studies remains at the forefront. Similarly, it is equally important that individuals or organisations engaged in the field of research are aware of their own prejudices and preconceptions during the data collection stage, its interpretation and when suggesting recommendations in comparative studies. One should shun ethnocentrism (i.e. judging another culture based on your own values) while analysing cross-cultural data. It is important that the researchers acknowledge their own socio-cultural background and how it can influence the perceptions and assumptions they make when undertaking any cross-cultural study.

## 7. Accessibility issues

Data collection involving comparative studies in some parts of the rural and urban world, where basic amenities are compromised, is often troublesome. Some of the important considerations would be: unfavourable climatic conditions; lack of means of transport and communication; lack of awareness of the local context; hostile attitudes of people; lack of law and order; and lack of trained personnel to undertake data collection. These factors may hinder accessibility to the data and further complicate research in such areas. For example, in a study being undertaken by Mooney et al. (2013) analysing the impact of nutritional levels on the academic achievement of middle school children in Nepal, data collection was delayed due to unfavourable climatic conditions and the unstable political situation in Nepal.

Having considered some of the theoretical and methodological issues that comparativists face, the issues faced in comparative research are not insurmountable. Further, the value of this research for influencing policy, behaviour and understanding is too important and would be an area that will continue to grow, expand and find prominence in the educational research context.

---

### Research box

### equity and quality of education in South Africa

Frempong, G, Reddy, V and Kanjee, A (2011) Exploring equity and quality education in South Africa using multilevel models, *Compare: A Journal of Comparative and International Education*, 41(6): 819–35.

Following the apartheid years, there has been educational reform in South Africa to ensure all students irrespective of their background have the opportunity to succeed. The researchers sought to investigate whether students' success in schools was dependent on their backgrounds, i.e. did going to high quality schools compensate for the achievement gap by those students who were socio-economically disadvantaged?

To investigate this research question, the researchers surveyed 34,015 Grade 6 students (around 12 years) in 998 schools which covered South Africa's nine provinces. The students were assessed on their language, mathematics and natural science skills. Further, data was also collected on the students' home background characteristics. The schools were also assessed based on their students' socio-economic status (SES) and their efficiency. Schools' efficiency was measured based on the number of students repeating grades, donations received, its internal school communication, the functioning of the school governing body, and support received by the Department of Education.

*(Continued)*

*(Continued)*

Using a statistical procedure called regression analysis, the researchers tried to model what factors were significantly affecting the students' achievement levels. The model was able to predict 75 per cent of the variance (i.e. the cases) and found that the significant (i.e. critical) factors in predicting achievement were the quality of learners; and their parents' engagement and participation in the schooling process. The researchers found that there was a statistically significant positive relationship ($p < 0.05$) between the school's SES and the school's achievement level, i.e. the probability (p) of this not being true was less than 0.05 which is 5 per cent). Therefore, as the school's SES increases (more affluent schools) so did the school's achievement.

These results suggest that policies need to be created to ensure a provision of quality education for the poor and may start with policies to encourage parents' engagement and participation in the schooling process.

## Summary and conclusions

With the increasing globalisation of the world, interest in the field of comparative education has been revitalised. Despite its long history, there still seem to be complexities linked to this field of study, which are compounded by the influence of the various disciplinary fields it encompasses. This makes it difficult to identify an ideological perspective that is unique to comparative educational research. We have attempted to present a brief overview of some of the issues linked to the field of comparative education. The chapter brings to the fore the difficulties in comprehending the very nature of comparative education. It assesses some of the uses and the potential abuses of comparative education. There is ambiguity around the ways studies should be conducted in this field and the complexities that arise from the problems faced by comparativists in undertaking such studies. We have in this chapter, identified and examined some of these substantive issues that present perpetual challenges for the comparativists and require critical attention. This critical analysis of some of the theoretical and methodological issues linked to the field of comparative education should not dissuade you from a study of comparative education and of the research in this field. This is particularly important considering the sensitivity comparative education research attaches to the various socio-cultural factors that shape the education systems at local, regional and national level in this increasingly globalised world.

To conclude, in the words of Noah (1984, p.561): *comparative study is a most desirable way of approaching an understanding of education. The challenge is to do it in ways that are valid, persuasive, practically usable and above all, enlightening.*

## References

Adamson, B (2012) International comparative studies in teaching and teacher education. *Teaching and Teacher Education,* 28 (2012): 641–8.
Alexander, R (2001) Border crossings: towards a comparative pedagogy. *Comparative Education,* 37(4): 507–23.

Bereday, GZ (1964) *Comparative Method in Education*. New York: Holt, Rinehart and Winston, Inc.

Bray, M (2007) Actors and purposes in comparative education, in Bray, M, Adamson, B and Mason, M (eds) *Comparative Education Research Approaches and Methods* (15–38). Hong Kong and Dordrecht, Netherlands: Comparative Education Research Centre and Springer.

Bray, M (2010) Comparative education and international education in the history of *Compare*: boundaries, overlaps and ambiguities. *Compare: A Journal of Comparative and International Education*, 40(6): 711–25.

Bray, M and Thomas, RM (1995) Levels of comparison in educational studies: Different insights from different literatures and the value of multilevel analyses. *Harvard Educational Review,* 65(3): 472–90.

Bray, M, Adamson, B and Mason, M (2007) Different models, different emphases, different insights, in Bray, M, Adamson, B and Mason, M (eds) *Comparative Education Research Approaches and Methods* (363–79). Hong Kong and Dordrecht, Netherlands: Comparative Education Research Centre and Springer.

Broadfoot, P (2000) Comparative education for the 21st century: Retrospect and prospect. *Comparative Education,* 36(3): 357–71.

Bunnell, T (2008) International education and the 'second phase': A framework for conceptualizing its nature and for the future assessment of its effectiveness. *Compare: A Journal of Comparative Education,* 38(4): 415–26.

Carnoy, M (2006) Rethinking the comparative – and the international. *Comparative Education Review*, 50(4): 551–70.

Chabbott, C (2003) *Constructing education for development: International organizations and education for all*. New York: Routledge Falmer.

Clarkson, J (2009) What is comparative education? in Bignold, W and Gayton, L (eds) *Global Issues and Comparative Education* (4–17). Exeter: Learning Matters.

Crossley, M (1999) Reconceptualising comparative and international education. *Compare: A Journal of Comparative an International Education*, 29(3): 249–67.

Crossley, M and Watson, K (2003) *Comparative and International Research in Education: Globalisation, context and difference*. London: Routledge.

Eliou, M (1997) Le comparatisme dans l'éducation comparée: une aventure ambiguë, in De Clerke, K and Simon, F (eds) *Studies in Comparative, International, and Peace Education: Liber amicorum Henk Van daele* (107–116). Gent: C.S.H.P

Epstein, EH (1994) Comparative and international education: Overview and historical development, in Husén, T and Postlethwaite, TN (eds) *The International Encyclopedia of Education* (918–23) (2nd edn). Oxford: Pergamon Press.

Frempong, G, Reddy, V and Kanjee, A (2011) Exploring equity and quality education in South Africa using multilevel models. *Compare: A Journal of Comparative and International Education*, 41(6): 819–35.

Halls, WD (1990) *Comparative Education: Contemporary Issues and Trends*. London: Jessica Kingsley/UNESCO.

Harkness, S, Blom, M, Oliva, A, Moscardino, U, Zylicz, PO, Bermudez, MR, Feng, X, Carrasco-Zylicz, A, Axia, G and Super, CM (2007) Teachers' ethnotheories of the 'ideal student' in five western cultures. *Comparative Education*, 43(1): 113–35.

Higginson, JH (1999) The development of a discipline: Some reflections on the development of comparative education as seen through the pages of *Compare*. *Compare: A Journal of Comparative Education,* 29(3): 341–51.

Kendal, I L (1936) History of education and comparative education. *Review of Educational Research*, 6(4): 400–16.

Kerawalla, GJ (1995) Comparative education, in Buch, MB (ed.) *Fifth Survey of Educational Research* (660–69). New Delhi: National Council of Educational Research and Training.

Mallinson, V (1975) *An Introduction to the Study of Comparative Education* (4th edn). London: Heinemann.

Mazuro, C and Rao, N (2011) *What ARE the differences? Indian and UK students' perceptions of degree studies,* Conference presentation at British Education Studies Association, Manchester, 30 June–1 July 2011.

Moin, V, Breitkopf, A and Schwartz, M (2011) Teachers' views on organizational and pedagogical approaches to early bilingual education: A case study of bilingual kindergartens in Germany and Israel. *Teaching and Teacher Education*, 27(6): 1008–18.

Mooney, K, McCauley, M, Rao, N and Sharma, AL (2013) An investigation of the academic performance and nutritional status of middle school children in Nepal. *Educational Research at Hope*, 1:56–7. Available at: **www.hope.ac.uk/educationalresearchathope/** [accessed 5 April, 2013].

Noah, HJ (1984) The use and abuse of comparative education. *Comparative Education Review*, 28(4): 550–62.

Noah, HJ and Eckstein, MA (1969) *Toward a Science of Comparative Education.* New York: Macmillan.

Phillips, D and Schweisfurth, M (2008) *Comparative and International Education: An Introduction to Theory, Method and Practice.* London: Continuum.

Sadler, Sir M (1900). How can we learn anything of practical value from the study of foreign systems of education? Reprinted 1964 in *Comparative Education Review*, 7(3): 307–14.

Smithers, A (2013) *Confusion in the Ranks: How Good are England's Schools.* The Sutton Trust. Available at: **www.suttontrust.com/public/documents/1confusion-in-the-ranks-smithers-league-tables-final.pdf** [accessed 3 April 2013].

Vidovich, L (2004) Towards internationalizing the curriculum in a context of globalization: Comparing policy processes in two settings. *Compare: A Journal of Comparative Education,* 34(4): 443–61.

Watson, K (1996) Comparative education, in Gordon, P. (ed.) *A Guide to Educational Research* (360–97). London: Woburn Press.

Wilson, DN (1994) Comparative and international education: Fraternal or siamese twins? A preliminary genealogy of our twin fields. *Comparative Education Review*, 38(4): 449–86.

Wolhuter, CC (2008) Review of the review: Constructing the identity of comparative education. *Research in Comparative and International Education*, 3(4): 323–44.

## Further reading

Bulle, N (2011) Comparing OECD educational models through the prism of PISA. *Comparative Education*, 47(4): 503–21.

Clarkson, J (2009) What is comparative education? in Bignold, W and Gayton, L (eds) *Global Issues and Comparative Education* (4–17). Exeter: Learning Matters.

Phillips, D and Ochs, K (2003) Processes of policy borrowing in education: some explanatory and analytical devices. *Comparative Education,* 39(4): 451–61.

Phillips, D and Schweisfurth, M (2008) *Comparative and International Education: An introduction to theory, method and practice.* London: Continuum.

Schweistfurth, M (2013) The comparative gaze: from telescope to microscope. *Comparative Education,* 49(2): 121–3.

Soudien, C (2011) The challenge of comparison: understanding global educational standards. *Compare: A Journal of Comparative and International Education*, 41(1): 131–9.

Srivastava, P (2006) Reconciling multiple researcher positionalities and languages in international research. *Research in Comparative and International Education,* 1(3): 210–22.

# Chapter 20

# Global citizenship education

## Feng Su, Andrea Bullivant and Victoria Holt

### Introduction

In recent years, there has been a growing interest in global citizenship as a concept and its implication for education. This increasing interest in global citizenship education has been partly due to the ongoing process of globalisation and the fact that people are becoming more interdependent and interconnected. The promotion of global citizenship education seems to be a way of addressing some of the global issues we face today, such as environmental issues, social justice, poverty, and human rights. What does 'global citizenship' mean? Is there a universal definition for it? How do we approach it in education? What are the challenges of introducing it in education? In this chapter, we explore how global citizenship is conceptualised and how it has evolved over time; the challenges of facilitating global citizenship education; and different approaches to global citizenship education at different stages of education.

## What is global citizenship?

Global citizenship is the idea of citizenship in a global context, and is a concept which is highly contested and not straightforward to define. Some argue that global citizenship is based on moral identity, which implies that everyone has a moral obligation to care about each other, regardless of geographic locations or nationality. Others believe global citizenship can only be achieved through the leadership of global institutions, such as the United Nations, or through involvement in non-governmental organisations (NGOs) (Dower, 2002). With such contrasting views on 'what makes a global citizen', it is near impossible to prescribe a singular definition.

Heater (1997, p.36) suggests interpretations of what it means to be a global citizen:

- a member of the human race;
- to be responsible for the condition of the planet;
- an individual subject to moral law;
- to promote world government.

These interpretations can be placed on a spectrum where the opposed ends are 'vague' and 'precise'. The 'vague' end of the spectrum centres on moral responsibility, while the 'precise' end focuses on realisation of global citizenship through global governance.

Nussbaum (1996) and Dower (2002) consider global citizenship to be a moral obligation, proposing that a global citizen is expected to feel a moral responsibility to all human beings around the world. According to Dower,

*When someone says of himself 'I am a global citizen', he is making some kind of moral claim about the nature and scope of our moral obligations. That is, he accepts that he has obligations in principle towards people in any part of the world; for instance, help alleviate poverty, work for international peace, support organisations trying to stop human rights violations, or play one's part in reducing global warming. And if someone says, of people in general and not merely of herself, that 'we are global citizens', she means to say that people generally have these kinds of obligations, whether or not they are currently aware of them or accept them.*

(2002, p.146)

However, the above description of global citizenship still seems vague and difficult to apply in practice. As a leading international NGO, Oxfam (2006, p.3) characterises the global citizen as someone who:

- is aware of the wider world and has a sense of their own role as a world citizen;
- respects and values diversity;
- has an understanding of how the world works;
- is outraged by social injustice;
- participates in the community at a range of levels, from the local to the global;
- is willing to act to make the world a more equitable and sustainable place;
- takes responsibility for their actions.

What Dower and Oxfam's interpretations both seem to emphasise is the 'moral' and 'action' dimensions of global citizenship.

*Pause for thought* | global citizenship

Using the bullet points above to assist you, what do you think are the differences between 'vague' and 'precise' interpretations of global citizenship? Can you think of anyone that is considered to be a global citizen? Why do you feel they are a global citizen? Why would a global citizen be outraged by social injustice?

# A historical overview of global citizenship education

While global citizenship continues to elude precise definition, global citizenship education and some of the issues it raises can be better understood by considering some key historical developments.

The idea of global citizenship is not a new one. Groups such as the Stoics, from the ancient Graeco-Roman world, believed that human beings were part of and had obligations to a global community beyond the local, national or wider regional communities in which they were located, and the concept of a 'universal ethic' has been part of religious and philosophical movements for centuries (Dower, 2002, p.6). However, the concept had tended to fall in and out of favour until its re-emergence in the twentieth century.

During the early part of the twentieth century a series of initiatives took place in the wake of the First World War, which sought to promote 'education for international understanding'. These included the League of Nations Union, the Council for Education in World Citizenship (CEWC) and the United Nations Educational, Scientific and Cultural Organisation (UNESCO), and they laid the foundations for different educational movements which emerged in the UK between the 1960s and 1980s, although similar movements were also taking place elsewhere in the world (Tye, 2003). Each of these educational movements took a different focus in terms of the 'issue' they were aiming to address and the following section will focus on three areas in particular which have influenced the concept of global citizenship education as it might be understood today.

## Global education

World Studies was the original term used by educators who led a series of projects during the 1970s and 1980s, providing training and resources for a large number of teachers, teacher trainers and NGO educators. The World Studies Project led by Robin Richardson (1976) and colleagues at the University of London Institute of Education was the first of these to provide a model for exploring global issues which emphasised the need to explore the economic and political context of such issues, the role of values in education and opportunities for action. The project was also highly influential in introducing alternative teaching approaches which promoted learners' active participation in the learning process. These drew on the work of radical educators such as Paulo Freire, and continue to play a key role in global citizenship education today.

As Richardson's ideas developed in later projects (Fisher and Hicks, 1985; Pike and Selby 1988), the term 'global education' became more commonly used, reflecting influences from educators elsewhere, who were also attempting to grapple with, define and measure a 'global perspective' (Hanvey, 1976, p.2).

## Development education

Originating in the campaigning work of NGOs, such as Oxfam, Christian Aid and the locally based network of Development Education Centres (DECs), development education was another field emerging from the 1960s onwards. Initially, development educators focused on teaching *about* poverty in developing countries, or what became referred to increasingly as the 'global south', but over time they have adopted a more holistic and critical approach, linking poverty with issues like climate change, social justice and human rights, and examining the social, economic and political causes of inequalities. However, as development educators shifted towards a broader conceptualisation of their work, the term 'development education' fell out of favour. Oxfam began to use the term global citizenship and devised an action-orientated framework, which continues to be used by schools today (see Case study 1, p.238).

Other 'issue-based educations' (Hicks, 2007, p.5) also emerged from the 1960s onwards. These ranged from environment and peace education to lesser known fields such as futures education. Some of these fell out of favour, for example peace education came under particular attack from right-wing commentators and politicians in the 1980s, during a general backlash against what was perceived as a form of political indoctrination in schools. Different issues also became subsumed into over-arching terms such as global education and global citizenship.

## Race, diversity and citizenship

Anti-racist education was another area which came under attack from those on the political right during the 1980s. However, events like the racist killing of Stephen Lawrence and the inquiry that followed, and more recently the London Underground bombings in 2005, have maintained a national debate about issues of race, diversity and national identity. Schools, along with other key institutions, were required to address these issues through legislation such as the Race Relations Amendment Act (2000) and the Duty to Promote Community Cohesion (2007), and when citizenship became a statutory subject in the UK National Curriculum in 2002 it appeared to be a response to the concerns raised by these issues, although critics have argued that it remained too focused on the nation state (Osler and Starkey, 2003); a tension we will return to shortly.

## The 'global dimension'

Whereas citizenship has featured in national curriculums, global citizenship education has never acquired the legitimacy of becoming a statutory subject. It continues to take place in a variety of ways ranging from international school linking and fund raising for charities, to drawing in global themes within subjects, using local contexts to explore global themes of diversity and sustainable living, and promoting participation and 'pupil voice' through student councils. Yet, despite these activities, the extent to which it is promoted in schools can depend on whether or not it finds favour with the government of the day.

Since 2000 there has been growing support for a 'global dimension' in education both in the UK and countries like Australia and Canada, often influenced by the work of NGOs and DECs in collaboration with government departments responsible for education and awareness raising for international development aid. In the UK, this resulted in a series of guidance documents being issued to schools, including *Developing a Global Dimension in the School Curriculum* and *The Global Dimension in Action*, the latter proposing that:

*The global dimension explores what connects us to the rest of the world. It enables learners to engage with complex global issues and explore the links between their own lives and people, places and issues throughout the world. … It helps learners to imagine different futures and the role they can play in creating a fair and sustainable world.*

(QCA, 2007, p.2)

While Oxfam and others continued to use the term global citizenship, the global dimension became another overarching term, encompassing many of the 'issues' which had previously been fields of education in their own right and encompassing similar themes already part of the discourse around global citizenship *related to responsibility, awareness and engagement* (Schattle, 2009, in Marais and Ogden, 2010, p.3).

---

***Pause for thought*** | Oxfam

Oxfam sets out the following key elements for responsible global citizenship from which they have developed a whole curriculum framework:

| Knowledge and understanding | Skills | Values and attitudes |
|---|---|---|
| Social justice and equity | Critical thinking | Sense of identity and self-esteem; empathy |
| Diversity | Ability to argue effectively | Commitment to social justice and equity |

| Knowledge and understanding | Skills | Values and attitudes |
|---|---|---|
| Globalisation and interdependence | Ability to challenge injustice and inequalities | Value and respect for diversity |
| Sustainable development | Respect for people and things | Concern for the environment and commitment to sustainable development |
| Peace and conflict | Cooperation and conflict resolution | Belief that people can make a difference |

(Oxfam, 2006, p.4)

Reflecting on your own experience of education or what you know of the education system currently in the UK, to what extent are these 'elements' of knowledge, skills, and values and attitudes part of the educational experience of young people? Can you think of specific examples of subjects or teaching pedagogies which promote any of these? You may also want to reflect on very recent debates in education about the demand for education to focus on acquisition of knowledge, a debate recently addressed by Bourn (2012) in *Global Learning and Subject Knowledge*.

# Challenges of facilitating global citizenship education

Having identified some key developments and themes in the emerging concept of global citizenship education, we now turn our attention to key challenges. Some of these are due to on-going uncertainty about the precise meaning of global citizenship both in theory and practice, while others relate to tensions about *who* is defining *what* and for what purpose, and all of this of course within the context of rapid globalisation with all its opportunities, challenges and contradictions.

## Balancing unity and diversity

While the rise of citizenship education has to some extent promoted exploration of global issues in schools, critics have argued that the way it has evolved is too distinct from developments in global education and that rather than becoming a hybrid of the two, citizenship needs to adapt and respond to globalisation to build a new kind of education (Davies et al., 2005). This poses a challenge for citizenship education in a world where globalisation and nationalism co-exist, and where there are competing demands between recognising diversity locally and globally, promoting unity within and between nations and embracing an *overarching set of shared values, ideals and goals to which all citizens are committed* (Banks et al., 2005, p.7). One response to this challenge is the idea of 'cosmopolitan citizenship' proposed by Osler and Starkey, which recognises *multiple and dynamic identities, embracing local, national and international perspectives* and seeks to promote young people's engagement in issues such as peace, rights and democracy (2003, p.252).

## A coherent approach

A further challenge is raised by David Hicks who argues that while the concept of global citizenship advocated by DECs and NGOs offers very practical approaches for schools, it still tends to exist as an 'umbrella' term for a range of issues and approaches and lacks both theoretical underpinning and coherency, leaving it open to a variety of interpretations (2008, p.9). In recent years, global citizenship has been promoted through several agendas such as the Global Dimension, the Duty to Promote Community Cohesion and the Sustainable Schools agenda. These provided schools with frameworks and concepts they could use as a basis for planning activities coherently across the curriculum and wider life of the school (see Case study 1), although schools engaged with these to varying degrees (Bourn, 2012). More recently, attempts have been made to move beyond terms such as the global dimension and global citizenship to seek greater clarity through the concept of global learning, defined as *'education that puts learning in a global context, fostering:*

- *critical and creative thinking;*
- *self-awareness and open-mindedness towards difference;*
- *understanding of global issues and power relationships; and*
- *optimism and action for a better world.*

(Think Global, 2012)

This has formed part of a wider debate in which writers and researchers draw on the field of Education for Sustainable Development (ESD) to emphasis the need for clear learning outcomes which can enable young people to make decisions about how they act in the world (Scott, 2010). ESD has been promoted heavily by UNESCO, reflected in the UN Decade on ESD 2005–2014, and a significant body of literature has emerged around it in recent years. In a literature review conducted on behalf of UNESCO, Tilbury identifies learning in ESD as:

- *learning to ask critical questions;*
- *learning to clarify one's own values;*
- *learning to envision more positive and sustainable futures;*
- *learning to think systemically;*
- *learning to respond through applied learning; and,*
- *learning to explore the dialectic between tradition and innovation.*

(Tilbury, 2011, p.8)

Again, while there are overlaps with the definition of global learning provided by Think Global, this extends the debate about global citizenship education still further.

## Teachers' confidence to explore global issues

In a survey report by the Development Education Association (DEA) into UK teachers' attitudes to global learning the DEA concluded that, despite the vast majority of teachers believing that *schools should prepare pupils to deal with a fast-changing and globalised world* (2009, p.5), many lacked confidence to incorporate this into their teaching. Different studies have identified a number of factors involved in this:

- Teachers' perceptions that ability to teach about global issues depends on their level of knowledge about those issues.
- Teachers not being equipped or experienced in the kind of methodologies recommended for exploring complex issues.
- Significant differences in attitude towards incorporating global citizenship between teachers of different subjects. For example, teachers of humanities subjects being most enthusiastic.

(Bourn, 2012; Brown, 2009; Robbins et al., 2003)

Despite apparent, if variable, interest and support from teachers and the extent of activity going on through the work of DECs and NGOs, it is perhaps not surprising that teachers' confidence to deliver global citizenship in practice is low given its low profile in mainstream education. Government ideas about what education is for and what it should include can also influence teachers' motivation towards facilitating global citizenship education in schools. The current UK Coalition Government has promoted a 'back to basics' approach to education, which emphasises acquisition of knowledge in relation to a narrow range of subjects and minimises the relevance of the global context of young peoples' lives. This clearly poses a challenge for global citizenship education and its advocates, and has shifted the debate about its role in education yet again (Bourn, 2012).

## 'Soft' versus 'critical' global citizenship

Despite the challenges raised so far, Bourn (2012) highlights the extent to which global citizenship has evolved from its early focus on development issues, typically confined to subjects such as geography, to the range of approaches outlined earlier. However, what this wide range of approaches also exposes is both a divergence in perspectives about what global citizenship means and a tension that raises questions about how global citizenship should be facilitated. For example, activities such as international school linking are often as much about young people acquiring skills and competence to compete in a global economy as they are about promoting *learners to imagine different futures and the role they can play in creating a fair and sustainable world* (ibid). The challenge here is that if young people continue to see the world in terms of opportunities for trade and gaining competitive advantage, or what Alexander refers to as a 'contra-national' rather than 'international perspective', this perspective is likely to run counter to attempts to promote mutual cooperation, collectivity and redressing of inequalities (2008, p.123).

What this tension also exposes is a division between more or less critical approaches to global citizenship education. Andreotti defined differences between 'soft' and 'critical' global citizenship education where soft approaches emphasise poverty, 'lack of 'development' and the need to take responsibility for those who are helpless, as opposed to critical approaches which emphasise critical reflection on the history of power relations, and the way inequalities and dominant perspectives perpetuate inequalities (2006, pp.46–8). Equally challenging is Tully's argument that *the globalisation of modern citizenship has not tended to democracy, equality and perpetual peace, but to informal imperialism, dependency, inequality and resistance* (2008, p.17). These challenges have been taken up to some extent by organisations such as Think Global who argue that global learning requires critical thinking which questions understandings and assumptions, and recognises *how much is contested* (Shah and Brown, 2009, p.2).

In spite of these challenges, there is a persistent drive towards promoting global citizenship education which continues to take place in a variety of forms as will be demonstrated in Pause for thought below.

---

*Pause for thought* | imagine a scene

In the introduction to her article 'Soft versus critical global citizenship education', Andreotti describes the following scene:

*Imagine a huge ball-room. It is full of people wearing black-tie. They are all celebrities. You also see a red carpet leading to a stage on the other side. On the stage there is Nelson*

*(Continued)*

*(Continued)*

*Mandela. He is holding a prize. It is the activist of the year prize. He calls your name. You walk down that corridor. Everyone is looking at you. What are you wearing? How are you feeling? Think about how you got there: the number of people that have signed your petitions, the number of white bands on the wrists of your friends, the number of people you have taken to Edinburgh. You shake Mandela's hands. How does that feel? He gives you the microphone. Everyone is quiet waiting for you to speak. They respect you. They know what you have done. Think about the difference you have made to this campaign! Think about all the people you have helped in Africa...*

Bearing in mind Andreotti's distinction between 'soft' and 'critical' approaches to global citizenship education, why do you think she might find this 'disturbing' and what issues does it raise?

(Andreotti, 2006, pp.40–51)

# Different approaches to global citizenship education

This section explores different ways of implementing global citizenship education at three different educational stages: primary school, secondary school and higher education. Three case studies are provided to exemplify some of the approaches discussed.

## Case study 1: Primary school

Evelyn Community Primary School in Prescot, England, has been recognised for its high profile global citizenship provision, which is a main focus of its unique curriculum termed ARCS, A Real life Creative Skills based curriculum. Therefore, the school's ethos is very distinctive because it explicitly presents global citizenship as one of its key aims in its mission statement: *in equipping learners with the tools to be a global citizen in an ever-changing society*. The school has drawn on a range of global citizenship education frameworks such as Oxfam's (2006) *Education for Global Citizenship: A Guide for Schools* and has utilised the previous government's eight key concepts of the global dimension, listed below, which were taught across all National Curriculum subjects in the UK (DfID, 2005):

1. Global citizenship
2. Interdependence
3. Social justice
4. Human rights
5. Conflict resolution
6. Diversity
7. Sustainable development
8. Values and perceptions

These frameworks provided an active and participatory approach to global citizenship education, which the school addresses in its different approaches to teaching global citizenship education.

The school promotes global citizenship in a number of ways:

- Friday afternoons are dedicated to the exploration of global issues or world events, such as World Food Day or Diversity Day, which are discussed in the afternoon assembly. After the assembly the whole school, from reception to Year 6, go back to their classrooms to further explore the theme for the week by doing related activities.
- Global Ceremony is held by the school to celebrate and reward the achievements of pupils who have been involved in global citizenship projects. Parents and other people from the wider community are invited to this celebration, which again raises awareness of global citizenship education.
- The school is increasingly raising the profile of global citizenship education through the introduction of global, cultural and eco ambassadors. These ambassadors have the opportunity to be rewarded for their efforts by working towards bronze, silver, gold and platinum contribution awards. In addition, the school has a list, The Student Exit Profile, of what children have to achieve before they leave the school in Year 6, and one of these things is to win their Global Learner Award.
- The school understands the importance of awareness on a local and global scale; therefore, it send emails and a copy of the school magazine to the school and wider community to promote the global citizenship initiatives within the school. Additionally, the school hosts fair-trade coffee mornings and festivals.
- The school has recently become partners with a university's Confucius Institute, which has given the pupils the opportunity to learn about Chinese culture and visit the university for a Chinese Day.
- All the staff are heavily involved in raising the profile of global citizenship education, striving consistently towards sustainability through displaying their own achievements on the staff display board named the Eight Gateways of Sustainability.

Evelyn Community Primary School has had much success with raising the profile of global citizenship education. The school has been granted forest school status. The school also wishes to build on its success with the Ambassador and Global Learner Awards to raise the profile even more and make these awards an integral part of the school. Thus, this case study demonstrates how global citizenship provision can be integrated effectively into the wider school life.

(Case study is based on telephone interview with school headteacher, Ms Carole Arnold.)

## Case study 2: Secondary school

This case study demonstrates how a London secondary school can promote global citizenship education through implementing some of strategies discussed by Marshall (2007). Marshall proposes the following 12 different ways in which schools can develop a global dimension in their teaching practice (2007, p.177). However, these approaches are not exclusive to secondary schools. There is no single most effective approach to global citizenship education, as every school is different due to its contexts.

1. Appointment of global dimension coordinator
2. Partnerships with schools abroad
3. Staff development and exchange opportunities
4. Global dimension through the curriculum (e.g. through Citizenship)
5. Working with NGOs (e.g. Development Education Centres) promoting global education
6. Global days, weeks, conferences and outside speakers
7. Promotion and broadening of language learning
8. International visits and hosting international visitors
9. Promotion of values associated with global social justice
10. Development of global education policy
11. Offering the International Baccalaureate
12. Obtaining the International School Award

This case study shows how a London secondary school combines different approaches within its global citizenship education provision.

Notre Dame Roman Catholic Girls' School in London highly values and appreciates the importance of teaching global citizenship education in a diverse society. The teachers at the school believe that it is their responsibility to teach the pupils about issues that are happening in the world around us, and to empower them with the knowledge that they are able to change the way things are in the world for the better. The school has strong partnerships with other Notre Dame Schools around the UK, as well as having a long established collaboration with a number of universities. As a Notre Dame Catholic school their aim is to provide all pupils with a well-rounded education, and they feel that global citizenship education is integral to this aim. The school stresses how it wants to teach the knowledge, skills and attitudes that will enable the students to understand what their role is in an ever-changing world.

Global citizenship is promoted in four significant ways by the school:

1. The school has an elected group of 15 students called the 'Notre Dame Global Citizenship Group'. Once a year these students attend a Notre Dame Global Citizenship Conference either at Liverpool Hope University or in London. During this three-day conference, the students discuss global citizenship issues with students from other Notre Dame schools in the UK. In the past the conferences have been based on global issues such as Fairtrade, or Slavery, and the students work together to research and design presentations on these topics. It is a great way for the Notre Dame schools in the UK to make links with each other, and for the students from each school to discuss these issues in more depth and see things from different perspectives.
2. The school welcomes visiting university students from Liverpool Hope University, who come to the school and run workshops with whole year groups. In 2012, the university students delivered workshops to the whole of Year 8 and Year 9 on themes such as poverty, human trafficking, disability and stereotyping in society.
3. The school hosts a variety of activities that happen during the school year as well, an example being 'Lenten lunches' run by the RE department. During Lent, students can take part in activities that highlight global issues happening around the world during their lunchtimes.
4. The school also holds International School status, and many of the projects that it undertakes in the school, through which it gained this award, contribute towards global citizenship education.

In a recent Ofsted inspection in November 2012, London Notre Dame School was rated as an outstanding school which 'provides a range of activities for students to develop students' confidence, raise their self-esteem and prepare them extremely well for the future'.

(Case study is based on email interview with school global dimension coordinator, Ms Layla Froomes.)

## Case study 3: Higher education

Research box

### becoming a global citizen through studying abroad

Recent research (Su, 2011, 2012) shows that experience of studying and living abroad provides university students with opportunities to understand and appreciate the diversity of cultures and values. In his study, there was evidence that students who studied abroad had developed a social and cultural sophistication through their knowledge and experience of different cultural contexts. As a result, it contributes to their transformation of becoming a global citizen.

In the UK, many higher education institutions appreciate the importance of the development of students' capabilities of being a global citizen since it is central to university study. Service-learning has been recognised as an effective approach to global citizenship education in higher education. The term service-learning is a multifaceted pedagogical tool which directs students' classroom learning to address the needs of relevant communities, where reciprocity between the institution and the community partner is essential in formulating *proposals, solutions and strategies for meeting their organisational missions* (Ransom, 2009, p.215). Case study 3 demonstrates how service-learning is used to offer students opportunities for community involvement at local, national and international levels.

Liverpool Hope University is a post-1992 new university, and has an ecumenical Christian foundation. The university has a strong emphasis on developing students as global citizens through the curriculum design, school partnerships, its award winning charity 'Global Hope', and a unique student Service and Leadership Award. This emphasis has been clearly reflected in the university's mission statement. In order to achieve this goal, the university has purposefully embedded global citizenship into its academic practice at different levels:

- The university's BA Education Studies and BA (QTS) curriculum introduces students to the concept of global citizenship as an integral part of the courses.
- Strong school partnerships provide students with the opportunity to deliver group workshops on the themes of global citizenship and social justice to both secondary school and primary school pupils in Liverpool, Sheffield or London. This initiative aims to deepen students' understanding of contemporary issues by teaching others.
- 'Global Hope' is an educational charity established by the university to provide its students and staff with opportunities to volunteer in developing countries around the world. It uses the resources of the university to support the educational development of communities overseas. In particular this means using the university's expertise in teaching and learning, research and subject knowledge to effectively work alongside partners in developing countries to meet their educational needs appropriately. This approach is grounded in the principle of reciprocity. A commitment to these relationships over the longer term has enabled genuine partnerships to develop.
- The university has recently established a unique extracurricular award, termed the Service and Leadership Award (SALA), to provide opportunities for students to engage in service activity during the three years of their undergraduate study. It aims to provide students with opportunities for a well-rounded education that *shapes life and vision, such as intercultural learning, experience of other cultures and contexts, engagement in service and voluntary work both locally and internationally* as articulated in the university's Learning, Teaching and Assessment Strategy.

The use of service-learning has enabled Liverpool Hope University to engage students with its courses, and develop their sense of civic responsibility through participating in community projects.

## Research box

### interpretive pedagogies for global citizenship

Nixon (2012) argues that education for global citizenship is essential in a globally interconnected and interdependent world. He emphasises the need for what he terms 'interpretive pedagogies' that value plurality of viewpoint and opinion, and acknowledge the dialogical and interactive nature of all learning. Education for global citizenship, he further argues, is a public good that is of benefit not only to the individual pupils and students concerned but also to the well-being of society as a whole (Nixon, 2011).

## Summary and conclusions

While global citizenship may be perceived as a relatively new issue in education, this chapter has attempted to show how global citizenship has been part of educators' thinking over a long period, and has a particular history in the UK. Even so, *a passport for global citizenship does not yet exist* and the concept continues to be difficult to define (Bamber, 2011, p.56). This may be because it remains relatively under-theorised and under-researched, a criticism raised by Hicks (2008). It has also been conceptualised in a variety of ways, hence the need to understand the distinct fields of education from which it has emerged. The chapter considered three of these fields – global education, development education and citizenship education – and showed how in the course of these developments some key themes have emerged; themes such as awareness, responsibility, making connections (between ourselves and other people and places around the world) and action for the future. The chapter also sets out some of the key challenges and tensions in delivering these themes in practice. These included debates about what it means to be a citizen in a rapidly changing global context, what kind of learning outcomes global citizenship education is aspiring to promote for young people and how this process can be sufficiently critical and challenging to truly bring about social justice on a global scale. Many of the themes and debates referred to have been driven by individuals and groups working outside formal education, although in recent years attempts have been made to formalise the role of global citizenship education through agendas such as the Global Dimension. Despite concerns about a return to a 'back to basics' education system, the UK Government has just launched a Global Learning programme in which it is envisaged some of this work will continue to take place in schools.

## References

Alexander, R (2008) *Essays on Pedagogy*. Abingdon: Routledge.

Andreotti, V (2006) Soft versus critical global citizenship education. *Policy and Practice: A Development Education Review*, 3: 40–51.

Bamber, P (2011) Educating for global citizenship, in Gadsby, H and Bullivant, A (eds) *Global Learning and Sustainable Development*. London: Routledge.

Banks, J et al. (2005) *Democracy and Diversity: Principles and concepts for educating citizens in a global age*. Washington: Centre for Multicultural Education, University of Washington.

Bourn, D (2012) *Global Learning and Subject Knowledge*. Research Paper No. 4. London: Development Education Research Centre, Institute of Education.

Brown, E (2009) *Attitudes to Teaching Global Citizenship: Student teachers' perceptions of teaching complex global issues*. University of Nottingham CCCI 2009 Conference papers.

Davies, I, Evans, M and Reid, A (2005) Globalising citizenship education? A critique of 'global education' and 'citizenship education'. *British Journal of Educational Studies*, 53(1): 66–89.

Department for International Development (DfID) (2005) *Developing the Global Dimension in the School Curriculum*. East Kilbride: DfID.

Development Education Association (DEA/Ipsos Mori) (2009) *Our Global Future: How schools can meet the challenge of change. Teachers' Attitudes To Global Learning*. London: DEA.

Dower, N (2002) Global ethics and global citizenship, in Dower, N and Williams, J (eds) *Global Citizenship: A Critical Reader*. Edinburgh: Edinburgh University Press, pp.146–57.

Fisher, S and Hicks, D (1985) *World Studies 8–13: a teacher's handbook*. Edinburgh: Oliver and Boyd.

Hanvey, R (1976) *An Attainable Global Perspective*. New York: Centre for War/Peace Studies.

Heater, D (1997) The reality of multiple citizenship, in Davies, I and Sobisch, A (eds) *Developing European Citizens*. Sheffield: Sheffield Hallam University Press.

Hicks, D (2007) Responding to the world, in Hicks, D and Holden, C (eds) *Teaching the Global Dimension: Key principles and effective practice*. London: Routledge.

Hicks, D (2008) *Ways of Seeing: The origins of global education in the UK*. Background paper for UK ITE Network Inaugural Conference on Education for Sustainable Development/ Global Citizenship, London 2008.

Marshall, H (2007) Global citizenship in the secondary school, in Hicks, D and Holden, C (eds) *Teaching the Global Dimension: Key principles and effective practice*. London: Routledge.

Nixon, J (2011) *Higher Education and the Public Good: Imagining the university*. London and New York: Bloomsbury.

Nixon, J (2012) *Interpretive Pedagogies for Higher Education: Arendt, Berger, Said, Nussbaum and their legacies*. London and New York: Bloomsbury.

Nussbaum, M (1996) *For Love of Country? A New Democracy Forum on the Limits of Patriotism*. Boston: Beacon Press, pp.3–17.

Osler, A and Starkey, H (2003) Learning for cosmopolitan citizenship: theoretical debates and young people's experiences. *Educational Review*, 55(3): 243–54.

Oxfam (2006) *Education for Global Citizenship: A Guide for Schools* [online]. Available at: **www.oxfam.org.uk/~/media/Files/Education/Global%20Citizenship/education_for_ global_citizenship_a_guide_for_schools.ashx** [accessed 1 March 2013].

Pike, G and Selby, D (1988) *Global Teacher, Global Learner*. London: Hodder and Stoughton.

Qualifications and Curriculum Authority (2007) *The Global Dimension in Action: A curriculum planning guide for schools*. London: QCA.

Ransom, L (2009) Sowing the seeds of citizenship and social justice: service-learning in a public speaking course. *Education, Citizenship and Social Justice*, 4(3): 211–24.

Richardson, R (1976) *Learning for Change in World Society*. London: World Studies Project.

Robbins, M, Francis, LJ and Elliott, E (2003) Attitudes towards education for global citizenship among trainee teachers. *Research in Education*, 69: 93–8.

Schattle, H (2009) Global citizenship in theory and practice, in Marais, D and Ogden, A (eds) (2010) Initial Development and Validation of the Global Citizenship Scale. *Journal of Studies in International Education* published online 12 July 2010, p.3.

Scott, W (2010) Preface to My Response to the Consultation on the DFID/DCSF Consultation on a Strategy for Global Learning. Available at:**www.se-ed.org.uk/resources/news/ William_Scott_thoughts_on_Global_Learning_strategy.pdf** [accessed 2011].

Shah, H and Brown, K (2009) *Critical Thinking in the Context of Global Learning*. London: DEA.

Su, F (ed) (2011) *Chinese Learning Journeys: Chasing the dream*. Stoke on Trent, UK and Sterling, USA: Trentham.

Su, F (2012) The challenges of compliance: international students in a UK university, in Adamson, B, Nixon, J and Su, F (eds) *The Reorientation of Higher Education: Challenging the East-West dichotomy*. New York and Hong Kong: Springer and Comparative Education Research Centre (CERC) of the University of Hong Kong.

Think Global (2012) About global learning. *Think Global* [online]. Available at: **www.think-global.org.uk/pages/?p=3857** [accessed March 2013].

Tilbury, D (2011) *Education for Sustainable Development: An Expert Review on Processes and Learning for ESD* [online]. Paris, UNESCO. Available at: **http://unesdoc.unesco.org/ images/0019/001914/191442e.pdf** [accessed April 2013].

Tully, J (2008) Two meanings of global citizenship: modern and diverse, in Peters, M, Blee, H and Britton, A (eds) *Global Citizenship Education: Philosophy, theory and pedagogy*. Rotterdam: Sense Publications.

Tye, K (2003) Global education as a worldwide movement. *The Phi Delta Kappan*, 85(2): 165–8.

## *Further reading*

Bamber, P (2011) Educating for global citizenship, in Gadsby, H and Bullivant, A (eds) *Global Learning and Sustainable Development*. Abingdon: Routledge.

Dower, N (2003) *An Introduction to Global Citizenship*. Edinburgh: Edinburgh University Press.

Hicks, D and Holden, C (eds) (2007) *Teaching the Global Dimension: Key principles and effective practice*. London: Routledge.

Oxfam (2006) *Education for Global Citizenship: A guide for schools*. Oxford: Oxfam.

Shah, H and Brown, K (2009) *Critical Thinking in the Context of Global Learning*. London: DEA Available at: **www.think-global.org.uk**/

Sinclair, S (2011) *Global Learning: Let's talk about it*. Tide~global learning. Available at: **http://www.tidec.org/**.

# Index